women

OUTSIDE

Women Outside: Conversations about Nature, Art & Spirit
© Mary Olmsted Greene, 2010

Interviews used with permission of the women interviewed: Kristin Barron, Eileen Pagan, Sandy Long, Krista Gromalski, Jenna Snow, Amy Gillingham, Stephanie Streeter, Karen MacIntyre, Peggy Hamill, Dorothy Hartz, Elizabeth Kaye Kaminski, Druis Ann Iya Oshun Koya Beasley and Mother Joan LaLiberte.

Poems used with permission of the poets: Kristin Barron, Eileen Pagan, Sandy Long, Dorothy Hartz, Elizabeth Kaye Kaminski, Druis Ann Iya Oshun Koya Beasley, Lori Anderson Moseman and Mary Olmsted Greene.

Cover photos by Sandy Long

Photos used with permision of photographers: Sandy Long, John Ogozalik, Mary Olmsted Greene, Heron's Eye Communication and W Design, Gerard Manzi, Wes Gillingham, Bill Streeter, Alan McGill, Bolade Miles-Beasley, Episcopal Diocese of New York and Carrie Coil.

Painting used with permission of Ted Keller.

Greene, Mary Olmsted
    Women Outside: Conversations about Nature, Art & Spirit
    interviews by Mary Olmsted Greene;
    poems by Kristin Barron, Eileen Pagan, Sandy Long, Dorothy Hartz, Elizabeth Kaye Kaminski, Druis Ann Iya Oshun Koya Beasley, Lori Anderson Moseman and Mary Olmsted Greene.
    ISBN 978-0-9819267-9-7 (Paperback)
    1. Nature—Poetry—Ecofeminism—Spirituality.

Stockport Flats, 2010

1120 East Martin Luther King Jr. Street   Ithaca, NY 14850   (607) 272-1630

women

OUTSIDE

conversations about **nature, art & spirit**

by **Mary Olmsted Greene**

*For Elizabeth Whitney Greene and James Robert Greene,
who taught me to love the world.*

women *OUTSIDE*

Introduction

Journey Back by *Mary Olmsted Greene* — 4
"Mahls Pond Road" by *Mary Olmsted Greene* — 13

Earth's Daughters

An Introduction to Earth's Daughters — 17

Interviews
What Remains: *Kristin Barron* — 18
A Home at the End of the Road: *Eileen Pagan* — 30
Wild Silence: *Krista Gromalski and Sandy Long* — 44

Poems
"Tossing a Coin" by *Sandy Long* — 62
"Garden" by *Kristin Barron* — 63
"Snail" by *Kristin Barron* — 64
"If" by *Kristin Barron* — 65
"Lost Land" by *Eileen Pagan* — 66
"Moment" by *Sandy Long* — 67

Crossing Paths

An Introduction to Crossing Paths — 71

Interviews
Yard, Dump, Stream: *Jenna Snow* — 72
Sustainable Knowledge: *Amy Gillingham* — 82
Birds and Dirty Clockwork: *Stephanie Streeter* — 98

Poems
"Discreet, Flagrant Abundance" by *Lori Anderson Moseman* — 112
"Eat & Try Not To Be Eaten" by *Lori Anderson Moseman* — 113
"Bear" by *Sandy Long* — 114
"Four" by *Mary Olmsted Greene* — 115
"Doorways" by *Mary Olmsted Greene* — 119

Body Knowledge

  An Introduction to Body Knowledge   131
Interviews
  Camping and Other Miracles: *Karen MacIntyre*   132
  Crossing the Void: *Peggy Hamill*   146
  Mud Pies and the Order Beneath the Chaos: *Dorothy Hartz*   164
Poems
  "Driving into Town" by *Kristin Barron*   178
  "The Mimosa Tree" by *Karen MacIntyre*   179
  "Jimson Weed" by *Dorothy Hartz*   180
  "Dusk" by *Sandy Long*   182
  "October Nocturne" by *Mary Olmsted Greene*   184
  "Coast Guard Beach" by *Mary Olmsted Greene*   185

Answering the Call

  An Introduction to Answering the Call   189
Interviews
  Elemental Nature: *Elizabeth Kaye Kaminski*   190
  Ancestor Work: *Druis Ann Iya Oshun Koya Beasley*   206
  A Hard Calling: *Mother Joan LaLiberte*   222
Poems
  "Adrift" by *Mary Olmsted Greene*   240
  "How Far Two Birds Flew to Carry Good News" by *Lori Anderson Moseman*   241
  "Casting Lots" by *Druis Ann Iya Oshun Koya Beasley*   242
  "Stations of the Wind" by *Elizabeth Kaye Kaminski*   244
  "Biomimicry: A Blessing, A Binaural Beat" by *Lori Anderson Moseman*   245
  "White Bed, April Moon" by *Mary Olmsted Greene*   246

Afterword

  Publisher's Afterword by *Lori Anderson Moseman*   249
  Author's Afterword by *Mary Olmsted Greene*   253
  "Cape May, January" by *Mary Olmsted Greene*   257

Works Cited   260

Recommended Readings   262

Acknowledgments   265

"I didn't know where to go, so I went into the field of orb spiders. At first, as I walked in among their waiting webs, I was afraid. The mind is a wolf. Then the light shed down sharply golden and I began to think. Thinking saved me. Perception saved me. I saw that the spiders were just substance. Not bad, not good. We were all made of the same stuff. I saw how we spurted out of creation in different shapes. How for a time I would inhabit this shape but then I'd be the lace on my sister's shoe that had dropped off her foot onto the weeds and tamped grass, or I'd be the blue pot my parents argued about, or maybe something else... I tapped a loaded jewelweed and the seed flipped out of sight. Feral and silent as coal, the spiders ranged to all sides of me. I put out my finger and with the slightest of motions I stroked the back of a spider. I coaxed the biggest one, using a thin blade of grass, into my palm. Then I held it for a motionless time. It was a sun-warmed thing, heavy as a dirt clod, but light as a plastic toy. Poised, excited, it vibrated with cold breath, ticked swiftly in my hand. Hummed, sang, knocked away the edges of the world."

Louise Erdrich, The Painted Drum

"I am not after conclusions. Conclusions are meant to shut (from the Latin 'con' plus 'claudere,' to shut). The 'unconcluding' word, which opens the gates for the wild birds to fly again."

Rubem A Alves, The Poet, The Warrior, The Prophet

photo by Sandy Long

MARY OLMSTED GREENE

"This paradox, and the clash between wilderness and our human fear, avoidance, manipulation and stark lack of compassion for it, has led me down a trail with more questions than answers. In order to sort out my own beliefs, I set out to ask other women about their specific experience, a set of conversations that became *Women Outside: Conversations about Nature, Art & Spirit*. Here, I explore how women use a relationship with nature to heal or create or feel connected to spirit, and how that relationship changes over time. I am interested in the correlation between inner experience and external landscape."

journey **BACK**

Tony Soprano, head of the Di Meo crime family in North Jersey, wades into his swimming pool in a bathrobe, waiting. His broad pocked face is a study of attention. He stares intently at the stand of bushes at the edge of the yard. Suddenly, a flock of ducks bursts through, running toward the pool. They make the water with a slap of wing and settle there, quacking contentedly in circles. Tony has bread for them. He gives them the bread and they eat.

In this pilot episode of *The Sopranos,* aired on HBO in January 1999, Tony has an anxiety attack that he later describes as "ginger ale in my skull," which leads to a loss of consciousness. Right before the attack he is grilling pork sausages for his son's thirteenth birthday celebration, humming happily, watching the pool and the ducks. The babies have been trying to fledge for days and suddenly they do, rising straight from the pool and arrowing over the trees. Tony clutches his chest. Tony falls.

As a result, Tony goes for psychiatric treatment. When the subject of the ducks comes up, he weeps. He tells his psychiatrist, the female Dr. Melfi, "It was a trip having those wild creatures coming into my pool and having their babies." He tells Melfi, "My life is out of balance."

There is a word for it in psychiatric terms, and although it is not Tony's diagnosis, it could have been. Today, ecotherapists treat people for Nature Deficit Disorder, people who become depressed and nonfunctional because they are deprived of and disconnected from nature. Books such as Richard Louv's *Last Child in the Woods: Saving our Children from Nature Deficit Disorder* are written about the effects of nature deprivation on children. This might be funny, were it not indicative of how close to the brink we are sailing. Just as Tony's ducks might be funny if they were not so poignant and powerful a metaphor for what we lack—those damned wild ducks, bringing us to ourselves and to collapse.

1962. Mourning doves, cooing and calling on a bright June morning. Dew all over the grass. I feel sturdy and connected to energy and earth in PF Flyers. Enough sleep zings my body like a drug, making every moment sharp-edged and perfect. I am out of the house and running through the back yards of New Jersey. The wooden suburban fences are like horses. There is no separation between fence, earth, tree, sky, me. I run in my body and my imagination at the same time.

That morning, as we do every summer morning of my long childhood, my sisters and I do chores as fast as possible so we can head to the beach with our mother in our big white station wagon. We drive along Ocean Avenue next to a cement-and-boulder sea wall that hides the beaches and the surf. In winter, ocean waves sometimes crash over the wall onto our car. But this is summer, and the air is already white with heat. We change into our suits in locker number 144, which smells of salt and sun and old towels. We cruise into our world. There is the hot sand near the jetties where we bury ourselves. There is the little boardwalk with its smell of frying burgers and juke box that we stuff with quarters, dancing to the Dixie Cups and the Everly Brothers. There is the secret dead dog that we walk half a mile down the beach to visit, day upon day, until the maggots leave nothing more than a sheet of leathery hide over thin rib bones. There are sharks' teeth and clams and razor shells. There is ocean tar and colonies of big creepy ants that land—and drown—on the surface of the waves. There are jellyfish and rip tides. There are sharks and bluefish and dog fish. One morning, there is a whale, huge and dead and stinking on the beach. We watch as Sea Bright Public Works cuts it into pieces and carts it away.

There is always the salt water, salt drying our skin to tightness in the afternoon. There is the painful, nose-clogging tumble to shore under a wave that catches us unaware. Every day we bob in the water looking seaward, judging the size and progression of waves, which come in sets of seven, or five. We ride them to shore with our bodies or on red and blue air-inflated rafts. On calm days we play in the shifty gray Atlantic like it is a lake, digging for sand crabs and making kingdoms with pails of wet sand. In the distance, on a clear day, Manhattan rises above Sandy Hook, piling like children's blocks over the blue.

On our rounds of daily bliss, we leave the beach at 4:00: just enough time to stop at Sickles Market where my mother buys tomatoes or green beans or fresh corn for supper. I step into the shadowy store like stepping into another world. Stepping over a border, from sunlight into shade, a nether world of big-handed farmers that I know nothing about, breathing the dusty bins of potatoes and peaches, ocean water still running out of my hair. At night, wild street games of kick the can or sardines, the neighborhood kids staying out until it is too dark to see. Then, sleep: safety in the soft whir of the fan and my sister in the bunk bed above me, our mother singing "Taps" from the doorway. Day after day. Night after night.

This is my early world: not without its heartache and struggle, but overlaid with a glimmering sense of rightness and connection, brought daily on the sun and wind, the rain and birds, the weeping willow growing ever taller in the back yard. During these years, on good days, I experience a connection so profound and elemental that I never really consider it. I certainly never try to verbalize it. I assume it is something everyone experiences, off and on. *Women Outside* came into being out of a desire to explore this elemental connection with life that I felt while out in nature as a child.

"Nothing gold can stay," writes Robert Frost, and when I turn thirteen, the good world fades and another world appears, a world of skin and nails and school and time and hurt. It suddenly matters what I wear. The phone becomes a lifeline instead of a mere convenience. My friends turn on me with a viciousness that I turn back on them, when it is their turn to be "out." My mother morphs from a loving being with food and comfort to an unreasonable jailer, harsh and critical and hopelessly out of touch. As we all do, I leave the chrysalis of childhood, passing through high school and then college as through a dense, dangerous, tangled maze. You could say I enter the dark wood and lose my way, forgetting the connection to earth and spirit that once was a birthright. Why this happens is hard to say: turbulent times, family dynamics, my own stubborn unwillingness to get out of my own way.

For a number of years, it is not the prettiest of journeys. Jobs, marriage, affairs, divorce, drugs, poverty: six years in Minneapolis, the extreme, land-bound climate of the midwest deepening my sense of alienation, followed by a scant decade in New York City—exhilarating, but stress-ridden and terrifying too.

During my first week in the city, in the fall of 1981, I am, you could say, a bit green. Within seven days, I am mugged in my vestibule; my bicycle is ripped off outside the Met and my purse stolen from a Greek restaurant. This wakes me up in a big hurry to the predator-prey relationship. My instincts honed to knife-edge, I walk down the block with every skin hair alert to my surroundings. A group of boys approach. I can smell their threat a hundred feet off. I cross the street. They call me a yuppie, a cunt, a racist. I don't care what they say. I know the truth in my bones.

I stand in Washington Square Park and watch kids break dancing, spinning on their shoulders on the asphalt, tumbling and moon walking and finessing the gainer. I notice the older Puerto Rican and Dominican men who sit on the street all night, playing dominos as though they are sitting near the ocean. It is as though urban dwellers develop another sense—a quickness or ability—a blind talent that compensates for the lack of nature and wilderness in their lives. A raw alchemy that begins inside and ends up externally, in body or wit or art. I think a lot of street life is about that.

In my years in the city I concoct an alter ego: a ratty adolescent, sort of like the tomboy called Anybodys from *West Side Story*, androgynous, boyish but maybe female, with a baseball cap on backwards. She's tough. You really cannot break her. She's free, unbounded by gravity. She flies up and down fire escapes and in and out of windows; she is dirty all the time from roof-jumping and zipping down alleys in the rain. She is my wild thing. She is my wild.

Weekends, I go to visit my friend downtown. I ride my bike too fast from the Upper West Side to her neighborhood in Tribeca. I speed dangerously through traffic as the city changes from its midtown self to its downtown self, becoming more cavernous and mysterious, older, less predictable and planned. Often, I am going faster than the cars. The buildings rise from semi-darkness into darkness and light the darkness. Shortcut alleys are twisty and dark. My senses sharpen and I see men pissing into walls, rats running in orderly columns along the walls. The air smells like garbage and cement, the press of bodies, the bottled rank air of the subway and the ailanthus trees that line every block. I arrive at my friend's house, arrogant and windswept. I push a buzzer, step with my bike into an elevator, ride up to the fifth floor and step into her loft, an urban cage of space and steel and sky where anything might happen. Around midnight, I reverse the process, cruising past drug deals and stumbling women and families out too late. Ordinary Manhattan dramas. The ratty teen comes forth, grabs the handlebars and flies.

———

In spite of the fascination the city held for me, living there wore me down. My life was spinning quietly out of control, leaking all its meaning and connection. Day after day, I'd wake up to grey grit and feel that my blood, my heart, was equally drawn and colorless. Finally, at thirty-two, feeling worn out and stunted as a gnarly old pine, several miraculous things happened. I gave birth to a daughter, Cassandra Rose. I moved to a spacious neighborhood in Brooklyn where tulips bloomed, and that fall (1986) the Mets won the World Series. I took my daughter in her little front pack to the Manhattan victory parade, and somehow among the throng, my life began to pulse again.

I followed those tulips and the sense of expanse they gave me, and in 1990, when Cassie was three, we moved from the city to Sullivan County, a rural, wild, impoverished corner of upstate New York. Here, where I still live, there is no ocean, but there are stands of old pines, and trails deep in the woods, and winters that howl. There are black bears and flocks of wild turkey. There is a lot of land for the coyotes to travel. They travel like swift ghosts, yipping long into the night. And, there is the Upper Delaware River. Swimming the river is good enough to hear it again: the voice of water, the rhythm of sun and night and star and storm and season. I am able to remember who I am.

———

In 1962, the naturalist and author Hal Borland wrote that "countrysides are common and within the reach of almost everyone, but wildernesses have become rare and usually are remote." But what is wilderness? What is the wild? The ongoing debate about the specific character of wilderness and how best to preserve it is an old argument with a vast canon of literature behind it, beginning (in this country at least) with Henry David Thoreau's *Walden Pond* and Emily Dickinson's sharp, poetic observations of the natural world and its human counterpart. Perhaps the modern bell began to toll with Rachel Carson's *Silent Spring*. Other writers from the '50s and '60s, such as Borland and Lorus and Margery Milne, made careful, eloquent and sometimes judgmental documentation of the earth and its creatures in relation to people, as though to illuminate and preserve the ordinary mystery of it all. Joining the canon are contemporary poets and wilderness writers such as Annie Dillard, Gary Snyder, Linda Hogan, Craig Childs, Terry Tempest Williams, Doug Peacock, Wendell Berry and many, many more: voices that are passionate, angry, fierce—yet full of mourning, longing and tenderness.

Today, wilderness is shrinking faster than ever; biodiversity wanes and the human population explodes. Climate changes, global warming and our obscenely huge "carbon footprint" alert us to the very real possibility that our planet may outlive us. And still, the argument continues at gale force. Jack Turner, in *The Abstract Wild*, laments the loss of true wilderness for a tamed substitute, what he calls "our preference for artifice, copy, simulation, and surrogate, for the engineered and the managed instead of the natural." He chastises us for our "increasing ignorance of what we have lost in sacrificing our several-million-year-old intimacy with the natural world." So, it's not only what we've lost, it's that we don't even know we have lost it.

Compare this with the gentler Michael Pollan, who, in his book *The Botany of Desire*, writes that "Nature is not only to be found 'out there;' it is also 'in here,' in the apple and the potato, in the garden and in the kitchen, even in the brain of a [person] beholding the beauty of a tulip or inhaling smoke from a burning cannabis flower." He wagers that "when we can find nature in these sorts of places as readily as we now find it in the wild, we'll have traveled a considerable distance toward understanding our place in the world in the fullness of its complexity and ambiguity." He admits, though, in a similar vein to Turner, that "even the wild now depends on civilization for its survival."

This paradox, and the clash between wilderness and our human fear, avoidance, manipulation and stark lack of compassion for it, has led me down a trail with more questions than answers. In order to sort out my own beliefs, I set out to ask other women about their specific experience, a set of conversations that became *Women Outside: Conversations about Nature, Art & Spirit*. Here, I explore how women use a relationship with nature to heal or create or feel connected to spirit, and how that relationship changes over time. I am interested in the correlation between inner experience and external landscape. Special mention goes to *The Wild Within* by Paul Rezendes, wherein the author tracks a passage through wilderness with a twin passage through his own psyche. Rezendes writes that his book is "filled with adventures in nature that have illuminated my inward journey—adventures that have taught me about fear, life and death, aggression, compassion, direct communication, silence, the true nature of intelligence, and love." Oh. So it *can* be like that.

  The questions that are asked in this book took their framework from the first interview I conducted, with artist-and-activist pair Krista Gromalski and Sandy Long. I had the rather ambitious idea that the interviews would be conducted out-of-doors, lakeside or maybe on cross country skis. It was winter when I met with Krista and Sandy, and I packed my skis and backpack, along with my tape recorder, in anticipation of our visit. It was cold outside and it seemed like a wise idea to begin with a cup of tea beside their wood-burning stove. The tea morphed into wine, which morphed into small glasses of absinthe, and as the afternoon staggered toward evening the interview had lost its careful thread and became a sort of wild thing itself, unbounded and off the page (but caught on tape). We began quite spontaneously to talk about wilderness in relation to religion, to art and the eye of perception. The question of evil came up with regard to the harsh rules of the wild, and to human perceptions of God and nature. This conversation, which was better than anything I could have crafted out of a carefully devised set of questions and answers, set the tone for the issues explored in this book.

  Thus, I kept on asking women: what is nature? What is wilderness? How does it connect with evil, with spirit, with art, with the human condition? How do we as individuals find connection with nature and the wilderness experience? We engaged in conversations that often did take place outside, by a stream or a ridge top, or along a meandering forest trail. For some, connection with nature (and self) means climbing a mountain and traversing dangerously along its edge. For others, it means sitting in stillness by a pond. For some, activism is a prescription for love, a necessary way to sustain beauty and keep hope alive. For others, hope and beauty are found in the minutia of a meadow or a snowstorm. Inevitably, the conversations turn to the nature of God and spirituality. The two subjects (wilderness and spirituality) seem intrinsically linked. The question of evil—whether and in what form it exists—stuck as one of the themes we explored.

I have included poetry throughout the book to deepen and punctuate the ideas and questions raised. Originally, I had intended to create a small manuscript of poetry based on the interviews to be included as a subset of the book. However, having multiple poetic voices seemed a better, more interesting and more workable choice. Thus, we have my poetry, as well as that of Lori Anderson Moseman, who wrote the afterword and published *Women Outside*, and of contributors Kristin Barron, Druis Beasley, Dorothy Hartz, Elizabeth Kaminski, Sandy Long, Karen MacIntyre and Eileen Pagan.

I began researching and writing this book in 2000—soon after Tony Soprano had his adventure with the ducks. When 9/11 happened, I stopped cold for three years. I don't know why this was so, but I know that other people underwent similar affects and frozen states. The phenomenon of 9/11—the visual horror of the towers afire, crumbling into a cloud of dust that spread all over Manhattan like a nuclear wave, of the sudden thousands of deaths, people calling on cell phones and disappearing forever, burning up or jumping from the towers, the grime and exhaustion in the faces of survivors climbing over the Brooklyn Bridge to home, and all that took place (still taking place) in Afghanistan and ultimately Iraq in the aftermath of 9/11 was itself the ultimate raw, wild, fearsome, uncontrollable edge. It was somehow very hard to process, to carry on in any significant way, as though an invisible depressive blanket had fallen upon me and upon many others. I was finally able to resume the project in 2004, led on by the strength of the voices within these pages and my belief in what they have to say.

These are ordinary women. They are the women you pass in the grocery store. They are the hard working artists and activists at the grass roots level. They are the ministers in your churches and parishes. They are teaching your kids and nursing your elderly. They are hardy, forthright souls, trying their best to live at a sustainable level. And they are sneaking off whenever they can to grab a bit of the wild.

I hope they will bring it here, to you, within these pages.

Mahls Pond Road

Mary Olmsted Greene

Its curves lead me toward the shadowy shape
of the water. I pull the car into the trees.
Walk to the causeway where the pond spills
into the brook below. I sit a long time as night

becomes deeper—sit alone in a wild place
where Old Milwaukee cans and tangled lures
rust in the weeds. I lift my arms in a slow
arcing prayer, memory an ache with sharp

wings. Here in the wetlands—summer sweet
as it ever, ever was, where dogs bark some
place far off, where peepers fill the night with desire,
where the old camp house leans on its struts—

I and the wild woman I am attend with love
the mystery that overcomes this world.

earth's DAUGHTERS

KRISTIN BARRON grew up in the French Woods section of the town of Hancock in Delaware County, New York, where she currently resides with her husband, John Ogozalek and their two children. She graduated from SUNY Cortland with a BA in English and is also a licensed practical nurse. She has been a member of the Upper Delaware Writers Collective since 1996. Her poems have appeared in *The River Reporter* newspaper and other small press publications, and she writes a column for *The River Reporter*, "Root Cellar," about life in the Upper Delaware Valley region. Swamps are her favorite wild places.

EILEEN PAGAN was born in 1926 to progeny of North European immigrants in the Silk City of Paterson, New Jersey. She attended public schools in New Jersey, married and raised a family in Long Island, and later received an MA in writing from Goddard College in Vermont. Penning letters, journals, poems and newspaper reporting became essential early in her life and continued into her later years when, she said, "the challenges of story telling—in all forms—remain mysterious and satisfying." Eileen Pagan died on July 18, 2008. She was 81. Her favorite wild place, according to her daughter, Elinor Holland, is "the far field."

KRISTA GROMALSKI is a writer based in Pike and Schuylkill counties, in Pennsylvania. She occasionally paints and photographs. Krista has worked at the grassroots level in support of conservation-minded community planning, land protection and a balanced approach to development. She is a board member of the Delaware Highlands Conservancy. In 2006 she co-founded Heron's Eye Communications with Sandy Long. Heron's Eye has collaborated with community groups and creative professionals to create the *Shop Local, Save Land* guides to regional farm markets and forest resources. Krista's favorite place in the wild is the interior landscape.

SANDY LONG is a poet, writer and photographer who examines her world with pen and lens and is endlessly intrigued with what she finds. Sandy has developed a personal vision influenced by her environmental interests and interaction with the natural world. She currently writes for *The River Reporter* newspaper. Sandy's favorite wild place remains undisclosed in hopes of protecting its wildness. It is a place where golden light threads hemlock boughs, dances across the surface of a small stream and cascades over boulders studded with lichen and moss. It is usually silent enough to hear a thrush singing.

earth's **DAUGHTERS**

We are all of us connected with earth, every day—it is what sustains our lives. But many of us are not so keenly aware of how we are held up, fed and supported by the bounties of the planet. The women in this section, by contrast, have shaped their lives around considering the landscape, caretaking the fields and the wetlands and closely observing the movement and music of the earth. There are several pathways into this knowledge: it is acquired gradually, in middle and later years, or it is born of childhood experience, so deep at times as to be almost mute.

From Earth's Daughters, we hear of family histories that evolve into a landscape of Christian mythology and barn kittens, of country front yards left unmowed and populated by snakes. Or of a childhood raised in Patterson, New Jersey apartment buildings where gardening meant two kids planting petunias. Or even of a childhood largely unremembered. How do the deeper parts of childhood shape us? How do we travel along earth's pathways to become productive, passionate citizens of the world—to become ourselves?

It is both a romantic and highly pragmatic task to care so deeply for the earth, and the voices here reflect that. We come to ponder: how does one find silence within in a world of crashing noise? Why does fear overtake us when we are stripped of our comfort levels and are in a truly wild zone? How is the landscape changing as farms disappear? Does nature partake in cruelty and deceit? How can we describe the beauty of a patch of sparkling snow? These and many other explorations evolved during my conversations with these women, who all harbor a sense of devotion and responsibility for the earth.

Their journeys, and the meditations of poetry that follow, might instruct and inspire our own passion for the planet and our responsibility to become mindful caretakers of its fate.

photo by John Ogozalik

KRISTIN BARRON

"It's not so much now, but then, when people came, they'd comment on certain dates when they saw things, like bluebirds migrating and the weather. My uncle, say, would bring home a stick insect that he found in the woods logging. He had it in a coffee can in the refrigerator. They brought stuff home, the wood lilies, just to show us because they were pretty. They were good. Good at what they did. My parents didn't keep a lawn. They didn't mow the lawn. Occasionally my mother would complain about too many snakes and my father would take the tractor to it—maybe once a summer. Other people would cut their lawns, but my parents—they were unusual. My father was, like, back to nature before there was back to nature."

KRISTIN BARRON

Kristin Barron is a tall woman with long dark hair and large bones. She moves with the ambling grace of someone more at home in woods and swamps than in offices or meeting halls. She has an ethereal quality that is hard to pin down; inarticulate at times, she knows things most of us do not, and can speak freely on any matter of the natural world.

Kristin, the youngest of four, was born in Hancock, New York in February, 1966. She was raised on her mother's ancestral farm in the French Woods section of Hancock in rural Delaware County. Kristin married a high school history teacher and began raising her own two children within short walking distance of the farm where she grew up. She took care of her ailing mother until her mother's death in 2006—after her mother died, Kristin learned the little-talked-about piece of family history that her mother, who was Rh negative, had five pregnancies that resulted in still births or miscarriages. (Kristin was aware of three of them.) One baby, now buried in Brooklyn, lived a week. The children were all named, and three of the graves are on the land that she and her sisters now own.

At the time of our interview, Kristin's mother was still living; afterward, she and her sisters faced the difficult decision of what to do with the property. The old dairy barn had to be burned; it was a hazard for trespassers or youngsters who might find its tipping hay loft a tempting climb. And what to do with the rest of the swampy, hilly patch that, without the dairy farm and community life it used to harbor, has grown back into wilderness? Kristin is considering placing a portion of it into land trust.

Many days of the week, you will find Kristin at the houses of neighbors in need, or doing their grocery shopping, or taking them to a doctor's visit, or dropping off a clean load of laundry. Her kids already reflect the intellectual climate and old-world sense of belonging and obligation that their parents exhibit—and maybe, at times, the wild streak in their mother.

Kristin's poems come slowly. They are short, even terse; like the hard landscape where she lives, nothing is wasted. But when she reads them in her soft voice, the world grows a bit in both clarity and mystery. This wonderful, taciturn, at times funny, at times fragile woman has become a leader within her family, hosting the family gatherings necessary when her mother died and, before that, when her sister died of cancer. She may not always be able to put into words what she is thinking, but you can be sure she is thinking. Her intelligence is a sharp lamp lighting any path she's on, and illuminating the lives of those fortunate enough to grow close to her. I count myself among those lucky few.

WHAT REMAINS:
Interview with Kristin Barron

Swope Road and Nearing Road, French Woods, Hancock, New York
October

Tell me about this road we are walking on.

Where we are walking is where I grew up—in French Woods. We can walk past the old farm house where I grew up. Originally, when my mother's family came here, they build a log cabin up in the corner of the property. Then they built the house down where I grew up, which in its day was thought to be kind of modern—the spring brought water down and they had it run in the house.

My father, Robert Barron, was from Brooklyn—Flatbush. In the '30s, they had the communist union, and he was very interested in that. He was also very "back to nature." He wanted to be a farmer. That's what he wanted to do. He met my mother, Catherine Ann Dirig, after the war. They were both in the army. My mother was an army nurse.

My father's car broke down somewhere around here and her brothers hauled it up to her house to fix it. That's how they met, even though they'd been on the same ship, and he'd been in a hospital branch where she worked. They missed each other all through that. So—anyway, they moved here. That's what he wanted to do. I think my mother would have been better off in the city. She grew up here through the Depression. There were eight kids. Her father died when she was 13. It was not easy.

My father's father also died when he was 13, but they had a little more money. And, they lived in the city. My father did all that kind of Boy Scout, natural history stuff. There was a *New York Times* article that we had for a while— I don't think we do anymore— about how he found a black widow spider in Brooklyn, or it may have been Staten Island.

My parents shipped milk, originally. They had a dairy farm. In the '50s there was a pretty bad drought locally and everybody sold out, just about. In the '70s, when I was in kindergarten, he started getting Holstein calves again.

My mother really wasn't interested in farming. She and my father were, in many ways, at odds. They both were Rh negative and she had a lot of trouble having children. She had some stillborns and one baby that lived a week. At the time, they didn't have Rogaine. Transfusions were how they dealt with it then. She had to go to Brooklyn to have all her baby care.

How many children were in your family, then?

Four of us who lived. I'm the youngest. When I was born my older sister was eighteen. My mother was forty-seven. That's quite a thought, isn't it? She had had it, by then.

Did your mother ever hold a job outside the home?

She did a lot of kinds of nursing. She was a "scrub" operating nurse in the hospital that used to be in Callicoon.

My father retired from Bendix when I was in fourth grade. Then he put full time into farming. It was rough because he got asthma. First he had this whole prostate problem which set off all the rest of it, seems like, to me. He got sick.

The neighborhood had to come and do all our haying, one year, which was very exciting. But my parents weren't really community-minded people. You were very frugal, just stayed in your place. It was almost taboo to have friends over. It was a real strange dynamic, there. We were very family oriented. Cousins could come, but friends? They were suspicious. It was a weird thing.

Do you find that continuing as you are grown and have your own household?

I love having people over. So does my mother, actually. This came from my dad. Anyway, it was very isolated. I had my cousin Matthew, who was a year older than me. He lived across the road from where I live now. His father's still up there, my mother's brother, who was a logger.

As I said, my father was very interested in insects, in natural history, environmental causes. It's not so much now, but then, when people came, they'd comment on certain dates when they saw things, like bluebirds migrating and the weather. My uncle, say, would bring home a stick insect that he found in the woods logging. He had it in a coffee can in the refrigerator. They brought stuff home, the wood lilies, just to show us because they were pretty. They were good. Good at what they did.

My parents didn't keep a lawn. They didn't mow the lawn. Occasionally my mother would complain about too many snakes and my father would take the tractor to it—maybe once a summer. Other people would cut their lawns, but my parents—they were unusual. My father was, like, back to nature before there was back to nature.

What are your first memories of being in nature?

First memories. Wildflowers come to mind. It was a big thing, every year, to go and look for them. Little tiny yellow violets, I don't know what the proper name was for them. We called them little yellow roosters. May apples. Orchids.

Another memory is of a live fish (a trout, I think, rather large) that someone had caught on a Thanksgiving Day and had brought to our house. It was in a kind of plastic wash basin on a chair in the kitchen. It was glistening and beautiful but frightening because it thrashed around a lot. It was frantic and didn't have enough water. It also had a healed scar where someone or something had hooked or hurt it. I don't know what happened to it but it was the most interesting thing, probably, to happen that day.

I remember my father telling me about a time when I was a little kid and I went up in the field and got a blackbird's nest. Up in the swamp area. It was covered with lice. And I brought it home. I was happy: I had this nest, and it was just crawling!
I don't remember that, really. It's very vague. But he used to tell me about that.

What year did your father die?

1992. I had just come back to this area.

From where?

Upstate—Cortland, where I went to school. The farmhouse where we lived was damaged in a chimney fire in 1986. Then they moved into the double-wide trailer, where my mother still lives.

My cousin Robert (I call him Bobby) was very active in 4-H; he did all the natural history projects, very advanced insect projects. Bobby was very influential. We would go all summer, just take walks all over the swamp down there. We spent a lot of time in the swamp. There was another swamp behind it, and another swamp behind that. We'd walk through along the edge.

We took the canoe down there a couple of summers ago. But now there is a golf course. It's definitely affected the swamp.

Anyway, Bobby was always around. We'd walk all over the place and stop and collect stuff. My cousin was very interested in lichens, too. We also belonged to 4-H and would exhibit our collections at the fair.

What is Robert doing now?

He works for Cornell, in the herbarium. He lives in Ithaca. He's writing a butterfly book. He's currently traveling up and down the coast to different areas to take photographs.

What did you study in college?

English. I liked writing.

I was really out of it in high school. I could have done tremendously better. I was just a mess. I didn't have any social skills whatsoever. I just turned off. I did not talk to people. It was quite strange to go through the day not talking to anyone. I just was very—outside. But I took my ballet lessons. I read fairy tales. I did my insect collections.

Now, you think, well—you don't really want to kill it [for the collection]. Ethel acetate and cyanide killing jars!

In college I really had to learn how to talk to people.

Do you recall feeling a greater affinity for the out-of-doors than you did with other people?

Yes! I have often felt at odds with the "larger community." At times I am proud of this and other times I just want to belong. I think I'm capable of great ambivalence. When I was growing up I always felt more comfortable out-of-doors (or alone) than with other people. I often feel I am traveling my many circles, taking in "the watch fires of my thousand circling camps," as the song says. Perhaps at the end of the day I can take what is good in each. And in the end we are all one.

How many acres do you own back here?

Almost two hundred. I feel very vulnerable with the old farmhouse. People come hunting without permission.

How does it feel to raise your kids on the same stretch of land you grew up on? What do you hope to give to them?

Well, it's very, very different from what it was. It's wild. You can't walk through things anymore. They've never been up to see the old foundations because you can't get through. It's too overgrown. It's much, much wilder.

When I was growing up I know there were coyotes. But we never saw them or heard them. Now, they howl at night. It's much wilder. I don't see my kids as much just running out and running all over it like I did. I'm more fearful, I guess. I hate to say that. I hate that attitude. But the kids are also just very young right now. I used to just take off all over. And even when I went away to college I'd just, by myself, walk all over. It was pretty dangerous, sometimes. My farm, and a lot of the farms, are more wild. There is only one dairy farm in our town.

Down from how many? Fifty?

Yes. There are some other farms, but they are not shipping milk.
My sister and my cousin are kind of anti-farm. They like to see things growing up. They want it to go back. It's their philosophy. They don't want it clipped. We have a farmer come take the hay from the field across from our house, which is building the field back up. My sister doesn't want him to come before certain dates, when we can get meadow larks to nest. Beaver dams! When we were young, when my cousin saw a beaver dam, he'd break it up. He didn't want the beavers building on it. They dammed it but he thought they shouldn't have dammed it. They should have just left it.

Do you agree with that?

No—I'm not that radical. But there is a lot of development going on around here.

Are there two contradictory things going on, with development and also re-wilding?

Yes. We consider putting our acres into a land trust, because it is going to become much more built up here. You need to preserve something of it. Notes come on our old farmhouse all the time, people from Manhattan who write, "If you are thinking of selling this, please call me."

Around here, there is still a very "us and them" attitude between local people and "outsiders" from the city or wherever. I don't really prescribe to that. I don't think that way. But when I was a little kid I knew about "us" and "them." It's always been that way.

How else do you see the changes?

There were many, many more hunters when I was young. Now, it's really diminished.

Your son Sam is seven. Does he share your interests?

Yes.

What about Lil, who is three? Do you see the same spark in her?

I do, although right now she's afraid of bears, and rattlesnakes. Which is probably good. She's more finicky about things.

How do you show them the natural world?

Just walking around. What you see. The natural changes of the year.

What about the snail you brought inside?

Ah, yes, the snail. I loved the snail. My only pet. We kept the snail just to watch it, I guess, look at it. It seemed happy, and thriving. It ate lettuce. The kids liked it. A few times it tried to escape. I returned it in the fall.
Farm people have a very different relationship and attitude toward the animals than people who just have pets. It's very different. Less sentimental. Farmers are not bad to animals but if they die, well, they die.
We had a dog. We had kittens a lot, barn cats. I remember raccoons eating my kittens. We had all kinds of caterpillars. I remember cecropia moths.

Do you expect that your children will stay in this area when they are grown?

Probably not.

If not, what do you hope they will get from growing up here?

It's a beautiful, wild place. A relationship with nature—knowing things come from an essence.

What kind of writing do you do?

Poetry.

Did you keep journals when you were growing up?

I did. My cousin and I had a story club. We were entrenched in red, blue and white ribbons from the fair. So we'd make our ribbons and award our stories.

How old were you?

Junior high. I remember reading *An American Tragedy*, by Theodore Dreiser, about the guy who drowns the girlfriend in the Adirondacks. I named kittens after the characters—Clyde, and Roberta and Sondra.

Did you write poetry when you were at Cortland?

Yes. I ran the literary magazine. I was the editor.

Was college a different experience for you than high school?

In many ways, yes.

The curse of high school didn't follow you up there?

It did. I had a hard time too, after a while. I had a breakdown, more or less.

Did you come home for that?

No. My parents never knew.

Did you have to get on medication?

Yes. I never took it because I drank. I got really crazy. I was more desperate than crazy.

You were living right on the edge?

Oh, yeah. I tried all the usual things.

Drugs?

Yes.

Sex?

Yes.

How did you work yourself out of it?

I came back here. I got a job.

Did you finish your degree?

Yes. I took Master's classes up there for a while. I could do that.

So you have a BA in English Lit?

Yes. Then I came back here and got a job at a newspaper.

Your poetry has a naturalist perspective. When you are writing, how does the nature perspective come about?

It's there. I don't know. I start with a pretty strong image and it builds around that. I don't seem to be able to write about an idea.

Your sister died of cancer last year. She was quite young when she died, just about to begin enjoying her retirement when she got sick. Does her death make any sense to you in terms of fulfilling or following a natural cycle or season, as we see in nature?

We thought she was going to get better. And then it became apparent that she wouldn't. There came a point where it was better for her to be dead. She wasn't getting better, she wasn't well.

It hurt, a lot. And that's how it is for everywhere, not necessarily with that level of pain. I'm constantly telling Lil, well, everything dies, eventually. Every living thing will die, and they go back, you know. It's a cycle.

Does her death feel unfair?

Yeah, there's some of that. It makes me question, a little. She had a Catholic service. She was very religious, in the traditional sense. But she was a reasonable person. We grew up in a strict Catholic, but also somewhat religiously eccentric, family. I have (and had) many priest and nun relatives. (This has not been carried on in my generation, however.) While I still attend church I don't think of myself as dogmatic at all. I especially despise Catholicism's stance on homosexuality. It can be very insulting to sit there sometimes. But I still get something from it I can't exactly explain. I like the prayers. I need something from it. Sometimes I think I don't know how long this can go on. It drives me crazy so when they burn me at the stake I'll send an invitation.

Do you believe in God?

Yes. One of my earliest ideas of God was of a fireman. I think I got it from a Little Golden Book about firemen in which the bald, fat fire chief is standing on the top floor of the firehouse with his hands spread out in a sort of "giving" gesture. I used to like to draw copies of nativity paintings—especially "Flight into Egypt" by Giotto. Incidentally, we used to play "Flight into Egypt" as a game as kids. My pictures always had two stick figure hands in the sky at the top of the page, like in "The Baptims of Christ" by Andrea Del Verrocchio and Leonardo Da Vinci, or "Virgin Adoring the Child" by Fra Filippo Lippi.

But I think I had a much more diffuse, cross-cultural idea of God even as a small child. My father seemed to have had some interest in Hinduism and he talked about it. He was a character—a bit of a clothes horse of ideas. I like to think "God is love." A connecting spirit of goodness. And often just leave it at that.

Do you believe in a force of evil in nature?

I don't believe that nature does evil things. No floods, Tsunami or hell to rip our children from our arms for our sins. I hate that. How we respond to such events is the important thing. Where God is found, in humility.

Would you say living this close to this particular piece of land has taught you anything, has created an element in you that wouldn't be there otherwise?

Yes. I do. I have some misgivings, here and there. But I love this area. I love the people. I think about moving sometimes—what that would be like. I think I'd be afraid. I don't like to drive in cities. Everything is there in the city, too; you just have to find it. It's a different habitat. It is rooted for me, here. My mother's family has been here since the French Woods settlement started. But, it's all changed. I don't have anybody who can baby sit my kids. People who have these families—you think they are all able to help. But it's not like that for me, at all.

Do you still feel isolated here?

Somewhat. Yes. What my husband likes about it here is that the people are individuals. There is a certain kind of independence that people have. And, it is beautiful, and it is safe.

Do you ever feel restless here?

Yes. I do. I'll go back to work at some point.

You're a trained nurse?

Yes. I like the idea of home health in a rural area—of going out and taking care of people. My mother was a traveling nurse—she walked around Brooklyn. I've always liked that idea.

With regard to your writing, do you have ambitions to have a collection someday?

Yeah. I think so. It'll be a while.

Your poems are often very short. Is that just a lack of time or do you think that is your natural voice?

My poems are very often very short. I think that's just my voice—what I have to say.

You've been compared to Emily Dickenson now and then. Do you agree?

Yes, I kind of like it.

photo by Mary Olmsted Greene

EILEEN PAGAN

"I used to use the word 'healing' a lot. I draw back from it now. I don't quite know what it means. It's become one of the funny words. I'm in transition about it, I don't know. 'Spiritual,' sure. There is the wonderful cosmic connection I feel when I stand out there, when I go to the waterfall and listen to the water. And that line of larch trees, over there—there are two or three days in October when they turn marvelous colors, purple and green and gold. I find the colors of the larch trees on those special days as difficult to describe as the rainbow. I am still trying to write about the rainbow."

EILEEN PAGAN

When we conducted our interview, I had known Eileen Pagan for about ten years. She found her way into my writers group and became the senior member, impressing us with her calm, measured, wise-woman ways.

Eileen was born in 1926 in Paterson, New Jersey. Her parents were left-wing urbanites with Communist leanings, as was not uncommon among some Jewish and Eastern European populations around New York City during the Roaring Twenties and the Depression era.

At the time of our interview, Eileen lived in a small log cabin on forty acres that she inherited through an unlikely set of circumstances. She came to the area from the suburbs and immediately set about learning how to grow a garden, bring in wood for a wood-burning stove and hike over all the lakesides, brambly banks, forests and open fields of her land. When we spoke, she was nearly eighty and embarking on a "sabbatical" from her active life of poetry workshops and other pursuits to do some reading and questioning into matters of economics and politics. Eileen had held liberal beliefs all her life, but she'd begun to wonder if they were correct after all. I don't know what conclusions she drew; she'd promised to tell me when her thinking ripened, and when the time was right, but unfortunately, time ran out. Eileen Pagan died of lung cancer in 2008.

Although Eileen always took the gift of her life on faith, she never once stopped questioning how best to live. I, and others, often felt as though we were children seated about her proverbial knee, waiting to see what she said and did next. She was true blue, a person of deep, unflinching honesty and integrity. She was a fine writer, an expressive thinker and a pearl of a person. Her gifts live on.

A HOME AT THE END OF THE ROAD:
Interview with Eileen Pagan

Sackett Lake Road, Forestburgh, New York
February

I expect the reason you thought of me in the context of your book is simply because I live here in this cabin.

Yes. I see you as rooted here. Your every day reality is interacting with your land, with your house.

It makes me think of sitting out on the porch, four years ago, when my neighbor came to live there. We were just getting acquainted, asking each other questions about our lives, and he said, "Do you think you'll ever move away from here?" It startled me! I said, "No! I couldn't exist anywhere else, I said, looking out at the pond..." Wow, is that true? That's true!

I would have a hard time not being able to get up in the morning and check the trees, check the color of the sky. I love to look up the road; I love when people come down it, they come down that curving road, you know. That's all part of it.

How did you come to own these forty acres?

It was a gift from a man named Tony. The story goes this way.

Katie—my lesbian lover—and I came in 1978 and rented the cabin. A lady owned the whole of the one hundred and twenty acres—Eva was her name. She grew up around here. She showed us a picture of herself as a young woman holding up two long rattlesnakes with a shotgun in her other hand. She killed a snake down here.

About the snakes, I say, "Let them go; they're happy here." Minding their own business. I don't see any intersection between those snakes and me that are going to cause either of us any harm. The bear—when she has her three babies—that's another story. Some years I don't see bears at all. But if I do, I stay in the house when they are out there. The last bear I saw was in August, walking through eating the blueberries.

So, anyway, Eva died and left all the property to Tony. Tony was her companion. No sex, so I guess we say companion. He'd tell us, "I agreed to no sex." He was a character. Where do you find a man like that?

He agreed to sell the land to three of us. There are three people, and I'm one of them, who bought portions of the one hundred twenty acres from Tony. I had a mortgage; I made mortgage payments every month. Along the way, he had a will drawn up, and made it so that when he died, the mortgage would be released. He died! I never expected it. We loved him; we all loved him. Anyway, this land became mine.

Going back to your childhood, what was your relationship with nature? How did that manifest in Paterson when you were growing up?

During my childhood we lived in various places in Paterson, little houses, and then into flats—you'd call them apartments—but they were in a house, on a floor of a house. There was always a yard with flowers.

I remember as a kid, being nine or ten, with Georgina. We planted petunia seeds, and we went around to houses actually selling bunches of the petunias. God, we were thrilled with some pennies, probably. But nobody in my family ever had a garden. I really was not involved—it was just those petunias.

Georgina was a good friend, my buddy. We learned to stand on our heads together. It took us all summer and we were so thrilled when we succeeded. The two of us just kept at it, holding each other's feet up.

She didn't finish high school. She got married and I lost track of her. I don't know what happened to her. But there was no one in the family who gardened, and I didn't have that kind of model in front of me. I didn't do any of that until I came here. This was all new to me, to have a garden and get my hands into the dirt.

Can you think back to those first few summers when you were experimenting and learning how to garden?

I got right into it. I loved it. That garden out there, cultivated over the years with the various flowers. I was talking with somebody at the library the other day. She was burning off some part of the asparagus patch. She was telling me that the little red bugs come on, and you have to burn them off. I said I had asparagus. It used to come up every year for about three or four years. I never had any little red bugs and I never heard of burning it off. I never used to cut it down or anything, I just let it flop, and in the spring it would come up again and it was wonderful and healthy.

After three or four years I just dug it all up. "Dug it all up!" she said. "Asparagus? You wanted to get rid of asparagus?" I said, "Yah, because I have limited space, and I wanted to put something else in there."

I used to do that. My neighbor gave me Norwegian primroses. A beautiful yellow color, intense; I want to say buttery. They were beautiful. They came up every year. After three years I wanted to plant something else. I forget. Maybe iris. That was part of the thrill, planning, and changing the designs of the colors of the flowers.

The first third of my life was in Paterson, New Jersey. The second third was in Levittown, Pennsylvania, in the suburbs, raising three children. The last third is here. The only thing I ever planted until this last third were those petunias. And every year, when I lived in Pennsylvania, I would plant morning glories somewhere by the house, so I could look out the window and see those beautiful flowers.

That garden out there was all trees and rocks and broken beer bottles. Before me, hunters used to come here, and rent this cabin. I had to dig all that up. It took three or four years to get rid of all the broken glass.

There was a big pine tree there. I cut it down, sawed it down, dug up the roots, and it was all an adventure. I was only working part time so I had the time to do it.

What does wilderness mean to you?

One of the qualities that defines wilderness for me is that sense of quietness, being with water, trees, rocks and sky, and knowing that there are living creatures of all the various sorts that are out there. The foxes, for instance, which I rarely see. I do see the little chipmunks, and snakes, and raccoons, and groundhogs, and all the millions of little creatures in the water in the summertime. Those beautiful flying neon—what are they called? Darning needles? Down by the waterfall they are magnificent.

That's all part of wilderness to me. Sitting on the rock by the waterfall, the cool rock and the dragonflies flying around and a million little creatures in the water, God knows how many more underneath that we don't see.

There is a quietness that comes with my sense of wilderness, but it's full of life. They're not talking like we do, and shooting guns and all the rest of that. But they are cruel. There's a lot of cruelty, murder, rape going on. Out on that pond? Every summer? Do you know what goes on? Oh . . .

When you say cruelty, are you assigning intent?

Yes. A couple of winters ago, in February, in the middle of the night, I heard, out on the pond, this terrible shrieking and howling and screeching. Boy! I knew from the sound of it that something pretty nasty was going on. With clear intention! And the next day, the bones of the deer was all that was left.

Those coyotes, barking and screeching—what was that about? Was it clearly about food?—which is one reason creatures kill each other. (We're creatures.) I think, you know, there is something about a mob mentality that takes over. I think the coyotes kind of enjoyed it—God! The snow was all covered with blood and the deer's hair.

Of course, I stood out here screaming and yelling at that same deer because he was eating my morning glories off the fence.

Well, is that about wilderness? I mean, I think of wilderness as being up in Alaska, you know, some vast expanse of quiet— it's the thing that creatures don't talk—

They don't analyze, and judge—

Well, but they do, no, they do. All the time. They've got to figure out how to survive. They're figuring stuff out all the time. Who to eat next, and how they can make their way, but it's quiet. It's quiet, it's not like us.

Does something happen within you when you put yourself in a wilderness setting?

I feel like I'm at home—I'm where I should be.

What about loneliness, living out here alone?

No. People say that, but I don't have enough time every day to think about and do all the things I'd like to do. I'm not conscious of being lonely.

I have these books, right? If I get lonely, I pull down a book of Virginia Wolfe's letters, say, and I'm gone! Or my history book, my favorite little *History of Western Civilization*.

Here, I just made another little friend, *The Road to Serfdom*. A woman, Kathleen King, did the drawing on the title page. Look! Chains! She designed this, and look what's on the spine! A whole row of chains.

This is the original publication, published in July 1944. The author, F.A. Hayek—he's an economist. He's expressing the opinion that the socialists have an illusion about what can really happen, and the real effects of that form of government. Last week, I got out a book by Sigmund Freud in which he says exactly the same thing, using the word "illusion." I'll spend the evening, until my eyes get tired, and it's exciting. It satisfies my soul.

I like people too, though. I just spent two weeks with my grandchildren. One is a senior in high school and the other is graduating eighth grade. It reminded me of back in the '50s, driving them to this lesson and back, the Scout meetings and all. Adam takes tuba lessons. Well, the tuba's a big thing, so I have to drive the tuba to school and pick it up the next day. He had four basketball games that I attended and cheered.

So I was back and forth, meeting all these young parents. I helped with food at the dance on Friday night. I met so many new people, which I love doing. I found myself saying to someone, I feel like a hermit up there! In the Catskills, all by myself, in a cabin in the woods. I love both. I do love being alone and being able to do this kind of reading and thinking by myself. I couldn't live without that.

You define your life in three stages. You did have a very active life, very social, raising the kids.

Oh, absolutely.

It's not that you are in retreat from that?

Oh, no.

Do you walk your property a lot?

I used to, a lot.

How many acres do you have?

Forty-seven. They're interesting, because there are swamps. We are on a migratory route, so we get a lot of birds. I regret not walking as much, but that has to do with age, and my body. I wish that were not true.

I really long and dream about having some companion. I've even thought of hiring a young person to come and walk with me. I've tried to work it out at different times, with different friends. At the time it seemed like they had some extra time and they would be interested in walking. But, things came up and they got too busy and that's how life goes.

I used to spend a lot of time walking by myself. I can't do it anymore. I don't feel agile enough. If I trip and fall, I could break my hip and not be able to get back. I hate that! The most I do is walk out to the waterfall, and I go to the other side of the pond. But, I'm doing it less and less.

From the days when you did walk, does an adventure come to mind that you could share?

Years ago, when I first came here, I lived with a woman in this cabin, and the two of us would go with the "old woman" (as I referred to her) who owned the land. (Now I'm the old lady who owns the cabin.)

She owned 120 acres. We'd go with her every fall. It took us two days. We'd pack lunch and do the whole perimeter, putting up the new "No Trespassing" and "No Hunting" signs.

That always was lovely, to be able to see all the different shapes, the rocks and the different water formations. God! That was so much fun. We'd sit on big rocks and eat our lunch.

Those first five years, we'd go in the woods and saw up fallen trees with chain saws into logs. I used to fill the shed out there. If we had that filled, that was enough for the winter.

I don't have the wood stove anymore. It got to be too much, and it's dusty. I have emphysema.

Were you a smoker?

Forty-five years, morning 'til night. I loved it!

Would you categorize your walks in nature and your relationship with your pond as healing in any way, or as spiritual?

I used to use the word "healing" a lot. I draw back from it now. I don't quite know what it means. It's become one of the funny words. I'm in transition about it, I don't know.

"Spiritual," sure. There is the wonderful cosmic connection I feel when I stand out there, when I go to the waterfall and listen to the water. And that line of larch trees, over there—there are two or three days in October when they turn marvelous colors, purple and green and gold. I find the colors of the larch trees on those special days as difficult to describe as the rainbow. I am still trying to write about the rainbow. One of the first things I wrote, back in the '70s, was a poem about the rainbow.

There is a third thing, too: to try and describe how I see the rainbow colors on the snow in the morning, when the sunshine hits. All those crystals, and you see all the colors of the rainbow, every one of them. I never have found a way to express what happens for me when I look at that.

Even now, with the little bit of snow that's left, it happens. When I walk out to the car I have to stop and just look at it. Talk about beauty! So available. Rich, poor, short, tall, fat, thin, stupid… it's available for all of us. I almost want to say, "All God's children." Sometime you find something that you think you revere, and it's only available in special places, or with special people, or it costs too much money. But this absolutely astounding beauty is just right here.

Does it lead you to thoughts of God, of a creator?

Just. . .wonderment. It's all wondrous to me. It remains a mystery. Who knows! I heard some people on the radio talking about what came before the big bang. Was there time before the big bang? Was there a beginning? Is there an end? I haven't the slightest clue. I just take a deep breath and take the next step.

There is a line in one of your poems about how you were given this land, and the line is: "Even though I was not always good," Can you tell me what that line means to you?

It seems like such a reward, to have come here and had this experience of feeling at home here, surrounded by this wilderness quality of life, able to connect with the earth and listen for the animals and look at the birds—my God, we have an eagle, right out here! We also have a black cormorant. It seems like some kind of marvelous blessing, a reward. So, I think: what did I do to deserve it? That's the simple question.

I've done much good, but I've also done lousy things, things that I have a sense of guilt about, that I haven't totally learned to accept in my life.

Can you give an example of one of these lousy things?

Writing my memoirs has made me think that the cruelest—or the most unrational—unreasonable—the most off-centered thing that I have done in my life is to have not found a way to value myself enough. As I look back I see how I cooperated with the negative kind of energy coming my way. How I swallowed and cooperated in behaving like the unworthy person that, because of circumstances, I was portrayed as by parents, by the adults who were in charge of me.

They told me I wasn't worth very much, and I accepted that and incorporated it in my being. Now, I'm free to see that in a whole different way. And I think, wow. How much good energy I wasted being caught up in that negative kind of network—the alcoholism of my father and my brother, the insanity. They were wrapped up in that addiction. It is such a relief for me now, but it took me this long to learn it.

There are people who go through their whole lives and don't change their attitude toward themselves. They live and die feeling like a piece of shit.

How were you able to change the script? What brought about your sense of freedom?

I don't know. I don't know. I have the ability to just keep going, and just keep hoping. I don't know where that comes from.

Have you ever encountered what you could describe as evil in the world?

Well, everything has an opposite. The opposite of evil has to be something very good, very life-sustaining. I think of evil as something that interrupts the flow and the joy of life. The torment of young life, of children—young girls being abused, boys telling about priests abusing them—and always it's the feeling of diminishment, the cutting off the flow of life. Life in all its forms. It gets multiplied on a grand scale. The deer taken down by coyotes, that's not a single event. That kind of stuff's going on all the time. I read a book about pond life—everybody's eating everybody, everybody's murdering everybody out there.

Which makes us not so different from the natural scheme of things?

No, indeed! It's multiplied and there are all these wars. Right now the divisions seem to be about what we call religion, different views about religion, and property, and power. We're all part of that. That's all part of life.

Do you think that evil is part of our world, in a natural sense?

It seems to come with the territory. That's the best guess I can make. It's going to keep popping up, just like the tulips in the spring, in one form or another. You just have to do the best you can.

I understand you are currently engaged in an inquiry into economics and politics. Can you talk a bit about how that came about?

As I was coming into my teenage years, the influence of the adults in my life was toward—liberal is not really the correct word, but it's the word that's used a lot: liberal and conservative, those are the two categories, right? Liberal used to have a very different meaning, and that's part of the fun of what I'm learning.

My first vote was for Harry Truman, but I had campaigned for Henry Wallace. When I got in the booth I realized a vote for Wallace would be a vote for Dewey, the Republican. I was influenced by active Communists at that time, living in New Jersey. So I always voted Democratic, I was always for the "good guys," for poor people and against racism—all the good stuff! Those "bad guys"—those rich guys who were controlling everything were not as humane as I am. It made me feel good that I was standing up for the underdog. I went along with it, and I surrounded myself with friends who felt the same way.

Seventy years went by, and it just became automatic. I really wasn't thinking about it very much or questioning anything.

Three friends that I talked with, maybe three years ago, felt differently, expressed very different opinions. They were conservatives! Some of the things they said, I started to hear. The question is why? I don't know. I've known these three people for many years, and they've been talking like that all along. Suddenly, I heard them. I thought: My God! Maybe they're right! Maybe the long-term effects of some of these political actions is not good, like socialism ending up a totalitarian government. Stalin killing millions of Kulaks—the peasants who wouldn't do the right thing with what they were growing.

Three people. I respect these people. I consider them valuable friends. And here, they have these very different opinions. One is my son. Another is a cousin my age, and the other is a very old friend who lives in the city. So, I said, I'm going to look into this. I'm just finding it very exciting. It's refreshing that I'm not just "going along." I may end up being the most progressive George Bush-hater of them all, but, wow! Is it exciting to entertain a different vision. It's refreshing! Fresh air!

I'd like to ask you now about your poetry. How does nature shape your images, metaphors, subjects and language of your poems?

I'm always trying to describe what I see here. The sparkles on the snow. The images, qualities of a cathedral, with those larch trees across the pond. Various flowers. Oh, the sky. Just take the sky! From morning until night, at night, during the night, the moon comes right up here. Sometimes there is a reflection of it on the water. I'm always trying to capture those images in words. And I never succeed.

What is your process? How do you begin a poem? How long do you work on it?

I don't know. I just pick up the pencil and I write on the blue-lined notebook paper. That's how it starts. Those blue lines! I like those blue lines.

Does it begin with an idea? an image? a story? a memory? a sensory kind of approach?

All of those things, at various times. Something going on in my mind, some idea. Then I see an image out there and I try and tie the two things together. The idea, like I say, that I'm still trying to write about rainbows. There's a quality about rainbows: they're suddenly there. Out of nowhere! And just as soon they are gone, not leaving a trace.

Ruminate . . . ruminate . . . putting an idea into some place in your head, and every now and then it says: hey, pay attention to me a little bit, here. Move me along. Then I put it aside to make soup, or something.

I start out in longhand. Now I'm beginning to go from there to the computer. It used to be the typewriter. A little Royal typewriter was the first thing I bought when I got an extra job.

How long have you been writing poetry?

I wrote a poem when John F. Kennedy was killed. I wrote a few poems when I was a young mother. I guess those are the earliest I remember. I got a masters degree from Goddard

College in Creative Writing and Feminist Studies. I was in a writers group. The first page of my thesis is a poem, dated May, 1974. *I did what I was told/ and acted like you said/ running all the while/ to keep from being dead.* I called it "A Love Letter to my Mother." Writing is just something on tap. It's always going. You plug into it when you have time.

I loved writing letters. Upstairs in the attic, I've got boxes. I have letters that my best friend Charlotte and I exchanged. God, back in 1943! Somehow I've managed to hold on to them. I've kept a journal all along. Even just writing down what I had for breakfast. It's almost like if it isn't written down, it's not real.

Anything else you want to add about your sense of nature, of wilderness?

It's a sense of connection, really true connection, with the cosmos, with life, that I can feel without interruption, for periods. It makes it worth all the effort, all the crap you have to do to stay alive.

It's certainly not the same in the city, with all the cement and glass and plastic. However, there's also a special current that happens in an urban situation; even suburban, where my daughter lives. They are off at the end of a small road, long driveway. They are up on a hill, and when you look out their windows you see only one house. You're surrounded by woods, but still, there are the sounds of traffic, not far away. Here, there is just me and the moon.

Do you ever get a sense of an animate sensibility or force that comes through, that might be termed love, or goodness? Hope. Renewal. Something that is not random, that is alive?

Yes, I have some sense. I would talk in terms of beauty, rather than love. There is great beauty to be experienced, to be felt, to be seen, to be breathed. By beauty, I mean harmony. Yes! Definitely.

I felt that beauty, harmony for little segments of time when I was with the two growing grandchildren. They are both so beautiful, and accomplished, and, Jesus, he's six feet tall! So handsome, and a particular girl was watching him. And my grand-daughter is eighteen, and marvelous. She's the principal bassoonist in the Bergen Youth Symphony Orchestra. We went to a concert and she had a little solo.

The excitement there was watching her emerge from her room. One day she'd be with pigtails and jeans and a sweater, and the next day a white skirt that came just above her knees, and she had sewn on all these sparkly spangles on it, and some outrageous sweater that didn't go with it at all, the craziest, you know! She's an artist, and every morning she'd emerge! Goodness. Yes. There is a sense of harmony and beauty. I feel it with my two daughters. I felt it when we had the women's circle, talking, trying to communicate with one another. Beauty is the word that comes to mind. The opposite of that is ugliness, and that is the good and the evil. The dark and the light.

photo by Heron's Eye Communications and W Design

SANDY LONG (left)

KRISTA GROMALSKI (right)

"I think greed is in our genes. The taking and acquiring may be cultural. What does all this mean related to wilderness, though? If it just means that we are totally lost, where is our wilderness? Not just in the places that we're losing, but where is it inside of us? Do we even have an appreciation for it? Are we afraid of that part of ourselves? Because if we really take a look, we're going to have to realize that we're not in control of everything, we don't know all the answers and we're going to have to be okay with that."

Krista Gromalski

KRISTA GROMALSKI and SANDY LONG

Krista and Sandy live in a small house across the street from Greeley Lake, in Pennsylvania, a house they lovingly converted from a dark cubbyhole heated by wood to a two-story dwelling with a spacious and well-lit studio on the top floor. Everywhere along the window sills and surfaces are objects from the wild: rocks, shells, feathers, sticks and bones. Shelves are crammed with books and photos, paintings, poems and sketches done by the pair as they explore and celebrate the natural world and our human place in it.

Krista and Sandy are passionate about doing their part in a world that could be folding from excess and abuse. They often engage in grassroots organizing related to conservation initiatives such as better community planning and a balanced approach to development, and have written insightfully and informatively about their work. As a vehicle for their activism and writing, in 2006 they founded Heron's Eye Communications, which received a 2008 Pennsylvania Governor's Award for Environmental Excellence for its work on the public television documentary *Nature's Keepers: A Community of Conservationists*. The mission of Heron's Eye is to foster awareness and positive change on issues related to community and environment.

Both women have written for and edited regional newspapers and magazines, sometimes uncovering deep investigative information that has become recognized as source information nationwide on environmental issues such as gas drilling in the Marcellus Shale. In her office, Sandy is the resident naturalist, and once even tried to save an errant cockroach that had somehow made its way from the city upstate. She was overruled in that attempt.

Sandy and Krista also know how to live life. They are generous, spirited, unsentimental and charming. They hike out in good weather and bad with their Tibetan terrier mix, Buddhawg. They tell a good story and are not afraid to laugh at themselves. They're fun at a party and relish their fair share of microbrews.

The pair now keep a small coal stove percolating in their home all winter. Krista has never, on some elemental level, drifted far from her Schuylkill County roots in the heart of the anthracite coal mining region. Sandy grew up in Luzerne County in Wilkes-Barre, also part of the coal region, rooted in the labor of harvesting anthracite and characterized by a mix of ethnicities and cultures. Krista and Sandy come close to being an iconic symbol for this nation. They are Northeasterners, but identified more with the hardsoil blue collar Northeast than the prep school socialite or sophisticated urbanite; they are college educated and self educated, self effacing, hard working, committed to each other and to their community. They live outside the boundaries of societally sanctioned family life, although they are vitally connected to their families. They are easy to love, and they change lives. They changed mine, and I am grateful for their lively friendship.

WILD SILENCE:
Interview with Krista Gromalski & Sandy Long

Greeley, Pennsylvania
February, May

Krista, when and where were you born?

     I was born on December 19, 1969. I was raised in Mahanoy City, Pennsylvania but I was born in Pottsville, Pennsylvania—home of Yuengling beer.

Sandy, what about you?

     I was born on February 4, 1962 in Wilkes-Barre, Pennsylvania.

Sandy, I know you often work with a camera to document what you see, and you also write poetry. Can you talk about the relationship between the two?

     [Sandy]
     I use the camera as a way of seeing. It's a device that helps me find the words.

What comes first, words or pictures?

     [Sandy]
     It varies. Sometimes walking brings a word or a phrase. Other times, it's progressional. A lot of my photographs tend to be close-ups. I have an interest in minutia, in smaller, miniscule things that are also huge things. Very two-sided, coin-like things. When I am looking at the little curl of sweet fern down there, I'm also into something that is a lot, lot bigger. Psychological or mental territory or terrain that is down there.

     The book that I'm working on is called *Portal*, and I think the natural world is one of the most valuable portal opportunities that exist for humans. It's that thing that you can get to the other side with.

     It is very mystical, how you get there. I don't know if you can specifically identify any sort of process, except to say, "Well, I walk," or, "I have my camera when I walk," and then there are poems that come out of this thing, distilled out of the whole experience.

What is the "Portal" of your book title?

[Sandy]
There is a portal that can, and is, being destroyed or irreparably harmed. There is wildness, there is wilderness in a dandelion. If you are in a city, your experience might be a dandelion in the crack of a sidewalk. But to reduce the possibilities for wildness and wilderness down to only that—that's a grave thought.

Do you think that people in cities find it possible to lose their connection with this portal, this way inside?
[Sandy]
Yes.

And then what happens?

[Sandy]
I think that produces a lot of problems in our society. There are a lot of outcomes that result from losing that "other thing." Booming car stereos just raving away any silence that could possibly exist. The crush, the frenetic energy, the constant drive forward… when you get caught or swept into that thing, there's barely even the hint that there is something lost. There's a vague sense that something's wrong, but it is what is.

What does silence have to do with it?

[Sandy]
Silence is one of the most neglected things that we're losing, that we have no, or little, awareness that we're losing.

[Krista]
Sandy has a poem about this, called "Losing Silence." It goes, in part:

"I shot your foot to keep it still
for I've grown tired....
No more can I sit idly by unable to hear the trees moan low
A million feet tapping with impatience take their toll."

[Sandy]

It has to do with the idea that we're making huge noise without even being aware that we're doing it. And so, we have to do something drastic. I need to just shoot your foot to keep it still, because I've grown tired of saying, "The silence is going." In the poem, I ask, "If a sound cost you something . . . would you make it?" So if this is what it takes, I'm the little toll collector in the booth, collecting the toll.

Can you remember any childhood experiences in nature when you felt connected, and how that relates to your relationship to nature now?

[Sandy]

My childhood is a very subconscious, or subliminal, experience for me. In a conscious way, it's almost vacant. I have few specific recollections of what I was as a child or what I did or where I went. I know we did spend a lot of time in the natural world because my parents liked that kind of setting. My parents didn't really hang with other people. We didn't do social circle things. We came up to the lodge and hung out there, and we hiked in the woods, we picked up rocks, we had campfires.

When do your memories begin?

[Sandy]

Early teens. From before that, I can remember playing at the base of a certain tree in my yard, a rose of sharon tree, and feeling just good.

Has your relationship to wilderness changed over time?

[Sandy]

It's getting deeper all the time. I feel like it's some sort of... trust, something trusting, and deep, and mystical. What does define reality, and where does truth lie? That is related to truth-seeking that I'm doing with myself. It's very based in the natural world, and it's informed by that. The natural world is my partner in this process.

In *Winter Hours*, the poet Mary Oliver talks about a particular forest area that she has, for years, just cruised. So much of her poetry has come through and from that. Eventually, it was made into a national park, and access to it is now gated, and she can't actually enter it until the sunlight comes up. Her portal is now restricted. Who could understand what a terrible,

[Sandy]
terrible loss that is except for someone like her? How do you say, "that's loss," to a general public that doesn't really even hike anymore?

One of my poems is called "Bear Fear" and it's about a bear encounter that I had with my dog Sadie. We were hiking on a trail. There were bear droppings on the path but I really didn't give it the awareness that I should have. Suddenly I heard cracking and swishing sounds. We came around the bend and here were four cubs, sliding down a tree—I have a picture of the last one. Sadie ran toward them and brought the mother back on us—on me. The last thing I saw before I started to run was the mother bear coming toward me.

Did the bear chase you?

[Sandy]
She probably did; I don't know how far. I didn't look back; it was just blind terror. I ran off and got myself lost. I was somewhere I'd never been before. I couldn't sense my way back, and it was starting to be dusk. I stopped. I couldn't run any further. My heart was beating out of my chest and my lungs were exploding. I heard something crashing through the underbrush. This time I thought, the only thing to do was stand there and face it.

Did you have Sadie on a leash?

[Sandy]
No. She was separate from me at this point. So I hear this crashing, and I'm standing, and panting, and the brush parts, and it's Sadie!

But it didn't end there.

I had to find our way back, and I was having a lot of trouble. At one point I stopped to get my bearings, and I heard another crashing. Total irrational fear: I thought the bear had found us or I had circled back around her. It turned out to be a deer. We continued on, down a hill. I was trying to follow what I thought were the signs. But it was a really opaque sky, too, and it wasn't helpful.

I went to step over a log and—honest to God—there was a rattlesnake, coiled on the other side of the log. I never see snakes there; we haven't seen a rattlesnake at the lodge for twenty years. Now, on the same day, I see five bears, a deer and a snake. It was just unbelievable.

I caught myself, but here comes Sadie, flying up past me and I grabbed two fists of fur

[Sandy]
and yanked back. "Don't go there!"

Afterward, I thought: "That snake was asleep. It didn't have any awareness of me." I could have taken its picture, I could have looked at it, but I was so... lost. Lost, literally. When we finally came out of the woods, we came out on the road a good half mile below the lodge, when I was thoroughly convinced I was coming out a quarter of a mile or so above the lodge.

When I first started out onto that walk—and this is one of the things I find so interesting about the wild—in a naïve kind of way, I had said to the thing out there: "Show me what you want me to know, give me that sense, out there, of nature, and wilderness."

And it did! It was so big.

It was one of those altering experiences where you wake up hard, really hard. And it's different once you wake up. The experience moved me from some sort of fairy tale, naïve sense of nature to that whole sense of silence, death, finality—that is all the same thing, and I had to learn that.

For awhile it left me scared, it left me fearful. I was doing tamer trails, and every sound was catching my attention. I had to work my way back through. It was like swinging from one extreme to the other. And I had to work toward some realistic way of seeing it.

But again, what is realistic about that? What is real?

[Krista]
The book *Tropic of Capricorn*, by Henry Miller, was transformational for me. He writes about being in the city, but how the wilderness was inside him. He says:

"I was like the lighthouse itself—secure in the midst of the most turbulent sea. Beneath me was solid rock, the same shelf of rock on which the towering skyscrapers were reared. My foundations went deep into the earth and the armature of my body was made of steel riveted with hot bolts. Above all I was an eye, a huge searchlight which scoured far and wide, which revolved ceaselessly, pitilessly. This eye so wide-awake seemed to have made all my other faculties dormant...

"I wanted the eye extinguished so that I might have a chance to know my own body, my desires. I wanted to be alone for a thousand years in order to reflect on what I had seen and heard—and in order not to forget. I wanted something of the earth which was not of man's doing... to feel the blood running back into my veins, even at the cost of annihilation. I wanted to shake the stone and the light out of my system. I wanted the dark fecundity of nature, the deep well of the womb, silence, or else the lapping of the black waters of death. To be of night so frighteningly silent, so utterly incomprehensible and eloquent at the same time... To

be human only terrestrially, like a plant or worm or a brook. To be decomposed... variable as the molecule, durable as the atom, heartless as the earth itself."

I think that we have those experiences where you see crisp stars in the sky, or the moon, or the crowns of trees that you love on the hill. And something happens inside that allows you to get to that wilderness place, some sort of magic, or, mystic, place. It's not human. You have to get yourself out of the picture in order to be open to feeling that kind of imagery. There is a piece of writing that I have called "The Godball." It explores my sister's death in abstract prose. But it ties into the natural world and that thing that goes on inside yourself. That place, which is like the green man, that allows you to grow, and destroy, and grow, and destroy, over and over again throughout your life.

How did your sister die?

[Krista]
Joanne was killed in a car accident, in a collision with a deer. Her husband was driving and she was in the passenger seat. This is a photo of the car.

Why does the car have snow in it? It doesn't have a roof?

[Krista]
That was the car my sister was killed in. Here's the snow, here is nature happening already. Here is the cross that she hung on her dashboard, thinking, "If I just believe in God, if I have the right life, if I do the right thing, I have some control over this." But you don't have control over anything.

Wilderness, for me—it's not a pretty place, not an easy place. It's beautiful, but I don't think that beauty is necessarily pretty and soft. It's more like so awesome in whatever it is, that it's beautiful. Death is beautiful. I saw my sister dead in the morgue; we had to go there and see her. And the first thing that I thought when I saw her was: "She's beautiful." She was laying there with her mouth and her eyes open, and she was just looking—she was beautiful, right then. It was terrible. I thought, "Oh my God, oh my God," you know. There was nothing else you could say about it. I don't know, it was just—that was that place.

The abyss?

[Krista]
The abyss.

Do you think we have to lose control emotionally, or intellectually, to go to a place that's connected to wilderness, or wildness?

[Krista]
Yes. You have to get past the ego, the part that thinks that what you "produce" is wilderness. Wilderness, the green man, nature, whatever, it's so "other" than the part of you that thinks that it has control. You have to let go of that, let that bleed away.

That thing inside—the eye inside—that's the place. You want your inner eye to see, so that you can see that wild place. You have to wipe your real eyes away, in order to do that.

In art, too, it applies—that "other" thing. You might think you're doing one thing, and then you stand back and you're like, wow. It did this "other" thing, while "I" had no idea. And why is silence important? It's because you can't hear that other thing, the thing that connects us, when there is so much noise.

That uncontrollable thing is not necessarily evil, but I might think it's evil, sometimes. It comes into the process, it's that thing that's beyond our control. It happens no matter what. Let me show you: here is a painting that's not finished, but here is the chrysalis, breaking open. This is me, hanging, a shadow of me hanging with my hands tied behind my back and my ankles tied together, sort of like dying. And then, the beginning of the butterfly, here.

So, when we are talking about doorways, or portals, are we really talking about an altered state, something that's beyond our rational, every day, get-up-and-go-to-work self?

[Sandy]
Yes. Which many people aren't comfortable with. A certain amount of intensity can be a turnoff. Within my family, I'm always trying to bring them where I am and they don't want to come.

I learned a process of self-editing to deal with that, in terms of language. My dad used to ask me, and he meant it in a completely loving way: "Why do you have to use such big words? Just talk like other people talk." He was trying to say, "You're going to alienate yourself. People are going to think you are trying to be above them."

And I figured he was right. So using my vocabulary was a private thing that I did in my writing. I kept the words for my writing. I didn't use them so much in my speech. But now I'm trying to say what I want to say, and if the word is too "big," oh well. Words are really important to me, and different on very subtle levels.

Does the wilderness have to do with the void?

> [Krista]
> Yes.
> You buy some land, you own some land, and then you go up and sit on the hill, and you hear the cars, and a plane goes over. There is no place that is void of sound and things that are of the world. You just can't get there, really.
> But even if you're in the middle of the city, even if you are in the middle of noise, the middle of whatever, there's always that thing inside of you that you can go to that doesn't have anything to do with all that.
> People want that kind of inner intensity, but they can't let themselves do it, so they make it a place where only artists can go. It's like there are only a few people allowed to go there, who are allowed to actually experience that state. And the rest of us get there through their experience.

What about this evil force you refer to? This evil thread?

> [Krista]
> It's the same thing that Sandy is talking about when she says, "Show me what I need to see," and then she goes out, thinking, like, "nature," and the bear comes down the tree and all of a sudden she's in fear of her life.

But is that evil?

> [Sandy]
> No—absolutely not.
> Did you hear about the woman who was jogging in Yosemite or somewhere, and the cougar leapt onto her back and took her down, and it was interpreted as such an evil, horrible act? There were two incidences of cougar attacks near each other, and it brought all sorts of human attention to the matter. And now we needed new restrictions, and now we needed solutions. There was nothing even remotely evil about that. There was simply a jogger, and a cougar that was hungry and pregnant, and it needed a meal, and the person happened by.

But when does the rattlesnake hiding behind a rock, the bear protecting her cubs, become predators? Is that evil? Is there an evil that enters the world, that subverts a process?

[Sandy]

Ultimately, no. While it may be honest, it isn't evil. It is a brutal honesty, though. Evil is a label for a set of circumstances that transpires.

[Krista]

It's the judgment that you put on what happens.

[Sandy]

Right. Because, only because, we're attached to this particular human existence. And if there is some way to not be attached to this particular time around, then that becomes not evil. It is neither evil nor good. But it's almost impossible for a person, raised with a set of human values, not to judge it that way. Or it takes a huge, huge leap of faith—faith that there are the million other realities out there. And you're bound for another one after this one, and whatever it is, it's just going to be something else.

[Krista]

It's just this thing that's always dancing with everybody else who's dancing, and one day you bang into it. And one day somebody else does. Every day a million times, somebody does. One day it's closer; one day it's not as close. But it's always there.

In addition to your creative and artistic leanings, you have been involved in a number of projects having to do with the environment. Could you talk about that?

[Sandy]

Well, one of the initial triggers was the day that the spray-planes started flying over our home and treating the forest around us with chemicals for the neighboring camps. It sort of brought it home, pun intended. And as we explored this, we discovered that there was really nothing we could do about it.

Why wasn't there anything you could do about it?

[Sandy]

Because the camps purchase this. It's a private spraying, and the most we could do was ask them to avoid our house, which, of course, is pretty impossible; with any kind of breeze, it just drifts across.

Did they actually fly over your house?

[Sandy]
Oh yeah. We took pictures because it was so shocking to us. And the plane is visible. If you look out our front window you can watch it fly across the lake. That woke us up to some of what was happening right around us. Pike County is one of the fastest growing counties in the state of Pennsylvania. 9/11 really increased the development because of the people moving here to get out of the city, so that kind of spurred our next involvement.

[Krista]
As soon as you start to take a step, you have to keep on going. Once you start doing things like that, it's hard to shut down awareness. So, you kind of keep going forward.

[Sandy]
It really comes down to what your community looks like when you think about how you plan for future growth. If you haven't protected those resources ahead of time, it's too late, you know, when the developer is already looking through the door.

As you continue to do the work, is it an act of faith or is it more like screaming in the dark?

[Krista]
Both.

[Sandy]
Like Krista said: once you start, you can't just walk away. It can become all-consuming, and there's a struggle to find some sort of balance. While you're so busy calling people to get them out to vote for the referendum, two weeks of life have gone by and you have missed all sorts of things happening in the natural world, where you really want to be. But ironically you're fighting to save that and make it possible for that to stick around. So, it seems like you can do some things, but you can't save everything. It does become some sort of compromise in the process.

[Krista]
But every individual has to decide what they are comfortable with, what level of participation, or non-participation, or even ignorance.

Is it a justifiable position for individuals to choose not to get involved, to choose instead to grow their little garden and read, watch TV, spend time with their families and whatever, or is that one that you would challenge?

[Krista]
It's fine, if that's what they want to do and that's what they're comfortable with and that's how they connect with the world. Some people don't feel comfortable going out and being political, or even being involved with a group. Some people just don't want to be out there publicly.

[Sandy]
Whatever the role is, I do think everybody needs to do a little something. I would love nothing better than to just be in my garden. The problem is, while your nose is down there with the weeds and flowers and bees, the next threat is creeping up behind you.

[Krista]
Even being the activist and doing everything, you know, will not always stop four hundred houses from being built behind you.

Development is one piece of it, but the other thing is while you have your head down smelling the weeds and the flowers and the bees, you turn around and there are no more bees.

[Krista]
Well, that's true.

[Sandy]
Right.
But it may be enough just to be a voice for it, like the poet Mary Oliver, who is not an activist. It's a matter of finding your way to the thing that you're best at, or where your contribution can most help out.

[Krista]
You can't put someone down because they just want to work in the garden. There's nothing wrong with that. They may be teaching someone in their family, passing that appreciation along to someone else.

What works to help people and communities change their perspective, in your experience?

[Sandy]

When something hits home, people think, "Oh, now I have to do something about this," when it affects them personally, and it's sometimes too late. But sometimes that can spark an activism that they then may carry on.

Is that what happened to you?

[Sandy]

We've always had that activist bent.

Where does that come from, that ability or that urge to translate your life into action?

[Sandy]

I think there are things that trigger it, dreams, maybe. I used to have dreams about the lodge and they were dreams about development. I mean, I would be at the lodge and there would suddenly be people building homes all around it and roads coming in and cars and things. And that was back when I was still a teenager.

Have those dreams come true?

[Sandy]

Not for that particular place, but there has been a lot of development in that area.

What's been the most frustrating aspect of this work for you?

[Sandy]

You have an opportunity to practice setting aside your own hostilities. You learn that the opposition has their objectives too, and in order to get to a goal together, you're going to have to come closer to some point where you can agree.

[Krista]

I can't remain idealistic.

I would think the greatest frustration is misinformation. I mean, development is going to happen; that's fair. We can't preserve and protect everything. Where would we live? Where would we go to school? Where would we drive our cars? But when people purposely put out incorrect information or manipulate information just to confuse an issue or to spread fear, that's really hard to come up against; it's just craziness.

[Sandy]
It's not necessarily what's true; it's what people believe to be true.

[Krista]
Yeah, what's true?

What is the most rewarding aspect of this work?

[Sandy]
The feeling that you've at least tried. The worst thing would be just standing by watching it happen and having some excuse for not doing something.

[Krista]
And the people we've met and the stuff we've learned along the way—I mean, it's like school.

So you do see your activism as continual?

[Krista]
I think the ability to be involved comes in waves because your life changes as you go along. Sometimes you need to give attention to other things; sometimes you have more time to be out there in the community. As long as you're willing to admit that you have this awareness and not just bury it somewhere, you'll always be involved in some way.

Do you have hope for our planet?

[Krista]
No.
I don't know, I mean, yes, there are many hopeful things.
But we need a tremendous change of perspective. Is that possible? I don't know. Are we all going to stop driving and using gas; are we going to stop using electricity? Probably not.

What is the role of overpopulation in all this? The "population explosion" was a term coined in the '60s, I think, and we're still exploding.

[Krista]
Oh yeah. But we think we need so much.

So you think the problem is not so much the population, but consumerism?

[Krista]
It's both. We want everything to be a limitless resource for our taking, whether we want it, need it or otherwise. We're accustomed to that. And so, therefore, we gather, whether it's at K-mart loading up the cart or loading up the SUV with gas. The biggest change we would need to learn as a society is to resist, to limit ourselves.

Is it something in our genes, do you think?

[Krista]
I think greed is in our genes. The taking and acquiring may be cultural. What does all this mean related to wilderness, though? If it just means that we are totally lost, where is our wilderness? Not just in the places that we're losing, but where is it inside of us? Do we even have an appreciation for it? Are we afraid of that part of ourselves? Because if we really take a look, we're going to have to realize that we're not in control of everything; we don't know all the answers and we're going to have to be okay with that.

The interesting thing about climate change, whatever its cause, is that it's forcing people to realize that you can lose everything at any second. It's all over the Weather Channel. People have lost control of their environments.

And yet, we feel entitled to continue building in flood plains and on beaches that are certain to erode. Then, when that home is taken by the sea, we mourn. How crazy is that?

Do you think it's possible that human beings are just really slow learners?

[Krista]
I think it's more like defiance. We want to build where we want to build, and not have nature trump the situation. But nature always can trump the situation.

[Sandy]

I do have hope, mostly when I see people taking action for their small place. But, honestly, when I venture to cities and urban areas, I find it really distressing; my hope is dwarfed, because I see so much in those environments that seems so insurmountable. So, I kind of rise and fall in the hope field.

[Krista]

I'm not an optimist by nature. I have no idea if there's a big plan or not. I don't know if there's an afterlife; I don't know if there's a God.

I know there is a spirit, I know there's goodness, so there's the capacity for good, the capacity for evil and people can choose. We're shaped by all kinds of things.

It's easy to feel hopeless, but that's kind of dumb. We'd just kind of fall into depression and what's the point of that? I believe that life is sacred. And we've been given life, so we're sacred beings. We have to try to not waste that gift. And how we don't waste that gift is the hard part, not to waste it out of certain despair.

Is there anything that you would like to add?

[Krista]
We hit a turkey today. Or the turkey hit us.

It was flying low?

[Krista]

Yeah, right across Route 6. There was no swerving or slamming on the brakes or anything, I was just, "Okay. I hit this turkey." I thought it was going to come through the windshield.

[Sandy]

And the sound was really loud when it hit, too. And we just both opened our eyes and said, "Oh my God, the windshield is intact!"

And the turkey?

The poor turkey? No.

Tossing the Coin

Sandy Long

Grey sky again,
and the winged Buddhas
nestle in the winter mulch.
Not much choice on a day like
this dramatic day of
weeping and gusting,
heavy universal sighing
catching unaware the
bursting orange robins
struggling to lift bellies
from the wet macadam.

Airborne,
the toss goes,
and comes
down again,
landing like it will
on every throw.
We study this side,
knowing how the other side
sits at odds
to this,
knowing the blue spheres
bursting toward sun are,
even today, lifting
over snow-mucked wings.

The other side
is this same side
comprising just one
one.

Garden

Kristin Barron

A stillness
on this bright green day.
I stoop to pinch husk
and dead blooms from the pansies
purple and yellow
faces like newborn kittens
eyes still shut.
I think of leaves, seeds
handed down
dried on paper, saved
in envelopes
heirloom tomatoes
saved from frost
laid out on newspaper
to ripen in the back bedroom
their green smell.

Snail

Kristin Barron

All summer the snail
Graced our kitchen table
In the glass wedding bowl
Eating leaf after leaf of Black Seeded
Simpson

We admired the swirl of shell
The eyes on stalks
That surveyed the delicate shadows
Of our sudden mornings—
Sam swooping down in Batman pajamas
The baby contemplating cup and spoon

We returned the snail
To the woods, before winter
And I imagine it now
In the rot of the leaf mat
Its rich, bright world

If

Kristin Barron

If I could I would be a swamp
festooned with Spanish moss asway
through the trees with gnarled trunks
crusted with the lichen of infinite beauty
as it is I inhabit my own swamp mind
hung with grief and bluff

My mother had a closet full of noodles
I found after her death—a funny thing
to open the sliding closet in the back bedroom
a crucifix, scraps of Christmas wrapping paper
and a wardrobe full of noodles
wal-mart bags hung on hangers
filled with elbows and dumplings and ramen pride
saved for famine or war or just
forgotten, a boon
for the mice who scurry them away in neat piles

At autumn's edge I watch
the flocks of grackles gather overhead
their clatter
like glass breaking through trees
roiling and excited
the aspen leaves flicker
a ribbon of flight

that I might be like the wings of birds

Lost Land

Eileen Pagan

even though I am not always good
even though mostly poor is my lot
acres of land have come under my wing

        this land is my delight
        the woods, the stillness,
        birds, ponds, mists, baby otters

I stand on this land at midnight
and look up
a throbbing universe of lights
connects hello
I chuckle aloud, an owl hoos

        on this land I heal
        and reheal
        in the magic
        of inexhaustible change

If I lost this land
I would cry my eyes out
and make a flood to drown in
like in wonderland

Moment

Sandy Long

Yard Buddha crumbles to dust.
Black paint flakes into
white saint at rest

on rotting stump,
peaceful reposer
cradling striped stone

flanked in forget-me-nots
whose almost unearthly
squeaks of blue punctuate

rich mounds of moss,
trumpeting hosta
twirling into feathered stroke.

Overhead, rusted bell
chides the supplicants.
Grubs begin to vibrate.

A dandelion,
wild at its birth,
carols yellow at the sun.

crossing

PATHS

JENNA SNOW was born on May 20, 1992, and has lived all her life in Sullivan County, New York. She attended the Damascus School in Damascus, Pennsylvania and now attends Sullivan West High School from which she will graduate in 2010. She likes the sciences and plans to attend college in the fall. She plays volleyball and has worked making coffee and sandwiches at a local coffee house, and as a life guard at the pool of a local resort. Her favorite wild place is the beach.

AMY GILLINGHAM lives in New York's Catskill Mountains, where she and her husband Wes started Wild Roots Farm. She homeschools her two children and tends to her Icelandic sheep, Scottish Highland cows, milking shorthorn and chickens. Her work with plants in the vegetable and herb garden is a big part of her life, along with being a fiber artist using the wool from her sheep. She and Wes built a traditional half dovetail log home, with solar electricity and a Finnish Masonary heater. She loves living a half mile from the road, and her favorite wild place is above the treeline in alpine tundra. She also has a special affinity to native prairie.

STEPHANIE STREETER was born in 1948 and grew up in Allentown, Pennsylvania. She became a falconer in Massachusetts in 1979 and, with fellow falconer/ husband Bill Streeter, founded the North Quabbin Raptor Rehabilitation Center. In 1984, the Streeters were recruited back to their home state by the Natural Science for Youth Foundation's Natural Science Solar Center to begin a raptor rehabilitation and education program. When that program ended, she founded the Delaware Valley Raptor Center in Milford, Pennsylvania (dvrconline.org.), operating since 1987. Yearly, the staff rehabilitates over one hundred raptors and presents many education programs. As board chairman, Stephanie has appeared on numerous television programs, including *Animal Planet*. Her favorite wild place is the coast of Maine.

crossing **PATHS**

Animals are simultaneously commonplace in our lives and ever mysterious and unknowable. We accept the loyalty and affection of a dog, and we can understand to a limited degree such concepts as pack behavior and herding instinct. Yet there is much about even a tame and predictable pet that we cannot perceive or name. This sense of the unfathomable is multiplied manifold in the call of a wolf, or in observing a sea urchin slowly moving across a tidal pool, or in watching a hawk screeing and circling above a stand of tall pines, or in the sudden rush of seeing the dense shape of a black bear at the edge of a field.

So—animals create both a sense of connection and inexplicable otherness. We find in Crossing Paths that the women who are closest to animals exhibit a pragmatic lore and wealth of accumulating insight that allow their relationships with animals to prosper. During these conversations, we are brought to questions like: how does one rescue an injured hawk, exactly? What do you feed an Icelandic sheep? All white-tailed deer look alike—don't they? The task of caring for and about animals is gritty, full of physicality. Women who care so deeply for the creatures of the earth are tied to earth in intensely visceral ways. To feed an injured bird of prey, you must hack up frozen mice. To observe the creatures of the creek, you must get in the creek and learn to stand very still. Husbanding farm animals is not a sentimental activity—sometimes they are slaughtered (humanely, in this case) to become dinner.

In sum, what we find is that caring for and about animals means acquiring knowledge of a very specific and expedient sort. The conversations and poetry that encompass Crossing Paths will, I hope, animate and inform our own experience as we continue to encounter the wondrous spectrum of creatures that share our earth.

photo by Gerard Manzi

JENNA SNOW

"Last year I grew a sunflower—one big one like the tall one over there. There was only one sunflower that year. And when the birds went on it and they started to eat, they dropped some of the seeds. When the flower got old and it started to rot—it didn't really rot, it just got old and brown, and the head flipped over—we used it like a birdfeeder until the middle of winter. We'd fill it with birdseed. In the spring a new sunflower started growing."

JENNA SNOW

I first met Jenna Snow and her younger brother Johnny at the end of the 1990s when Jenna attended Penguin Camp for the Arts in Narrowsburg, New York, a day camp I ran from my home for six summers. She was a beautiful, self-assured child who wore her long brown hair tied back in a pony tail. Jenna participated fully and competently in our arts and writing projects, but always seemed to prefer a hearty game of capture the flag or an afternoon of berry picking from the highbush blueberry thickets behind the house.

With the generous permission of her parents, Joanne Snow and Gerard Manzi, I was able to interview Jenna for this book. At the time of our conversation, she was nine years old and as such, she is the youngest contributor to the book. I visited her at her home and we talked awhile on her porch, and then we took a walk so she could show me some of the local sites around her property, beginning at the dump and ending at the brook. She was fascinated by the idea of stuff left behind at the dump, whose corners and hidden treasures she seemed to know rather well. Ever observant, she could identify the deer in her yard by their markings, and she could tell you all about the physiology of the daddy long legs crawling across her arm or the water striders at the creek. Her best stories involved bear encounters on the front porch.

At the time of publication, Jenna was a senior at Sullivan West High School, part of the Class of 2010. She has plans to attend college in the fall. Her favorite subjects are biology and earth science. She is taking an Advanced Placement English course and has a creative way with language. In the eighth grade, she won first place in her region in the Patriot's Pen essay contest, and she placed third in New York State. Jenna spent her summer life guarding at the pool of a local resort. She still has her dog, Flash, and two cats named Gizmo and Caramel. Her brother John is now thirteen.

I feel most fortunate to have Jenna's clear fresh voice included in this work, reflective of her unsentimental outlook and close attunement to the land and its living creatures.

YARD, DUMP, STREAM:
Interview with Jenna Snow

Narrowsburg, New York
August

Jenna, how old are you?

I'm nine. I'm going into fourth grade.

When were you born?

May.

And where you you born?

Harris Hospital in Monticello, New York.

We are going to talk for a while here on the deck at your house, and then we will take a walk. All right? Will your dog Flash go on the walk to the brook with us?

She better. We have coyotes.

Have you seen them?

I have. They live up behind our grandparents' house, and sometimes they go down to the brook for a drink. Unless there's some source of water behind my grandparents' house, the brook is their main drinking source.

Have you explored behind your grandparents' house?

There is not anything over there; we found that out.

What do you do about the coyotes? Are you scared to walk down there?

No, we're not scared. Once, I went for a walk with my friend Lexi. We went down there and the woods are dark. In the woods there are so many trees, it's hard to see. But the coyotes can go into the underbrush and you can't see them.

Do they come out during the day and at night?

Me and my grandmother have seen them out during the day. And I have seen them walking back there during the night.

Sometimes, my brother Johnny and I take down hammers to the brook, because there are bears and there are coyotes. There are rocks so we could throw at them, but the rocks wouldn't do anything. So, we got the hammer.

What have you been doing this summer?

The day after school ended, we went to North Carolina. That was fun. We went swimming in the ocean and we went boogie boarding.

And my grandparents have a camp up in the Adirondacks, at Rainbow Lake, at Champlain. They live three hours away.

My best day this whole summer was the second day we were in North Carolina. We met Katie and her sister, and we played together in the pool, and we went to the beach and looked for shells together. Then, early in the morning, me and Mom got up together and we went shelling. We got some great shells.

When we were shelling, we picked up a small shell that wasn't broken at all. It was pretty much perfect. And the guy in front of us picked up a gigantic one. It was perfect, too.

A conch shell? The kind you can hear the ocean in?

Yes.

What do you like about being outdoors?

I like the breeze. It feels good on a hot day.

When you play outside, do you sometimes make up games?

Johnny and I bury each other in the sand, and we pretend like we're dogs in the sandbox. Sometimes we pretend we are animals, and one of us is a person. Say I'm a bird. I would dig with my feet, and he'd dig with a shovel. And we'd pretend to plant things, to grow a garden.

Last year I grew a sunflower—one big one like the tall one over there. There was only one sunflower that year. And when the birds went on it and they started to eat, they dropped some of the seeds. When the flower got old and it started to rot—it didn't really rot, it just got old and brown, and the head flipped over—we used it like a birdfeeder until the middle of winter. We'd fill it with birdseed. In the spring a new one started growing.

The birds would reach under and grab a seed. And then some fall off when they were landing on it, and that's how we got all those little sunflowers.

We didn't really grow a garden this year. We didn't really grow anything. But one thing we did grow was—I got potatoes home from school. I let Johnny plant one, so we planted a potato. And that one's growing.

We didn't plant the tomatoes that you can see over there either. They grew from last year's seeds.

What kinds of wild animals are living around here?

Bees. I got stung three times this year. I got stung by a hornet, at my cousin's. They are nesting inside the swing set. They go inside the holes.

And we got lots of deer. During the winter, right over there, usually, some grass is under the snow and when it's plowed the deer go over there. We have a picture of one deer; he stays there all day and eats. Sometimes we dig holes so he actually lays in there, in the little holes, and sometimes he sleeps in the hole by the grass.

You dig holes for him?

Yeah. They're pretty big.

How can you tell that it's the same deer?

Well, he's short for a deer and he's got a dark brown coat. Darker than normal.

I think it's a male but I don't know.

And we have bears.

Once, when we lived on Hilltop Lane in Narrowsburg, we came home after going shopping. It was windy and stormy, and we had a honeycomb on our porch, and a bear got into our porch. Johnny was a baby. He and Mom were the first ones to go up on the porch, and I saw it because you could see a little tiny bit of black over the door. He had trashed the whole porch. Mom opened the door and the bear came running out!

Wow! Who was more scared, your mom or the bear?

I think the bear was!

What other kinds of animals live near here?

We've got lots of birds.

Do you know their names?

Chickadees, blue jays, crows, and we've got red-tailed hawks. [Indicating a tree in the yard], I figure this is a tree that they would like best.

How do you learn all this?

I see it. The chickadees like the sunflowers. And then we got cardinals. We see them in the winter; they usually stay over there. They show up good then; it's easier to see them. On the white snow, they are bright red.

Have you seen foxes?

Yes.

Red foxes? And grey foxes?

Yes. And we've got squirrels and chipmunks, and raccoons.

Have you seen porcupines?

Yup. And, let's see, we got opossum. And we smelled a skunk, and once we really thought Flash was sprayed. "Flashy, sit! Good dog."

Let's take a walk. Jenna, where are you going to take us? Shall we go to the old dump?

    All right.

〖Walking to the dump〗

What other games do you play out here?

    Last night me and my cousin Mikey got our bikes, and Johnny and Joey were on their jeep, and we had races. Sometimes we play hide and seek.
    Oh, look it, it's a bee! I like honeybees.

What kind of feathers are those?

    I don't know.

Turkey, I think—baby turkey—

    Oh, yup. They probably are. There were a whole bunch of turkeys. There were big turkeys. Me and Johnny wanted to see them, and we wanted to see something funny. So we took Flash out with us. I told her to run up and scare them, and so that's what she did! She ran up there and it looked like the whole field exploded!

〖At the dump〗

What is back here at the dump?

    Car parts. Glass.

Who dumped this?

    I don't know.

This is an old truck. An old Dodge truck.

    And here is a tire.

Oh! Why is the tire cut like that? In a diamond shape.

    I don't know. At first I thought it was a bear trap.

Yeah, that's what it looks like.

We put these bottles up here on the tree stump. Sometimes we clear them out. We have some up there at the house; they're really nice, not broken. They are beautiful glass bottles.

Do you make up stories about who dumped all this stuff?

I have no idea, really, who dumped this stuff. But who knows, there might be some really cool stuff in here, covered in the leaves. It's nice having it back here. Some things, I don't know why they were dumped. There are glass bottles that could be used. And there's a shoe there!

Here's a pan. This looks like it could still be used, although it doesn't have a handle.

I see a light bulb. And look at this! It's not even broken!

Look at that, right there. Can you guess what that is?

A sink.

Close.

A tub.

Close. It's an old wringer washing machine.

It's a washing machine? Cool. There's a lot of cool stuff down here.

Let's head on over to the creek.

[Walking to the creek]

Look, here is an old plow. There used to be an old farm back here. That's why it's here. We got the seat somewhere, too.

Jenna, would you like to live in the city?

No. I like watching wild animals. I like the animals and there is a lot of room out here. In the city, if you have a house, your yard is like twenty or fifty feet on all sides. Plus, the driveway will take up a whole lot of space.

What about kids who live in apartment buildings? They don't even have a yard.

If they live in apartment buildings, they just learn to live there. They probably just learn to like it.

I like horses. I'm taking lessons. And in a few years, my parents might actually get me a horse. If you lived in the city, there would be no room for a horse. But here we have all this space. Oh—blueberries! I found some beetles—and blueberries.

[At the creek]

This [rock rubble here] is from where it floods. Sometimes it floods over the road. See, when it floods, this is all covered. This water is waist-high. Once, walking to the creek, we got lost. We were on a path, and we couldn't find our way back. There were so many roads to choose. We couldn't find which one to take. And once we got back from one, we couldn't remember which one we had already done.

What kind of bugs are those?

Water striders.

Are there any fish in the creek?

Yeah, we got minnows. See all the water striders, right here? They are making the water ripple. And see all the minnows?

What eats the water striders?

I don't know. We got those little lobster-thingys.

Crayfish.

Yeah, crayfish.

The water striders look like they have little suction cups on the ends of their feet.

Yeah, they can stand up on the water.

What do they eat?

I think algae from the top of the water… little tiny bugs, maybe.
There is a little waterfall right here. It's tiny. See, this is nice, up here.

It is. A little more open.

Yeah. And the water gets deeper. Oh, look at the worm. An inch worm! I'm trying to catch a water strider. Oh! I almost got one. I don't know where they go. They probably hide under water. Or under the rocks. They probably go under the rocks. Once, I caught a water strider, but I didn't want to keep it up out of the water because it would die. I found a daddy-long-legs! They are the most poisonous spiders on earth. Our skin is just too thick, but they poison other bugs. Wow! Look at this rock. Smooth. It's probably from being in the water so long. I'm walking in the water.

What's that?

A tunnel under the road. Oh, there's a frog! Don't touch him.

He is a little sluggish, isn't he? I think he is half asleep.

He's very active. I'm going to let him go. Little swimmer! Oh, I got him again. He's so cute. Oh! There he goes. Oops. Here he is. He's my special friend. "All right, we are going to let you go now, froggy. Bye bye!"

Jenna, do you like rain?

Yeah, but I don't like it when I want to go swimming.

Do you like cloudy skies?

Yeah. I like thunderstorms, because I like to watch the lightning. Especially when you are in a car.

Why is that?

Because the tires are rubber.

Do you like when it's sunny out?

Yeah.

Is there any kind of weather you don't like?

No.

Do you think God has anything to do with this world?

Yeah, lots of things. He created it. He makes everything what it is. He changes the seasons.

photo by Wes Gillingham

AMY GILLINGHAM

"My whole life, I've never done something just because someone said, 'That's the way you do it.' Little children need nature and wild places, gaining a connection to place. Nowadays, the perception is it's not even safe for kids to get on their bikes and roam the block or wherever they live. Children these days are very focused, concentrated right in their little houses. I want kids to be able to explore. They need wilderness, even if the wilderness is dandelions in the back yard."

AMY GILLINGHAM

One sunny but frigid day in January, I followed the directions to Amy Gillingham's house. She warned me that the half-mile-long driveway would be impassible with ice, and I should leave my car at the top. I cheated a bit, swinging my Honda Civic down as far as I dared and parking just in front of another truck parked at the side. I walked in over the icy patches with the help of a sturdy branch I'd found in the surrounding woods. The woods were white with old snow and sunlit, and very quiet. I was (I guessed) nearly there when I met visitors—a woman bundled in many colorful layers, walking with two very young kids.

"Hey," she greeted me. Then she asked, "Is your car blocking mine?"

Indeed it was. I turned around and walked with her back up the hill. Her progress was slow with the two kids, one of whom was tiny, and needed carrying from time to time.

Luckily for me, Amy's husband Wes appeared just as I was preparing to descend the drive again. He offered a ride in his truck. I was white-knuckled as we flew without traction over the icy bends, but it was nice to be out of the cold. It was, I think now, a fitting introduction to my interview with Amy.

Amy Gillingham is a slender, fit, talkative woman who brims with energy and ideas. Born in Kansas City, Missouri in 1973, she lives now in a rugged corner of Sullivan County, New York, on a hundred-acre farm that came down to her husband through his family. She and her husband's traditional half dovetail log house is off the grid. Energy systems for all their needs consist of solar electricity and a Finnish Masonary heater.

Amy possesses a formidable knowledge of sustainable ways of living. She is adept at growing crops and vegetables, raising animals for food and wool, home schooling her two children and harvesting wild foods for sustenance and medicine. She makes part of her living from the Icelandic sheep she raises, and she and her family also eat their meat. She chose the breed for its resiliency and its wildness, its ability to forage and survive in harsh conditions. From the wool of her sheep she spins and dyes, creating hats and clothing and art.

Amy became interested—passionate is a better word—about sustainability during hiking trips in her teens and twenties. Back packers, she said, need to get food from the supermarket, and somehow this got her on the track of thinking about and pursuing sustainability. She is the organic farmer who, with her muddy boots and vast knowledge of all things cultivated and wild, will lead us to find supper in field and forest, and among the animals, if the gas pumps do run dry.

SUSTAINABLE KNOWLEDGE:
Interview with Amy Gillingham

Livingston Manor, New York
January

[Walking outside on the grounds of Wild Roots Farm in Livingston Manor, New York.]

Amy, when and where were you born?

Kansas City, Missouri, 1973.

Tell me about your animals.

I have six sheep and three Scottish Highland cows, the ones with the shaggy coats and big curved horns. I also have a milking shorthorn cow. I have about twenty chickens, an angora rabbit, a ferret, a cat and a dog. I got the ferret for rodent protection in the greenhouse, when I was starting my seedlings. And it worked!

We have a Great Pyrenees guard dog. (She's more into the kids than the sheep.) We have three Scottish Highland cows. These two are females and the other's a bull.

Over there is the cabin we lived and worked in before we finished our log house. My kids were born in there. It served us well, but we were ready to move to someplace warmer!

[Down at the sheep corral.]

"Hey, Boomerang! Hey, Boomerang!"
These are my Icelandic sheep. They come from Iceland.

That's the best wool in the world, isn't it?

Yes. The one with the long curly horns... that's the ram. We don't get too close to him. But these girls—they are naturally short-tailed. They are less genetically manipulated than other breeds. They have the dual coat, so they have the inner thel and the outer, longer pog. I shear them twice a year. I use their spring shearing for the felting and the fall shearing for the spinning.

Icelandic sweaters, if you've seen them, have this fuzz that comes out. That is this outer stuff, that will kind of poke out.

Iceland doesn't let any other breed of sheep in. They tried it once and the new sheep got sick; they got diseases, they weren't hardy enough.

It's hard to get Icelandic sheep out, too. Now they send the semen straws. They don't ship the sheep.

I count five, plus the ram.

I had twenty-five this year. I sold some for breeding and we put some in the freezer. It's what we live on.

So you aren't very sentimental about them?

You can't be, because they multiply. We don't have that much grass, and then we're dealing with feeding them hay in the summer, and then you've got parasite issues.

This is Heather. She's our best baby.

Sheep don't have upper teeth—just lower. They chew their cud. They are ruminants—they regurgitate and chew, like cows.

I'm really big into grass-fed. I only grain them a tiny bit when they're lambing. We started raising our own beef and sheep because I want my kids to be eating grass-fed animals and I want to know what I'm eating.

The reason why I picked this breed is because they're so hardy. Like the dual coat—that's how wild sheep are. We have bred this hardiness out of other domestic sheep. But wild ewes have horns, so Icelandic guys have horns. They're so hardy that they don't need a barn. I don't have one—I have a little tiny shed.

It's the same with the Highland cows. We wanted really hardy animals.

The sheep are triple purpose: milk, meat, wool. The meat is delicious, even their stew meat. Many people don't like lamb, but this meat is so mild, just so good. And then the wool—I got this breed because I'm getting into felting, and this is a great wool for felt.

I like the way they look: skinny legs and wide bodies, like story-book sheep. I like their eyes, too; they're kind of iridescent.

They're a bit like a cross between a sheep and a goat. Their tendencies for what they eat are more goat-like. They prefer brambles, trees; they'll run through a patch of clover and pasture and go straight for raspberries.

With these small farms and this marginal land, these breeds are hardier. You don't need to de-horn these animals. It's cruel. And with horns, it's easier to handle them.

Do you make your own yarns?

Yes, I spin yarns.

From start to finish? From shearing to finished product?

I don't do the shearing myself. That's one thing I don't do. I'm hoping to learn.

Do you have a loom?

I have a loom. I wash the wool, I card it and I spin it. Then I either knit it or—as soon as my workshop area is all set up, I'm going to set up my loom. I've only done a few things on the loom because I'm home schooling. It's really neat when I have my bags full of wool. I start with that and I think about it a lot. I even dream about it.

Do you dream of patterns and things?

Yes, and just—textures.

How old are your children?

Iris is seven and Roan is five. Roan is a Gaelic name, means a little seal or fiery one. And Iris Fen is named after the wild iris and fen that we have right down through the woods here.

[Walking to a spot in the field.]

This covering over the ground here, this is an old rock foundation. This opening was our root cellar. For eight years, we sold vegetables out of there. We had oak pallets covered with hay and we stored our vegetables.

We think this was the original house on the homestead because of the three foundations that were here, it's the only one that had cut bluestone. We pulled the bluestone out and the top of our chimney is made from it, and the top of our masonry stove also. It's neat, bringing the old house into the new house and making that a part of it.

How long have you lived here?

My husband Wes's family bought this as a hundred-acre lot fifty years ago. His mom grew up on a dairy farm near Utica, New York. They were living in Long Island at the time and they wanted to have a place in the country. They bought this for a thousand dollars, maybe two thousand dollars.

They started coming up on weekends. Wes roamed the woods with his Alaskan Malamute, Stormy. He got to know the land so well and it taught him about natural history. Before I even knew him, his family let him move here and it became his home base. So when it came time for us to decide where to live, we were looking at Maine—I'd farmed a little in Maine—and I'd lived in Vermont and farmed a little. But, you know, it'd take Wes another thirty years to get to know a place like this. I thought there was something really special about that relationship.

Now, after the ten years that we have been married, it would be hard to leave and start over because you just get to know land.

We were on the National Audubon Expedition Institute, a traveling college program where you travel around and visit these resource people. The ones that touched us most were these people who had a connection to their community. They'd been there for a long time; they knew something really well.

Is that a conscious goal that you have? To stay here, to homestead here, get to know your land and the community well?

Yes. We both love farming. I think Wes probably would've chosen to be a dairy farmer. But I love plants, so we ended up doing vegetables.

What kind of relationship did you have with the out-of-doors when you were a child?

I was involved in a lot of stuff, especially sports. But my best memories were running around Brush Creek, which is the creek that runs through Kansas City, with my neighbor, catching tadpoles and stuff like that. We had a place at the lake in the Ozarks and I'd go fishing with my dad a lot there. I always was very drawn to that, although it was very much a city lifestyle.

I went to an Outward Bound camp in Colorado for six weeks when I was a sophomore. I backpacked for a month in the Sangre de Cristo mountains. I realized there was life beyond Kansas City.

I started thinking about, "Well, where are all our resources coming from?" And all of a sudden, sustainable living made a lot of sense. When you're backpacking, you're dependant on grocery store food. You're not as sustainable. So there's kind of a balance there—you're nomadic, living out of your backpack. My goal was to learn more about where my resources come from.

【Visiting the pond.】

Is it a natural pond?

We had this dug, actually. We ice skate here, although not much this winter—its been too warm. In the summer, we swim here every day. We water our greenhouse from here too. It's fed from our spring, our old well where we used to get water. So we knew there was a lot of water here.

We planted a few grains of wild rice that matured one year. We have cranberries. We had some arrowroots and different plants. I tried planting watercress.

This spot reminds me of Maine a little bit.

Well there are a lot of hemlocks. All the evergreens …

We looked at other farms because this land is so poor. Too poor, really, to farm. But it was hard to compete with the wildness here, the hemlocks and all.

When we decided to try farming vegetables to sell, we leased a Class One soil plot down on the flats in Youngsville, New York, about five miles down the mountain from here, for our vegetables. Up here, we planted some apple trees. We have blueberry bushes, and our home garden. But our living came from the organic vegetables in Youngsville.

And then this year, we got flooded. We lost so much soil. It was devastating. Rather than continue to stay on river bottom with global warming happening, we're going to move our energy up here and see what we can grow. I'd like to get a whole bunch of blueberries in the ground and do some greenhouse greens for off-season.

Will you try to grow the same summer and all-around crops?

For us we will, but not for sale. The soil is not conducive. Soil-wise, I'm going to have to re-learn some things.

How many years did you grow down on the flats?

Nine years. After nine years, we had it finally figured it out.

And then the floods of 2006 came.

Yes. We also got hit with Hurricane Ivan [in 2005] pretty bad. After that hurricane, we did a lot of drainage work. But this last flood was so big, it didn't matter what kind of drainage we had. There was five feet of water all the way across our field.

[Walking up a slight hill to another part of the farm.]

Up here, I have grapes, blueberries and gooseberries. We made eighty jars of jam this year.
We put so much energy in the field in the flats that we never really got to finish projects here. I'm excited to clean out wood piles and take a year to get our bearings straight.

Do you have greens growing in your greenhouse now?

Yes. In about a month, we'll be eating from them.

What is the temperature inside the greenhouse?

It got up to maybe 70 degrees today. It doesn't hold the heat at night, but the greens are so hardy that they can tolerate it. My second greenhouse, over there, is full of big water barrels. Those will hold heat, for tomatoes and peppers.

These greenhouses are where I start everything. We run the generator for watering so we don't drain our solar batteries in the winter.

This here is our orchard that we planted the year that we got married. You can see how slowly these trees are growing. To improve the soil, we'll lime it. That's the kind of stuff we've neglected here because everything went to the field on the flats, where our income came from.

Do you and Wes work from sunrise to sunset? Do you work all the time?

Not this time of year. This is our slow time.

In season, sunrise to sundown, yes. Usually past sundown. I get tired, but it's good. I like working outside. The problem is I like so much of what I do.

Here are the remnants from our winter Solstice party. We had a huge fire from the scrap lumber around. It was so hot! That's our annual ritual, our winter Solstice way of welcoming the sun back.

People ask me, "Do you have a routine?" I'm like, "Absolutely. The seasons dictate our routine. We celebrate the natural earth cycles."

Is there the idea of a supreme being or a creator?

Yes—the creator. I try to teach the kids about a lot of different beliefs. My general belief is that—the old Celtic religion, the goddess religion, Native American religion, Buddhism, Hinduism, Christianity, Judaism—they are all basically saying the same thing. It's just different words.

I want to convey a general respect for the land, for all other things and beings— "beings" meaning beyond just human. A big thing is just giving thanks, living in gratitude and being grateful. Being able to do that every day is important.

So much of our existence revolves around food. We're raising our beef, milking the cow, making dairy products. Raising the vegetables.

What do you buy from the supermarket?

I don't buy much. I mean, if we're out of parmesan cheese or whatever, but basically I order from a co-op once a month where I can get organic. We eat so much that I get in bulk. I might get five pounds of organic nuts, maybe some rice, although generally we eat mostly potatoes.

Do you grow any grains?

We grew rye and actually had a combine and tried harvesting, but it was a very wet year and it had ergot, so we couldn't use it. We were thinking that this year, if we weren't going to grow vegetables, maybe we'd grow grains and harvest them.

How did you decide to homeschool your children, and why?

I'm still struggling a bit; I still question, back and forth, whether it's the right thing to do. Intuitively, I feel that it is. But selfishly, I would love to do more with the wool and be out getting firewood and stuff like that without so much interruption.

My whole life, I've never done something just because someone said, "That's the way you do it." Little children need nature and wild places, gaining a connection to place. Nowadays, the perception is it's not even safe for kids to get on their bikes and roam the block or wherever they live. Children these days are very focused, concentrated right in their little houses. I want kids to be able to explore. They need wilderness, even if the wilderness is dandelions in the backyard.

Why get my kids up at 7:30 on these cold mornings, have them out for a bus and they don't get home till 4:30? That's a long day to learn how to sit in a chair and raise their hands. I want them to develop their imaginations, to enjoy and love learning without having negative feedback on that.

Homeschooling is a huge sacrifice. I'm aware of how much more we could've done with the farm. Our house would probably be done. But, children bring you other things in life—other lessons that you need to learn. I'm learning how to teach them without necessarily giving them answers to everything. Teaching them how to think and how to question, how to try to figure things out. They're going to learn to read and write. We read all the time. For them to establish a connection with the earth right now is crucial. They won't develop it in high school. And that's what our society is dealing with: kids who don't have that connection.

The generation that you are raising will have to face a lot of challenges.

They are. Iris knows more edible plants around here than probably people who have grown up here their whole lives. That's why we named our farm Wild Roots Farm—that was the most essential part of our existence, I felt. The wild food. Then we started growing so much that I had an abundance on my front porch all the time. I didn't have to pick as many dandelions.

How did you acquire your knowledge about wild foods?

I will say that people are drawn to different things. My best friend is a bird maniac. She can sing any bird song. My draw is plants. For Wes, it's trees. I remember getting a little jar of salve that someone had made of dried raspberry leaves and I was like, "Man, I can make this." So I got really into herbs and herbal medicine. When you are sick, you can make your own Echinacea salve. It's so simple.

My milking shorthorn sliced her teats really bad—she really should've had stitches. But how are you going to stitch up her teats? She'd kick you to death. I called the vet who said, "Well, just dry her out." I said, "I don't want her to get mastitis." The vet said, "Well, give her an antibiotic." Well, I wanted the milk. I just picked up my plantain sack and three times a day I coated the area. It healed.

The power of plants is so strong, and I've learned how to use them by just situations coming up. But it's taken a lot of years of delving into books and experimenting, having failures. Just learning.

Do you find that you have developed an intuition about how to do things?

For a while, I wished I had someone to teach me these things. I needed to find people who could teach me. I constantly asked questions and sought out people and read everything. Now what I'm realizing is that it comes in different ways. Obviously many people—ancestors—are there, guiding me.

I'm a fairly sustainable person. If something big and catastrophic happened, I would know how to hunt. I would know how to gut an animal. I would know how to cook it. I would know the important organs to eat so you were getting the vitamins. I would know wild plants. I would know how to build a fire. I would know herbs that would help us when we're sick. I would know how to make clothing. You know, a lot of basics that I didn't learn growing up, and yet somehow I have been given that gift of knowledge. That feels very powerful.

That's a lot of knowledge for your age.

Yes. I started young. I was committed. Having kids has slowed down my learning process in some ways. In other ways, the kids have connected me to my femininity, to the goddess.

Do you participate in women's circles?

Yes, there's one great one that I go to. We gather every full moon.

I started another one about five years ago. It's changed and evolved, and now it's about thirty women. It's more of a wise traditions group—we do a lot around food and celebrating women's work, crafts, cooking. We've made salves and that kind of thing. When we first started, it had a more spiritual focus. Now it's more about women and social awareness.

The full moon group is the power of women coming together and making our voices heard and giving thanks. I feel lucky to have found that.

I want my kids to be aware of the moon cycle and ways of celebration. We celebrate the Solstice and we celebrate Jesus. I'm not going to get into religion, but—it's important. I went to Catholic schools growing up.

[Returning to the house.]

I'd like to show you some of the wools, upstairs, if you'd like to see—

I'd love to see the wool. Yes.

This is some of the wool that I spin. This has a two-ply, so I'm getting ready to make a sweater for Iris.

How did you dye this wool?

I have different dye plants in the garden. Iris was out there with me one day and she was interested. So I said, "All right, let's dig it up." And she did it herself: dug it and washed it and let it dry, and then she put it in a pot and soaked it overnight.

So, felting?

Felting is just a matter of matting.

You get it wet and then it dries and then that's how it shrinks?

Yes. I do a lot of things with it. I'm making slippers and now I want to do cushions downstairs. And, I'm making felt balls, which sell in New York City for like $25.

This is my spinning wheel. It's a handmade cherry wheel that I got as a gift from a farm in Maine where I apprenticed. It's really one of the best wheels. And I have this more modern one.

These wooly rugs or blankets are sheep skin from your sheep?

Yes.

They must be warm.

Yes. Here, let's go down and have a snack, to warm up. I have some squash that I cooked this morning.

Is this for me? Oh, thank you. It's delicious. What kind is it?

It's Indelicata, a winter squash.

What do you think about global warming and climate change? Are we on the brink of catastrophe?

Well, in the nine years we've been farming, our season has extended pretty consistently on either end by several weeks. And the flooding—four floods in the past ten years. The last time it flooded before that was 1946.

How is it living off the grid?

Well, we really have everything we need. Earlier in my life, I worked on these little off-the-grid homestead farms and it just suited me. I liked sleeping longer hours in the winter because I didn't have light. I liked the rhythms that we kept. There were times I thought I could do something at night if we had lights, and now, here, of course, we have solar lights at night, but we have minimal lights compared to the average.

What happens to you when you are outside?

I get re-grounded. It's invigorating. You can get into a place where you can let go of all the questions and just let your mind kind of breathe and flow, and all of sudden you learn to listen to your intuition and let that guide you.

Do you think men have good intuition, the same as women?

Yes.

So the women's intuition idea is not really true?

Who says it's not true?

I'm asking you, whether women go by their intuition and men are more cerebral or logical, like their minds work differently.

I think our minds work differently.

Often, my intuitive feelings and my dreams actually seem more real than my real life. There's a realm of living that we're not taught to live in but it's very real. I'm learning to manifest my own life, trusting that that will happen. What I always find funny is that the time frame of how it works out is completely different from the time frame I had pictured in my mind.

I think our sense of time is also very interesting. Like, it's driven my family crazy that it's taken us six years to get out of that cabin and into our house here. For us, the process and the experience are important. Friends helped us build this house, and it has a whole spirit in itself because of the work that went into it.

My brother-in-law got back from Rome and he was like, "Hey, the Sistine Chapel took three hundred years to make." It takes a tree a really long time to grow. You see it standing out there through the winters and the storms and the summers and the droughts, season after season. It's strengthening and growing, and that's the backbone for my existence—lending support and being able to give that to others. It's all about meshing with different things.

Farming is a very domestic thing; I mean, we end up taking less walks in the woods. Luckily, our road has been fixed, but when we started we walked in and out all the time. I had two kids, one on my back and one on my front; I carried the bags and I walked a mile out to my car and down to the fields. Laundry? Put it on the sled, pull it around me, one baby on my front, one on my back. It was really intense. When I look back it was, wow—

No wonder you were glad to go to sleep at night.

Yes! But, I liked it. It was my choice.

In doing those mundane things, you sometimes can feel the most grounded. A physical life style works for me. I love splitting wood. I like to be out there using my body. I don't want to die with my body all intact and in good shape. I want to die with champagne in one hand, chocolate in the other.

It's a fear-based world right now. "We have to do this because of terrorism, blah, blah." Our whole medical system is fear-based; you have to do every test imaginable because no one wants to be sued. In our schools, fear: if your kids don't pass the standardized test, they will fail. It makes parents fearful. And I think people have a fear of wilderness, from not having experienced it.

Is there any conflict for you between cultivating domestic plants and collecting wild plants?

I think they both work really well together. There are times when it's really wonderful to nurture and cultivate, create a soil and start a little seedling and plant it and work with that. That's what got me working with plant spirits, where everything has a spirit. It's the magic of that, working with elements that you cannot necessarily see.

I love doing that and I also love harvesting. There are times when my own cravings are for something out of the garden, and other times when I just need something wild.

Look, here are my ramps—wild leeks—that I dried; I've strung these in little handfuls, for soup or whatever. It doesn't take very much to flavor it, and I'm getting the essence of the wild leeks.

May I taste one?

Sure.

These grow everywhere?

They're in patches, yes.

I love harvesting like this. It takes hours to clean it, cut it, put it on a rack, but I pull it out when I need it, and it feeds something more than just my belly. I have my pot of broth out on the porch; I'm constantly making broths.

Plant broths?

Yes, and meat broths, because we have our Highland bones. Making a lot of dense, nourishing foods, butters, butter broth. A lot of the old traditional cultures had foods like sauerkrauts or Kim cheese, and they had their broths, their salts and their properly prepared grains. They soaked their grains; they soaked their nuts and roasted them. For me to learn how to do that has been really important.

I mean, dinner can be literally, come home, cut the roasted chicken out of the bag, heat it up, cut the salad out of the bag. But is it necessarily such a bad thing to cut vegetables for an hour? Again, sometimes the mundane and simple things make our life the richest. I think that's the real point of life: to have this richness. It's just that we're looking for it in the wrong way. I was harvesting nettles down at the brook. I was harvesting with a friend, and she said, "You know, this is the best day I've had in a while."

I just love that: go out there, put on your rubber gloves and harvest. I think it is human nature, or women's nature, to want to be harvesting and gathering.

What about harvesting and gathering in the mall?

That's essentially the same act.

photo by Bill Streeter

STEPHANIE STREETER

"My parents were outdoorsy people who, although in middle age, still presented a vigorous and enthusiastic appetite for life. If we weren't camping, then we were hiking. We were outside and we were gardening. We canned all of our food. It was a shock for me to go to a friend's house and realize that when they talked about canned vegetables, the vegetables actually came in a can! I thought that everybody's canned vegetables were the ones that I ate, meaning in the Ball jars."

STEPHANIE STREETER

Stephanie Streeter and her husband, Bill Streeter, rehabilitate birds of prey. They came upon this unusual passion in 1979, while Bill was completing a masters degree at the University of Massachusetts in Amherst. They attended a program on birds of prey and "were just blown away," says Streeter. "To know that you could work with birds, experience them, not just at a zoo, or even, as I love to do, watching them migrate, but have a more intimate relationship with them—it was life changing."

Stephanie soon got training to become a falconer. She was the second licensed woman falconer in Massachusetts. (Her friend, Julie Ann Collier, was the first.) A year later, her husband became a falconer as well. As a falconer, Stephanie soon learned that people were finding and picking up injured birds of prey, but at that time, there was very few treatment options. Few veterinary schools had what is called "exotic medicine." So, she and Bill became licensed as wildlife rehabilitators and founded a rehab facility in Massachusetts that was incorporated into the environmental education that Bill was doing there. Soon after, Tufts University opened up its Tufts Veterinary School Wildlife Clinic, and the couple had the use of the veterinarians there.

The couple returned to Pennsylvania in 1985, although, says Stephanie, "we had no intention of coming home." They came at the behest of the Natural Science for Youth Foundation, which had a center in Milford. They were asked to head the environmental education department and begin a program with birds of prey. And when the Natural Science Center folded, they remained. The Delaware Raptor Center became their own non-profit corporation and labor of love.

The center rehabilitates a full range of birds of prey every year, and the birds that cannot be returned to the wild are used in the center's education program. The center visits festivals, museums, schools and bird clubs to educate the public about the magnificent birds of prey native to the Upper Delaware River region. In a typical year, Stephanie and Bill run one hundred and seventy-five or one hundred and eighty programs.

Standing before a crowd, wearing thick gloves and controlling a golden eagle or a great horned owl, is the glam side of the business, says Stephanie. "But ninety percent of what we do is real dirty clockwork. Let me tell you, it is not pretty. The glamour part is what you see at a program; the bird has been trained and you stand there and view close up that marvelous bird. It looks glamorous and it's appealing. But that's just a very small part of what we do."

The work is a calling, and she demonstrates the rough joy she takes in it as she calls her wounded birds by name, cage by cage, clucking and cooing and encouraging them back to health and the wild.

BIRDS AND DIRTY CLOCKWORK:
Interview with Stephanie Streeter

Delaware Valley Raptor Center, Milford, Pennsylvania
March

[Stephanie Streeter and I began our interview outside in the bird enclosures, where she introduced me to many of the birds in her care. The Delaware Valley Raptor Center has two buildings, one for program birds who are used for education and cannot, for medical or other reasons such as imprinting, be released into the wild; and the other for birds that are being rehabilitated for release back into the wild. I was given a tour of the program bird building.]

(Talking to birds:) "Hello Pandora, hello sweet girl, I know, I know darlin', hi, hello sweet, we'll be over in a minute. Hello, sweetie, you're so gorgeous. Ace, hey, you!"

Ace is a peregrine falcon. This is the bird that we pretty much wiped out in the Northeast, the whole eastern population with DDT.

The reintroduction program was remarkably successful, so successful that the Peregrine was taken off the endangered species list. Ace is one of the wild bred peregrines. Unfortunately he tackled a car and lost.

Most of the birds we see tend to be impact injuries.

How long have you had Ace?

About two years now, I believe.

What do you feed him?

Quail. These are bird-eating falcons, so we try to keep their diet as true to what they eat in the wild. We feed him quail but he also will eat rodents, mice and rats, as well, and chicks. He's a program bird so, you know, he's an ambassador for endangered species. People get to see this bird who at first looks rather small, but can hit two hundred miles an hour in a dive, coming down at prey, pretty mind-boggling.

A lot of states have cameras on their breeding sites so that you can watch Peregrines breeding and raising their chicks. They're ledge nesters, and rather than going back to their natural habitat, they started nesting on skyscrapers and city bridges, which actually makes perfect sense because it puts them into the same position that they are in their natural habitat, overlooking a lot of prey, in the case of cities a lot of—

Pigeons?

Yes, pigeons. Smorgasbord time.
These are the New York City nesting birds. In fact, there is a nesting pair of peregrines on every bridge from New York City up the Hudson River to Syracuse; I've been told.

When did your interest in birds begin?

I've always loved birds and I've been taking care of them since I was a little girl. My father used to introduce me to people and say, "This is my oldest daughter; she's feather-happy." We lived near Hawk Mountain, in Kempton, Pennsylvania. Lots of years the family would go to watch the migration.
I started taking care of song birds that were orphaned. My parents would help me to raise them. Nobody was licensing then, nobody thought about that. I'd get feather mites, which are just real tiny little things but you find them in almost all nests, and as soon as you touch a bird that has feather mites they're all over you. My mother would look at my father and say, "Your daughter has feather mites," and my father had to take me and shower me down.

What is that bird there? Is that a falcon?

That is Pandora, a gyrfalcon-peregrine hybrid, nothing that occurs in the wild. I'm not a big fan of captive breeding and cross breeding, but this was a bird that was a falconer's bird and it was cross bred, so it had some of the best characteristics of the gyrfalcon and the peregrine falcon. The bird was hurt when she was hunting and she can't fly anymore. She's a captive bird and she's imprinted. Imprinting is a socialization that happens when a human takes care of them, feeds them and raises them; they imprint on that human. It makes a social misfit. She's soliciting me right now. This is breeding season and she's running over to me, talking to me, she has no idea that she should be soliciting another bird. "Huh, Pandora?"
She will seek me out, but she is not friendly in a sense that a domesticated pet is friendly. She's a little bit more friendly right now because it's breeding season.

She will start laying eggs eventually, as will a lot of our birds. But they will be infertile. We don't allow them to breed. This isn't a breeding facility, it's a rehab facility. We try to get the birds back in the wild, that's the whole point. Here are barred owls; aren't they wonderful?

Sure are.

This is probably my favorite owl, one of the few dark-eyed owls. Oddly enough, they have found barred owls and spotted owls that have bred in the wild. They are closely related.

What happened to this bird?

This bird was shot, I believe. It is one of our program birds as well. You see the leather strap? That's how we hold them and control them.

How do you acquire your birds?

We'll get phone calls from the police, game commission and the park service, and just folks who find birds.

"Hi, Pretty girl." That's a red-tailed hawk. Our most common hawk, but you can't take them for granted; they're such glorious looking birds.

They're bigger than I thought.

This is a substantial bird. You see she's looking at you out of one eye and the other eye she keeps away? The eye that she can't see out of is the one that's facing you now. She fell out of the nest when she was young and evidently the nest was very near to the road; she was hit by a car and she lost the vision in one eye. Some of the eye surgeons at Boston General tried to give it a go, save her vision, and she was on Tom Brokaw's national news. Unfortunately, the surgery didn't work, but she had her fifteen minutes of fame.

And here's our beautiful Julia. She's a golden eagle. Probably the most gorgeous bird we've got in the United States. They have a nice body shape; they've got those incredible gold hackles coming down; look at the back of her neck and head, in the sunlight that just glows golden. They stretch out wings that are almost seven feet. These guys can fly straight out at one hundred miles an hour. She's a program bird as well—another victim of vehicle impact.

Are they native to Northeastern Pennsylvania?

They are not native, but they migrate through here. They are Canada birds and they come down here in winter along with the Canada balds that come down in winter. And we have one golden that spends most of the winter in the park service down here. We know it's there. Here is Lizzie!

Another beauty.

And another barred owl. She is clicking her beak to threaten you, uh-huh. Lizzie is aggressive for a barred owl. They tend to be rather sweet, laid-back owls. But Lizzie will always fly by and take a swipe at your head. Of course they're silent flyers, so she almost always gets us. But Lizzie will be going back to the wild, actually.

It's interesting the way she shuts her eyes like that.

Well, you see the white that goes over first? That's what is called a nictitating membrane; and some people call it the third eyelid. It offers protection.

Can she see through it?

Yes, although it's rather blurred, kind of an opaque.

What is this area?

Here is where we place food on the boards for the birds that have been newly released. If they're not hunting particularly well, they come back home to the boards to get some food till they finally get it right. And they'll wean themselves off of it. Some birds never use it; they're gone, that's it. But some birds will come back and use it.

And at a particular time each night, we'll put food out for the baby owls that we've released.

It's like a halfway house?

Yes, exactly! A halfway house for birds.

This area back here, this forest will never be developed, which is one of the reasons we bought our house. This is the Delaware State Forest. It's ten contiguous miles of land over to our other raptor center on the other side of town.

That must be a good feeling when you're releasing the birds out here.

As a matter of fact, yes.

Is there any bird that you would not accept, like if somebody tried to bring you a crow?

We're only licensed for birds of prey. So, hawks, eagles, owls.

We'd get them in touch with another rehabilitator, we'd make sure that the bird gets help, or the mammal for that matter.

Is that a saw-whet owl?

That's a saw-whet. Isn't that amazing? Aren't they wonderful?

They sure are.

They are Disney characters. But they're fierce little prey birds.

This bird here is a cooper's hawk

Cooper's hawks are bird eaters as well; they're extremely fast, they can take song birds very easily. They're called the accipiters. This is the mid-sized of the accipters, the goshawk is the largest, then the cooper's and then the sharp-shinned hawk. Often times they will fly full tilt into windows chasing birds and they can cut themselves badly or will break necks.

Are these the ones that hang around the bird feeders?

Yes.

Will red-tailed hawks hang around the birdfeeders too?

Not as much. They're not as fast and as agile.

Do bald eagles eat birds?

They will eat water fowl if they can get them.

That's a cooper's hawk that's not doing well and we won't bother him. He's got neurological damage, see? He's not standing well.

Yes.

You're going to have to believe me that there are screech owls in there, but they're sleeping. They're nocturnal, so they're in their little hole.

What are in these two little buildings?

Well, one has a kestrel in it. She's rather aggressive right now. She's got a strange story. Drug agents had a tip on an apartment they had been watching, near Harrisburg. They went in for a big raid, and took out all kinds of drugs, money, guns and one kestrel. Nobody could figure out what they were doing with a kestrel. They obviously took her illegally out of the nest; she was imprinted.

How do you get birds ready for release?

We start them in treatment cages inside. From there they move outside to a smaller enclosed building, and from there into a larger light enclosure. It's a gradual process.

[Stephanie and I move inside to her tidy split-level home and three dogs, where we continue our conversation.]

Where did you attend college?

I went to Moravian. I started there in 1965. I majored in music, but I didn't graduate.

Are you still involved in music?

Oddly enough, two weeks ago I bought a piano. Playing is one of those things that just takes you away from everything. Like these Zen moments; you get your mind completely blank.

Do you and Bill spend all your time with the birds?

My husband works full time. One of us has to earn enough money so that we can live.

So, it's a labor of love.

It is. You are not, certainly, going to get rich doing this. You're going to get rich as far as the experience in what you've done, no doubt about it. But financially, you are always scraping for pennies to do what you do.

What do you get from being close to the birds?

There's just been this fascination for me with the feather.

Is it because they fly?

I think that's part of it—the incredible freedom of these birds tooling through the air. I do realize that a red-tailed hawk that I help is not going to have an impact one way or another on the environment or on the species. But to me, saving that one bird matters a great deal to me and to the person who brought it to me, who found it. There's a deep sense of fulfillment. And if one of the birds brought to me is an endangered species, then I have really made a difference. We literally have to know how many are in our state, and I have saved one bird that can go back to the breeding pool.

What is your relationship with forests, or with other parts of nature?

I was born in the '40s; I was a war baby. We went camping for our vacations. At that time, you used army surplus equipment because that's what was available. The big camping thing hadn't happened yet, either. We went to one of our state parks on the Fourth of July when I was a little girl and there were ten other people in the park, ten. Now you've got to make a reservation a year in advance and you're lucky if you get a slot to put your tent up.

I started my daughter camping at eight months old. You set up a playpen and you put the kid in; she doesn't care where she's sleeping as long as Mom's there.

What is one of your earliest memories of the outside and nature?

Gosh, you know, I never thought about it, my first outdoor experience.

Even if it's just impressionistic, you know, something that comes back to you.

Walks in the woods. Some of the first walks were with my Polish grandfather. He didn't speak English. He was wonderful at identifying mushrooms. He would take me into the woods all day when I was a tiny girl and show me the ones to pick and put in the basket to take home to my grandmother. I still remember that. My grandfather had a pigeon loft in my backyard, and he had it simply because he loved to see birds fly. You know the way pigeons circle, they're wonderful birds. They don't get enough credit for the great birds that they are. They would circle and he would just sit back in his chair and glory and watch.

Do you remember running around when the fireflies came out for the first time, trying to trap them and having them in the jar and they'd light up and then letting them go? Stuff like that was so much fun. When Sailors Lake froze, we would drive from Allentown and spend the day there. We packed up hot chocolate and sandwiches and there was always a bonfire at the edge of the lake.

I can still remember the smell of the fall woods. We'd kick the leaves, the pretty colors and say, "How far can we go? How far can we walk?" There was a trail near our house. My girlfriend and I used to go on hikes, just on our own.

These days, all the parents drive down to the edge of the road so they can drive their children home from the school bus. They can't live more than a mile away. Can't these children walk? Obesity's got to be a problem because we don't get off our fannies anymore. These days, when I see kids outside playing I want to stop and say, "You're outside, good for you!"

We walked home for lunch. I realized times have changed now; mothers work; our mothers stayed at home. It was the Eisenhower era, mom at home, dad working, the ideal family. And you walked to school and walked home for lunch and you walked back to school and you walked home. By the time you were done walking, you had put in a couple of miles.

At dusk, you could hear all the mothers calling the kids, you know, all the names being bellowed up and down through the neighborhood.

Behind us were horses. Up the block was a chicken coop where I'd go and get the eggs from my neighbor. My grandparents lived a couple of miles away. The roads weren't paved at the time. Nobody was concerned that something would happen to us. I was ten years old and riding two miles on my bike to my grandparents' house.

Do you feel that there's a spiritual aspect of your relationship with the birds, with wilderness, with nature?

I think there's a hint of wilderness in everything and a spiritual bond with everything. Do I feel that in a religious way? Quite honestly, no. I feel this interconnectedness with the world. It is a spiritual feeling because everything that I do impacts the world.

Have your feelings about religion and spirituality changed through your work with the birds?

My feelings about religion have evolved over the years. I was, quite happily, raised in the church. I have no regrets about it and a lot of good memories from those years. But the older I got, the more ill-will I've seen, and so many bad things happening in the name of religion. We're still fighting religious wars, aren't we? How can that be?

I've seen the biggest hypocrites in the churches with the loudest voices, and some of the best people I've known are very quiet people living those blessings we were taught: "Do unto others."

Do you believe in the concept of good and evil; do you think evil exists? Do you think it's a force in the world? Do you think that good is also a force in the world?

I think there's good and bad, but I also think that you cannot do something bad, whether a small bad thing or a gigantic evil act, but that you will pay for it. What goes around comes around. And is there evil? Yes, I think there are some truly evil people. You can't explain them otherwise, can you?

I was taught, raised in a Christian church, you die and go to heaven, but the concept of reincarnation makes more sense to me in how people evolve. You do see truly evolved people, truly gentle people that do only good. You get a sense that they have knowledge from a previous life. You can't imagine a Gandhi having gotten to that point by just the lifetime that he lived.

So many of us wander away from one kind of life to another, like my very Christian, WASP upbringing. Let's face it, you know: White Anglo-Saxon Protestant—raised in the United Church of Christ, went to Sunday school, Daddy was a Sunday school teacher, sang in the choir, went to all the church groups, but the church didn't have the answers I needed. Where does it say: "Do not kill except?" No, you don't kill somebody for believing in following cows or having purple skin, anymore than you walk up to the rattlesnake and kill it because you're afraid of it.

What is your most memorable experience with the birds?

Probably the most unusual was when I got a call from the Honesdale [Pennslvania] police department. They said, "There's an owl in a hole in a tree." The tree was bending the power lines so it had to be taken down, and the workmen didn't want to take it down with the owl in it.

I drove to the site. They loaded me into a cherry picker and shot me right up to the top of the tree. It was two stories up. I could look down on all the houses in Honesdale. I could look in and see the owl, and I stuck my hand in and grabbed it. It was just a little screech owl, you know. All these big brawny guys and they stick this little lady into a cherry picker, throw her up to the top of the tree to get the owl out. I got down and I had all these big burly guys beside me, posing for a picture with this little screech owl.

Not a year ago, the day after the floods near Narrowsburg [New York], we got a call that there were two young bald eagles. The park service was there. They're large birds, let's face it; nobody wanted to pick them up. A truck had hit and killed one and the other one we brought back. As it turned out, they were just soaking wet. They had gotten so wet in those rains that they simply couldn't fly. Had they been removed from the side of the road, we would have had two alive.

What's the best approach for grabbing a live bird of prey off the side of the road?

We tell you on our website [www.dvrconline.org] exactly how to rescue a bird of prey. But if you have a towel or a blanket you can throw over them, that's fine; a pair of leather gloves, that's great. You have to secure their legs first. Ideally, you go over their back and get the legs. That's what they'll use to defend themselves. Most raptors don't bite. It's the talons you have to worry about.

Falcons are the exception. Falcons are biters.

Once you've got them, put them in a cardboard box. Don't lay them on their backs—just right on their feet or on their belly. Close up the cardboard box and that's it: give your wildlife rehabilitation center a call. It's a porous box; they'll be able to breathe through it.

And they won't try to fly out once you put them in a box?

No, raptors are very visual. In fact, that's why falconers have hooded them for thousands of years. As soon as you put a hood on and take away their vision, they calm down.

Do you think that women have a different approach to nature?

Women, in relation to the environment and the outdoors, have not gotten their due. We're out there, we're doing all the stuff the guys are doing. Rachel Carson, God love her, not only for what she did, but for the fact that a woman was the one that was sounding the alarm. I see more compassion in women. I see more patience in women; they don't give up and they will persevere. You know, if you have to get up every four hours one more night you're going to scream, and yet, women rehabilitators will persevere. They say, "Well, I've got to." I think it begins with the compassion that women feel for everything, what we feel for our children and what we feel for other people.

Does that translate in general, in how women relate to nature?

I think we're more aware. It's not all flash and boom and bang out there. Women notice the smaller things and it delights us. A spider web with dew on it is beautiful. Spiders I find most fascinating and I can sit and watch them. I like to watch toads. You know, I don't know that most men find all that much fascination in toads.

Women have an approach that is smaller, more intimate, more personal. Perhaps we see a little more, too, for that reason. You might see princess pine, and they're so tiny; you can pick them up and make a wreath. But first you have to see them. For a lot of guys, camping goes along with another activity. You're camping because you're kayaking the rapids to test yourself, or skiing a mountain to test yourself, or you're out there because you're going to fish this wonderful hole or go hunting. Women a lot of times just camp.

What about your daughter? Is she into birds?

She still lives in Massachusetts. And I don't know that she could tell you a pigeon from a peregrine. Isn't that weird?

But, if you ask about her strongest memory of her mom… well, when she was about sixteen she was working for a big antique fair. We were still in Massachusetts. She had to get up real early to get on the road to get to this fair. I had gotten up even earlier because I had young birds that I was feeding and the easiest way to do it was to stand out in the garage; there was a wood stove and we had this big stump. We were in the middle of the woods, the middle of nowhere. She walks into the garage, 6:30 in the morning, there is her mother in a pink housecoat with a hatchet in her hand, chopping up mice.

I'd take her to school when she was thirteen and fourteen and, I mean, if I saw a freshly killed squirrel, the eagles would love it, freshly killed rabbit? Forget it. I'd hit the breaks. This poor kid would get underneath the dashboard and she'd say, "Oh my God, Mom!" She'd hide under the dash until I would get back in the car and drive down the road like a normal mother.

Are you at all squeamish?

You can't be. Do I like it? Nah. But it's funny how people are affected. I had a park service ranger bring in a red-tailed falcon. This bird had just been shot, pepper-shot all through its body. He handed me the bird and I opened it up and started taking care of it, and it was just bleeding profusely. He took one look and I saw the guy going white.

When I get a bird that's injured, it's gruesome; it's awful. On top of that, the wound gets infested with maggots in the summertime and you've got to pull those out. It's just gross beyond words. What's peculiar is that Bill and I have been vegetarians for almost thirty years, but we take care of birds and meat is all they eat and we've got to prepare it for them.

Have you ever gotten ill from any of that?

We, no, none of us have. We've been extremely lucky.

Is there anything that you would change about your life if you could?

As Joseph Campbell suggested, I followed my bliss. In spite of long hours, no private life, low wages, etc. I wouldn't change a thing. I am doing what I love.

If you sit back and think about it, you can still smell autumn, can't you? You can smell what winter smells like. You can smell winter, certainly spring. I'm hearing the birdsongs now. It's really quiet and all of a sudden, it's going to be so noisy.

All your senses are involved, aren't they? You can see it, smell it, feel it, the mildness or the harshness of the air. The way the ground feels when you walk, whether it's frozen or muddy, like now. By April, end of April, we'll be looking again for rattlesnakes. There are some dens around here.

Discreet, Flagrant Abundance

Lori Anderson Moseman

留靈修兮憺忘歸
"Waiting for the divine one, I forget to go home."
                Qu Yuan from "Mountain Spirit"

She stands doves up outside
their towel-n-steel nest.
"Fledglings, feed yourself."
I get to watch them slop.
Later, she will wash them
not with soap or fire or any
four-letter configuration—
not "love" not "evil."

       *

Somedays zikr is birdsong:
multivocal warble, fingers
pulling prayer beads apart.
Still, I trade whirling
lessons for a boat
full. Tribe of 22, we sync
our paddles into wings
raise a dragon out of water.

       *

Old plot: a protester drowns,
and we race to a rescue.
Today, not a single word
twitters from Qu Yuan's
variable lines. Our tongues
tied. Stroke seat sets
a count we see before drums
quicken our torso turns.

Eat & Try Not To Be Eaten

Lori Anderson Moseman

last night

fox's story as told by a freckled-face
girl who knew when to use a ladder
to climb a beech so vista let her see
the vixen transverse the glen again

girl enters the door in the mountain:
burrows in moss, drinks run-off,
leaps gorge cliffs, scrambles scree,
wards off wolves, nuzzles fox cubs

she goes where vixen willingly leads
the leash, we know, is a mistake
as is fire and *playing house*. boxed-in
the fox lunges out a second story

window. girl must carry the wounded
wild back into the woods, walk away,
let little foxes lick its mother clean
let the vixen battle back on all fours

night before last

a flick, *Following*, about imprinting
(stalk, break, enter) murderous
end. again. a master manipulates
dedication and discipleship. curiosity.

man shaves to clean-up for break-in
takes one pearl earring then a million
bills he tapes to his body, hammers
the doorman-on-surveillance dead

such is the Marilyn-Monroe wannabe
model broad at a grand piano
doomed to be what she witnesses
body on a bloody carpet, throw away

rug another layer protecting nothing
blackmailer is surprised when she's double-
crossed. we distance ourselves
discuss jump-cuts and the slicing of time

one of my dogs watches growling
at sudden movement, sound track
triggers concern as does my tensing
my other dog sleeps until I weep

Bear
Sandy Long

She called me at work
end of the day,
to see if I wanted to walk.

Always say yes
when walking's in question,

unless you're dead—

like the bear we
stumbled up to,
stupefied at its dark
mass, its missing
head, its vast flanks
intact and tumbled.

The reducers,
busy at their buzzing tasks
made bone emerge,
paw, rib and spine,
while fat gathered
and dripped
from furred tips.

She moved off toward the water with the dog.

I drew my shirt up to cover my face,
and bent to look.

And bent to see.

Four
Mary Olmsted Greene

1.

A woman sits in a chair by a pond.
Early summer, early afternoon.
Hands small and freckled, fingers blunt.
Eyes closed, she listens to the woods
she's walked, mellow green mornings—

> *Walking into a flat mowed place.*
> *It was always very private. No one ever came.*
> *I was not an observer, not thinking, "how beautiful."*
> *I didn't go in a band of kids.*
> *I was a scientist, looking. Just*
> *a sort of walk, you know, going deeper.*

Bear across her vision
snuffles for ants, berries, beetles.

Black bear and black dog, hair rising.
The woman heads carefully toward
the porch. Here she sets out birdseed

on a straight plank of wood,
makes tea for her husband.

2.

In the city she says: I have one tree,
growing outside my window.
It is her voice and it says I have one tree, you see.

October. Scarlet leaves fall.
December. Branches black against white snow.
Summer. Dominican music coming from the corner.

The bus with its big wheels. The wheeling river.

Because we are not trees.
Is that what she is thinking?

My mother was a nurse. We lived
in a housing tract on the very edge of Albuquerque, below
the Sandia Mountains. Between civilization
and these mountains. Just a little walk, you know,
of the sort to make you go deeper

Take some twigs, tear off the bark.
See what's inside, how it could bend.

Never any real story lines

3.

By the time I found my father

> (and it was a long, long
> bus ride, sandwiches
> bought from a machine
> in Milwaukee)

he was dead.

> *and that's all you are*
> *chair facing the window*

So, long hair wreathed in cigarette smoke
I kissed my children goodbye.

I went to Sunday school
My grandma took me
sat there and waited for Jesus

> *roots in the earth*
> *just stand and breathe at the trees*
> *whiz whiz whiz*

Evil is a veil,
a covering.

Spend years pounding paper
against the wall with paint
allowed me to forgive myself

> *to be lifted*

4.

I walked through all
the stations of the cross
until my ego
died

Such power, every place
Every place is power

experiential
sluggish with earth practice
the point of it all to experience God

                        Get rid of myself into nature

                You sit down, you take a little piece of this
                        magic
                        unknown
                        random
and you put it there and you paste it on
and you understand something—a doorway

        Little self-portraits made with physical reminders:

connection between Reiki   *and little girl Indian—*

if you are searching   *something*

you can find the key   *that you recognize*

                             as yours

Doorways

Mary Olmsted Greene

> with thanks to Henry Miller's *Tropic of Capricorn* for certain
> of the passages stolen and stowed below...

one

Where's the bottle? she asked.

Don't you sometimes just want to drink all day?

She sat at her desk
and thought of eating pretzels.
Fingers handling words,
ears on the plastic and mouth at the wood
of pencils. Cliffs opened and crumbled,
the telephone barked and dusk fell.
Across the street, red neon glowed
and the sun left a drift of rose petals
against the gun metal sky.

It gave her back to herself.
It handed her over, inside.

She saw a wrapped cocoon, milky and silent.
It lay under the leaf fold as though there were all the time in the world.

It would climb oceans, if need be. To be of night so frighteningly silent—a worm a brook—heartless as the earth itself.

It was hot so she went up on the hillside to garden.
The sun, that old lover, beat her with yellow fists.
She took her bottle along—such company.
She put her hoe in the earth and turned the earth over.
Over and over, black dirt, tiny glowing seeds.
She was thirsty and had a drink.
The vodka was white fire,
the white dress of it set a sail for her
and the sky wrapped her up in blue silk.
She traveled over oceans and came upon a shore.
She lapped there, indolent, napping.
Did a lover come, whisper her name into her ear?

    Mountains opened into vistas of black eyes, steel rivets, roads.
    The natives caught fish and told their histories.

It was a continent of holdups, wild waves and fire from the nostrils. It was the same shelf of rock evolving ceaselessly, pitilessly. It wanted destruction, a change to fish, swallowing everything, alone for a thousand years to reflect and to forget—

Upon returning she watched her body, its soil and tear.
Her head, an anchor.

two

A car wreck and a woman lay dead in the morgue. *It was a deer, it darted across the road*, said the cop. The family came to view the body. An angular woman with grave gray eyes stood alongside her mother. She whispered to her sister's face: *you're beautiful*, to the lost warmth of her form, the innocent fall of hair, newly washed. She imagined her sister's mouth, opening toward the trees; the shape fast-forwarding out of the forest; the horned resistance, the great greenish head rising from the void; the night in black and white; the snow a secret message, falling from the sky; the secret of snow drifting over the car seats and the blue cross, swinging.

> *The Green Man dons his cap*
> *from a hollow tree in the hollow hill.*

three

The woman was out in nature, her dog Sadie was there, and she was searching.
for something—for a layer beneath a layer, a different view of the pines.
Nature, show me, she prayed.
A sign, a thunderstorm, a wild apple.

She knew the path, had traveled it often in childhood.
Her feet went unerringly into ruts and past the brook. Sadie
bounded along, sniffing everything, lapping thirstily.
They came round a bend and heard sounds: cracking and squishing.

A little further on. Curious. A big sound. What?
Striding on the familiar path into three black bear cubs,
tumbling in succession from a tree. The dog, running forward.
The mother bear, backing up, readying to charge.

       I ran off and got myself lost, said the woman later.
       It was blind terror.
       I stopped running finally, my lungs cracking.
       I did not know where I was.

She and the dog emerged from the woods, miles
from the camping lodge where they began. The bears were not
seen again, but on the path, several deer, startling them
with movement. And a lazy rattlesnake curled behind a log.

       She thought: that snake
       was asleep. It did not have any awareness of me.
       I could have taken its picture. Looked closely.

            I am the bear, I am running from the bear.
              My feet are sand and gravel and water.
            Out of conscious time, I am lightening, I am leaping air.
            I am the bear, I am running from the bear.

four

> I could give the danger signal
> But I was powerless to avert catastrophe
> Eye so wide awake it made all my other faculties dormant
> Wanted the eye extinguished so
> I might have a chance to know my own body, my desires…

Once, she took the subway by mistake into Harlem.

Everything was burned out, abandoned. She was the only white girl
in sight, no clue how to get out. After an eternity of walking

she remembered to follow the street signs south. 127th. 126th.
People understood, pulling their long arms away from their bodies

to point the way. A man stood in front of her
in plaid trousers, dancing. She did not look at him.

Back in her kitchen on 98th Street, she trembled with fear.
A mouse poked its city snout out of the burner, climbed up

on the ring. She screamed loudly enough
to wake the dead. Her scream, waking the dead.

> *Get yourself*
> *Get yourself out*
>
> *Get yourself out of the picture*

I walk up the hill. Up and back.
Up and back with a roll of film.
This curl of sweet fern against the snow,
a simple form, a pleasure
and part of something much larger.
I look for the dual sides of things.
The two halves of an eye.

There is wilderness in a dandelion in the yard
and in the rusting Buddha, sitting out its term among the mountains.
It rains, it snows, the clouds blow, the sun shines.

five

I don't recall my childhood. It is a subliminal doorway
that I was in for twelve years. My family tells me that we spent
a lot of time out of doors. We didn't do the social circle kind
of thing; we came to the lodge; we walked in the woods; we
built campfires. I remember sitting under a rose-of-sharon tree
in the yard. I felt good, sitting there.

I wanted to shake the stone and the light out of my system
I wanted the dark fecundity of nature, the well of the womb
Night diapered with stars and comets
Buds breaking in anguish
A starfish swimming on the frozen dew of the moon...

There is something deep and mystical and trusting.
This is my relationship to wilderness.
It grows deeper.

Behind the pane of reality, another reality, perhaps, and another and another.
It is our human form that disallows us to trust. We grow attached; values
Grow on us like new buds, like barnacles. Our form takes us walking over the earth,
Claiming its ravines and its cliffsides, zooming the sky, paving flowers.

six

It is early morning in a western park
A woman is jogging
There is a cougar up in a tree above the path

    The cougar is pregnant and hungry

        It is an early morning in a western park

    The jogging woman finds her death

People react, throw up their hands,
Look for ways to restrict the path
Of the cougar, of the wild hungry mouth.

        Perhaps
        there is no evil in the world,
        only a brutal honesty. Just

        a facet of something larger.
        The ice-cold life in the hollow
        of an atom, awaiting its hugeness,

        its spectacular otherness.
        Sometimes it dances a little closer.
        Sometimes a little further away.

        The woman on stage howls
        like a cow for what's been lost,
        a wind in the swirl of her skirt.

There are limits on the physical places people can go.
You buy some land, you own some land
And go up and sit on the hill
And you hear cars, and car horns, and brakes, and planes
Going over the mountain. And there is just no where—

> *In a sunrise, one of those altering*
> *experiences where you wake up.*
> *And when you wake up everything is different.*

—but in the wrap of wing
over the tongue. The silencing of these words.

body

KNOWLEDGE

KAREN MACINTYRE is director of Triad Dance Ensemble in Sullivan County, New York; and is owner and director of Green Space Arts Collective in Denton, Texas. Her work as a dancer and choreographer has been produced at Kennedy Center, Yale University, and many other national venues. She has received funding for and written five original musicals, including "Crazy Good Luck," which was accepted into The New York International Fringe Festival in 2009. MacIntyre holds an MFA in Dance from Texas Women's University, and a BFA from the University of Texas. Her favorite place in nature is floating down the Delaware River.

PEGGY HAMILL was born in 1951 in Washington, D.C. and grew up along the New Jersey shore. She received an RN in nursing from the University of Tennessee and settled on the Maine coast, where she worked as a county home health nurse and raised two daughters. She continues her life-long study of nature and wilderness, coupled with her study of Buddhist philosophy and mysticism, in Taos, New Mexico, where she moved in 2009 with her partner, Ted Keller. The Rocky Mountains are Peggy's favorite wild place.

DOROTHY HARTZ is a native of Sullivan County, New York, in the Upper Delaware River Valley, the source for much of her writing. She has a BA and MA in Literature from SUNY at Oneonta. Retired from a thirty-year career as a teacher of English, she has administered grants for the Delaware Valley Arts Alliance in Narrowsburg, New York and freelances for local publications. She is a member of the Upper Delaware Writers Collective. Acting, astrology, cats, cooking, gardening and the mysterious are also on her itinerary. Her favorite wild place is the River Road in Callicoon, New York that meanders along the Delaware River.

body **KNOWLEDGE**

For the women in this section, the body is the portal to connection with the earth, the wild, the self and the divine. The way of the body is the way of the senses. The list we learn in first grade—smell, touch, sight, hearing and taste—continue to lead these women toward meaning, knowledge and the comprehension of experience. As David Abram writes in "The Spell of the Sensuous," "the body itself is the true subject of experience."

As we are grounded in the body, so, paradoxically, do the conversations begin to take on a more esoteric tone. We are in a Zen state, traversing the narrow edge of a mountain. We are waxing philosophic about sex as a dissolution of boundaries. We are Artemis, channeling the ancient goddess through the ritual of dance. We are trying to define what "wilderness" is, exactly, and how the concept of DNA connects to the divine order.

This connection to nature and the senses make these women feel both ecstatic and bereft. A close connection to the body teaches us somehow about our separation from the All, from spirit. Being truly in the wilderness means sacrificing the veil of distraction that blankets everyday life for most of us, most of the time. Being truly aware means seeing the layers under the layers. Evil is looked upon by one contributor as "extreme laziness," by another as "insecurity and betrayal."

The conversations and poetry in this section remind us that authenticity must travel simultaneously via abstract thought and our giddy laughter; must be manifested by our terror or our unbounded joy or our need to push against physical limits. Connection comes sensually, with the sudden worship of a field of goldenrod, or the paradox of lanterns on the water, or walking into a forest grotto—the light and shade of a landscape that is within us and without us, pristine, familiar and—ultimately—part of the unknowable, dichotomous Other.

photo by Alan McGill

KAREN MACINTYRE

"I connect with fire at this point because it takes me back to this childhood place. I have been thinking lately about the feeling of homesickness. When I discovered, as a child, that I could experience feeling homesick in my own bed with my parents right there, it was a big heartbreak and disillusionment. Where is home, if not here in my bed? And then, realizing it may not even be a physical place, but somewhere inside myself. Being around a fire has always made me feel a sense of home. Staring into it, feeling a sense of sadness and melancholy and at the same time, ultimate joy."

KAREN MACINTYRE

Karen MacIntyre was born and raised in Denton, Texas. She graduated from the University of Texas in 1977, and two years later moved to New York to pursue her career as a professional dancer. Shortly thereafter, she married her college boyfriend (Peter Pope), who subsequently directed *Torch Song Trilogy*, which weathered long runs off-Broadway before moving to Broadway and winning the Tony Award in 1982. In 1984, the couple had a daughter, Bedarra, named after an island off the coast of Queensland, Australia, which they visited while Peter was directing a production of *Torch Song* in Sydney. Soon after, they bought a country home upstate in Yulan, New York where Karen and Bedarra began to live full time.

I first met her in 1990 when my daughter was Karen's student at The Homestead Montessori School in Glen Spey, New York. I noticed Karen's sturdy frame and long brown hair on the playground as she stood watch over recess. I was a bit intimidated by her clear, direct stare, and when I first heard the musical tones of her Texas-accented voice, I knew I wanted to get to know her.

In addition to teaching at The Homestead, Karen taught private dance classes at her home to my daughter and the kids of nearly everyone I knew. When our children were very young, Karen allowed me and the other mothers to sit on a sofa in her living room/dance studio and watch our little starlets under the guidance of "Miss MacIntyre." I was impressed by her patience and sense of playfulness. She was never critical or cross—there was no tapping baton in her room—she instructed by example rather than by correction. Her goal, she told me, was not to produce dancers with perfect lines, but to produce dancers that felt connected to their bodies and joy in their movements across the floor. Karen choreographed her own dances, bringing her background of Merce Cunningham's modern style to blend with Celtic and other folk dances that she knew. The kids had a ball, and they were beautiful, too.

Karen also founded Triad Dance Ensemble, a modern dance troupe that performs in my area regularly. I have had the great good fortune to collaborate with Karen more than once in multi-media performances involving dance, music and spoken word. She is a wonderful collaborator, coming up with the basic concept for our shows and running things with a steady hand, but also deeply interested in the process of collaboration and how the different art forms flow together. Often, as we worked, the words and music and movement coalesced in ways that are eerily "right" and powerfully lovely.

Karen and I also participated in women's circles together, she generally acting as our shaman by choreographing the movement and planning out the ceremonies. As in her children's dance classes, she had no interest in controlling the final outcome, but would allow the ceremony to take its own shape, falling in and out of focus, but ultimately finding its true design.

Karen has always been at home in the out-of-doors, and her relationship with dance and nature harkens back to childhood, to ritual and the meanings to be found in animals, landscape and symbol. Being with Karen is always surprising, and the stream of her voice (non-stop, she'd be the first to admit) is a rich concoction of music, metaphor, dream, observation, family history and what just happened a second ago. She is filled with a *joie de vivre* that is contagious.

In 2000, Karen moved back to Denton to reside in her childhood home. She continues to study and teach and choreograph dance into her middle age. Karen returns to her house in Yulan for a few months every summer, and vows to return to her home in the woods full time—one of these good fine days.

CAMPING AND OTHER MIRACLES:
Interview with Karen MacIntyre

Woods Road, Yulan, New York
August

Where were you born, Karen?

I was born in Denton, Texas, in a hospital, on May 30, 1954.

Do you remember, as a child, being out in the woods or in your yard, and feeling connected to nature?

The earliest memory that I have is one that I wrote a poem about, called "First Ecstasy." It's about a little girl who finds a pod and opens it and takes a seed out and plants it, and a tree has grown the next day. I must have been two or three.

I knew I had created this big tree, but didn't even go and show my mother, because I felt like it was a magical thing and I should keep it to myself.

What else do you remember?

I have a lot of outdoor memories of summer camp, where my dad was waterfront director and my mother was the camp nurse. Every summer we packed up for six weeks and went to Oklahoma, to Lake Murray. The camp's name was Sunshine, and I was the camp's darling. I have vivid memories of the big campfires, singing, crunching in dirt on the way back to the cabin, all the critters singing in the dark woods, being really afraid of scorpions. And seeing them! Quite often.

We had the back of the infirmary for our living quarters. We were one of the few people in camp with hot water. When I was three or four I got to go into the Brownie unit and stay in one of the cabins. Even though I was too young, they let me do it.

There's something about camp... you are free inside this place that's safe.

Yes—you can be a little unguarded at camp. I have fond, fond memories of the summer heat, the sounds and smells of smoke, and the crackling. I really connect with fires and lakes and dirt paths. When I get back in that environment again, it's like, whoa—it washes right over me. It's one of the reasons I chose to live here in the woods, even though it's nothing like the woods in Oklahoma. It's much denser and taller and older.

I feel a Native American influence in both places. I've always connected with that. I've got Cherokee blood. I just found that out a couple of years ago. I was so relieved—I'm not a poser!

What is your present connection to the woods?

The association right now is that it takes me back to a really good place in my childhood. I was very connected to nature. It could have been a bad memory if I'd hated the sand and dirt and bugs.

Some people are really bothered by bugs.

My mother was. Her favorite item at a picnic was the fly swatter. She was relentless. It was a terribly ungratitifying job because there were always more flies. I connect with fire at this point because it takes me back to this childhood place. I have been thinking lately about the feeling of homesickness. When I discovered, as a child, that I could experience feeling homesick in my own bed with my parents right there, it was a big heartbreak and disillusionment. Where is home, if not here in my bed?

And then, realizing it may not even be a physical place, but somewhere inside myself. Being around a fire has always made me feel a sense of home. Staring into it, feeling a sense of sadness and melancholy and at the same time, ultimate joy.

The camp circles were mostly women because I was at a Girl Scout camp—in fact, all were women but my father and brother, year after year, week after week, summer after summer. One of my favorite sights from those years—and I long to stage it and someday I will—is a floating campfire. You get two metal canoes, and you build a base of logs connecting the two canoes, and then between the logs you build a fire, far enough away that the people who are rowing don't get hot.

The last night of Girl Scout camp, we'd all gather down by the lake around our own fire. My father was often the one down at the lake who started the fire. We'd be singing, and all of a sudden you'd see the fire start to come from across the water. It would be illuminated in the water, and there would be the lapping—whooe—whooe—and the fire would be popping and sending up all these sparks, and you'd just see these silhouettes of the women, the counselors, the older girls who got to do it. Man, it was just so—they took their time, coming across the lake. Eventually the fire would fall down in between, into the water, and be gone. It would burn through the trees that it was sitting on. It was always this big—schwwwwwooooo. Fire becoming water. I don't have much fire in my chart at all. But I do have a fire sign for a daughter and a fire sign for a father. I'm the Gemini; that's an air sign.

Do you know what your moon sign is?

Taurus, so that is the earth. And then I've got Pisces rising, so that's water. But I don't have any fire in my major triad.

What about your connection to water?

Well, I've always been a good swimmer. I never was taught how to swim. They just threw me in, off the dock at the Girl Scout camp. I never cried, never was afraid. I have always loved swimming, the freedom of being able to turn in any direction, and have any limb down toward the core of the earth. It's a magical world under there. I like the sound of it lapping. I think I associate with lakes because I didn't grow up around an ocean; I grew up around a lot of lakes. And some rivers, but mostly lakes.

I am fearful of the ocean. I don't know the ocean well enough to feel at home there. I feel at home *by* the ocean, but I don't really feel at home *in* the ocean. It is a huge force, and I can really feel it when I set my feet in there.

Earlier, we were talking about your swim out at Martha's Vineyard, and the combination of joy and fear—wanting it, being afraid of it. Finally leaping in, meeting that place.

The edge of ecstasy and fright.

Water takes me to a magical place. The stream is the reason we bought our property. The stream is now dry, in the summer, but at other times of the year you hear it as you sleep. Spring and fall, it's running pretty good, and in the winter it gets all icicly and pretty. It's a little wonderland. The deer come, and they like it. It's a natural habitat for animals, which makes our property nice.

I have always felt that you are extremely rooted, grounded on earth. I guess it's because of the dance. You have balance, the ability to be on the earth. It's your art. I feel as though there are so many elements running through you, each strong in its own way. Your imagination is airy, and vivid, and light, and it flies a lot.

Oh, yeah, it does. But about earth, I have a vivid memory of earth from when I was in college. I was taking a psychedelic drug, and I felt a kinship with the earth, as though I was more plant than human. I was laying down in the yard at a drama party, after a show. Everyone was inside and they were dancing, doing their whole thing, showing off for each other, and my friend Judy and I went out and lay down in the grass because we wanted to feel the earth breathe. We were laying flat on our stomach and we were breathing with the earth, all spread out, nose to the grass in this yard in Austin. An actress walked by and said, in this very affected tone of voice—"Oh, the freshmen! They have already passed out and are going to miss the party!" But I had a real pleasurable feeling that meant more to me than what was going on in that house. Which said a lot about me, and the people I chose to hang with.

If you were sitting here alone, what would start to happen for you?

I would start keying into the sounds. The faraway sounds of humans start to really figure very loud: the train, pounding of someone chopping wood or, of course, gunfire—it seems three hundred times louder than in reality because you have gotten to a place where it's so quiet, and there's all this nature.

When you are not talking, you get really quiet, and you listen. And I would be doing that. I might sing a song I might know, like: "Mother, I feel you under my feet, mother, I feel your heart beat." Or, I might lay on my back, looking at the trees, a mosaic, with the light coming through. There are times when I would try, if I had the ability, to draw some of it. I might get really close to something and draw a leaf, or a little tree. I used to like to do a lot of painting and sketching, little works.

I'd like to ask you about dance and how it connects to your relationship with nature.

My dances are becoming more about relationships in nature, between nature; I seem to be moved by those subjects.

For example, my "Artemis" dance. I worked with water, I worked with fire, with earth. I worked with air. Each section was made trying to bring the power of the element into my body and then out in a visual impression for the audience. Working with Artemis made it really easy; I didn't have to stretch for that one. It was a very organic dance.

Before performing, I would stand offstage and call Artemis to me. I'd ask her to fill me up with her energy through my breathing. And then it would be like, boom! I performed it three times. Each time, I tried to take a moment beforehand and say, "The spirit that I called upon to create this dance should be with me when I performed it." 'Else it's an imitation; it's not real.

I like my piece, "Quartet," which again I used the four elements to create. Visually, it's the most beautiful piece I've ever done. Pretty soon everyone's going to say, "Oh, it's another one of those 'four element' dances." Well, you know, it's another one of those "four element" days!

How do you relate with your audience?

I have a lot of guilt about requiring an audience. There's a double-edged sword on this. I need people to notice how well I've done in acquiring my physical dexterity, my stretch and my strengths. I don't get paid very much for it, so I need the approval somewhere else. Then I feel guilty, like I'm begging people to watch me and needing their approval.

The other part of me says, no, this is a gift that you worked hard at. I had supportive parents who loved to watch me dance and helped me acquire the technique. I was always a dancer, even before I took dance. I danced around all over the house and made everybody watch my performance; I danced outside in the garden. I was always walking around on tiptoe as a kid. I loved pictures of fairies, on their tiptoes, about to take flight but not quite. I fancied myself a little dancing fairy.

When I go through periods of not dancing, I go through huge depressions. For years, I didn't really recognize it. I would start to get depressed, which would make me quit dancing, which would cause the depression to get worse.

At the time of the fire in our apartment in New York City, when I lost everything I owned, I was out doing a dance tour. The fire took everything except for one trunk that had all my leotards and tights in it. I lost my job in the dance company at the same time.

That sounds rough. What happened then?

I was married, so I came back to New York. I wouldn't have come back to the city had I not been married. But my husband was there. Back in New York, I didn't want to start dancing again. I didn't have the energy. I was extremely depressed, not doing anything with myself. A friend said, "Hey, when are you going to start dancing again?" She was a dancer, and she said to me, "Don't you want to feel good?" I was afraid to start feeling good again. If I felt good again, something bad would happen and knock me back down. So, I thought it was better to just not feel all that good.

My friend had auditioned a piece to be in a performance out in Brooklyn, kind of a prestigious thing. She had gotten her piece accepted but she didn't have anybody to do it with her. She needed me, so I needed to get in shape. I started dancing again. Ironically, she quit dancing. She doesn't dance anymore. And I do.

The large collaborative performances that you produce seem like such a gift that you give, to the audience but also to the other artists that participate. I'm wondering where the spark comes from that enables you to do it.

I don't really know how it's all going to fit together, but I like the magic of allowing it to take its own course—having everything happen separately, and then fitting it together. It's pretty fresh. I think that makes it exciting for the audience. It's not highly manipulated and honed in—it's wilder, more raw.

There's more room for error, and more risk built in, too. But in another way, it's less risky. The show is the show, instead of, "We didn't do it the way it was supposed to be done." Right now, I happen to be putting everything together that way. The last show I did in Texas was called, "At Your Own Risk." I think there was only one rehearsal before the show where we were all rehearsing together. And it was fabulous!

Where did the name come from?

I kept seeing: "Swim at your own risk." And at a papercutter where I was making xeroxes: "Use at your own risk." Everywhere I went, I saw these "At your own risk" signs. And I thought, well, of course, it's all at your own risk. Every day you wake up, it's your own risk!

Have you ever had an out-of-body experience?

The other day swimming when my fingers got so cold, I had a feeling like I could really leave my body. Like, die.

And I had this immediate homesickness for my father—to be with him.

My friend Pattie held my hands, and I shut my eyes. She said, "Your hands are so cold," and she kept looking at me, concerned. Her face looked huge. I was almost hallucinating. I was scared, because she looked so concerned. I really did feel like I could float away from my body.

I wasn't really ready to do that yet. I love my body. My body is a wonderful home for this spirit. I've been blessed with a body that will do lots of things. I really try not to ask too much of it, to not be unreasonable.

Recently I took a walk with Bedarra, my daughter. She was running circles around me like I used to do to my mother. I was really sore; I had a torn muscle. I'm walking really slow and careful, paying attention to where my heel is hitting the ground. Bedarra was running around, not paying any attention to how her feet were hitting the ground. Not having any feeling that she wouldn't always be able to do that.

Could I be strong enough to live if I couldn't walk?

I could probably lose my hearing, my sense of taste, my sense of smell—even my ability to talk. I wouldn't want to give up walking, or sight. Walking and seeing. I see such strength in other people who are physically incapacitated. In my case, I don't know but that I'd just want to say goodbye to the body and move onward.

What do you think love is?

Well... today, love is my dog. I love my dog, Rags, a whole lot. This morning I woke up and looked at my dog, laying there by my bed, breathing. He's ten. We are getting ready to go back to Texas, and I began to wonder what summer it is that Rags won't be able to come back here to New York again. I had to have a good cry, and hug him. Love in general—self love, romantic love, love for children—do I feel well-loved? Do I feel I love well?

I feel very well loved in my life, and I wonder if people really knew who I was, if they would love me as much—if I was as brutally honest as I would like to be, sometimes. I tend in general to be so outgoing that when I'm feeling inner, people often interpret it as being short or pissed off. When, really, I'm just doing what I need to do, which is pull it in.

You are an interesting mix. You are rather introverted, but all of your creativity is outward, and you are a social person, too.

It's the Gemini thing. There is one part of me that, like you, really likes to hibernate.

What is our role in nature?

We really can't control nature, at all. Man has no control over nature. Nature has total control. Man can hurt the earth and the water, but all in all, nature will kill us if she wants to.

The power of a tornado—

A plague—a war—

We bring that upon ourselves.

When you asked me to do this interview, I began thinking about my connection with nature. Nature is the balance that keeps me from spinning off the planet.

What do you think about the nature of evil? Does evil exist, and if so, what is it?

I think there is evil. I know there is evil. I've seen it. Evil comes from fear. Evil grows in the hearts of human beings who feel abandoned or disconnected or betrayed in life.

Are we born evil?

I don't know if people are born evil, or—because of chemicals and other man-made pollutants—people are born with an inclination to go in that direction. But, I think it comes from an insecure place, a feeling of betrayal and insecurity. And it comes out in this horrible force, so damaging to everyone. A main reason why I'm attracted to music and dance and the arts is because I feel that it compensates in the other direction. It helps people express those things that otherwise might come out in other ways. If you can draw it—write about it—sing it—drum it—dance it... we all are scared, and we are all feeling betrayed in some way or another.

But our society, the violent culture, reinforces that you don't have to be afraid if you have a gun. As if a gun could block fear.

Putting out energy into dance and music and goodness helps me feel I have a shield against negative energy. In reality, I know something bad could happen to me at any time. But it doesn't necessarily mean that everything bad is evil. If I was to have a car wreck, that would not be an evil act. Nothing evil would have happened to me. It may be stupidity or bad luck or not paying attention, but evil did not take me.

On the other hand, if a brutal man with a knife came in my house and slayed me, I would say I was facing evil. That is the face of evil. I've known personally two people that were stabbed to death, and one person who was blown up in the air over Locherby, Scotland. And then, of course, all the women who have been raped, and scared, and hurt.

It's born of fear—fear of people who have power that you don't have.

That's why I think so many evil acts are committed on women—because men fear our power, and they feel somehow if they can keep us afraid, we won't be powerful.

Some people do it to children.

What about people who do it to themselves, through addiction or other self-destructive behavior?

It could be a vein of the same thing. I have participated in self-destructive behavior, certainly, at times in my life, less with addiction to chemicals than with addiction to a certain kind of dark energy in other people. Wondering about that dark energy, flirting with that dark energy. Wanting to marry the Dark Lord.

Maybe the attraction to the darker element of humans is the feeling that if you embrace it, you won't be afraid of it. It loses its power over you.

I don't believe the devil is a red man with a tail. In fact, I was the devil, last Halloween. Lee Ann and I went as the devil girls. We both dressed like devils, and handed candy out to people, on the street. It was fun to be wicked, and move, dance like the devil girls.

The astrologer, Caroline Casey, says that if we don't release negative or dark energy or emotion, it can become crisis. But that we can use art to release and transform it into a positive force. She says: dance it, draw it, write it, or it becomes crisis.

In Texas I have TV. When I get up in the morning, in Texas, I turn on the TV. And I'm aware of what's going on in the world and I react to it.

Here, in New York, I don't have TV. The first couple of days of being back, I wake up and feel like, "Oh what am I going to do?" But I remember: "Oh, wow, I can read in the morning!" And I begin to read again, and just get an earlier start on my day. I have a lot of dances to create, so I use a lot of that morning time. And, I begin to do yoga again.

I'm not a preacher against television because I think there are positive aspects to it, but all in all, I think it has been a negative addition to our society because it has taken us away from some of those things that give us spiritual connection. We are feeding our heads full of other people's words, and other people's ideas, instead of voicing our own.

What happens when we die?

I was brought up in a Christian society (although my parents were really atheists; I don't think they had a lot of faith in some good power forgiving them for everything they'd ever done wrong). I didn't know the word "reincarnation," but as soon as I heard it, I thought, "Oh, so that's what it's called."

A leaf on the forest floor becomes the forest again—one giant circle. I always assumed that human beings did the same thing. I don't really ever feel, when someone dies, sad for them. When someone dies, it's sad for us, because they are gone, but they are existing in some other place. The knowledge of reincarnation, or the cycle, has been a calming influence. It certainly helped me through the loss of my parents, my grandparents and all my other ancestors. It's sad for me, but it's not sad for them. Maybe we will meet in another place. I never felt fear of dying. I would dearly miss my body, as I said, but nature is what gave it to me.

Some say that the gift—the wonder, the mystery—is that the spirit, our spirit, any spirit, has been allowed to live in a body. Has become embodied, and can experience the sensual wonder and delight of the physical form. I also read somewhere that humans were created so that nature could worship God, through us. If that's why we were created, it's amazing to think of where we are. Like creating a Frankenstein.

The monster, gone out of control!

Do you believe we come across the same souls, over and over?

I think we do. There is knowledge that comes to us that is physical: the blood and bone of things. I feel, absolutely, that the reason I can play the penny whistle is because I have a lot of Irish relatives. That's why Irish music makes me feel a certain way, and why Native American stuff makes me feel a certain way: why I connect so much to Native American drums and when I go to pow wows I feel like: "ahhhh... hooow."

There is certain knowledge in our blood and bones that we pass on to our children, and they pass on to their children, and that's the physical aspect of it. I also think there are other lives on other continents that may not have anything to do with our blood and bones. There is other information, other lifetimes, which have nothing to do with these physical bodies. We meet up with certain spirits again in other bodies, in other lifetimes, because we need to. When we see them, there's something that we react to; we recognize them right away, in a smile or a look, or the way they move. It's not so much the color of their eyes, or the shape of their hands; it's the gesture, and the gaze.

Can you speak about the Goddess rituals that you lead?

After the last ritual I led, in early August with a circle of women, everybody told me, "Throw away the books; you are really there, Karen. This is the best one yet. You've got it."

I thought, "I am not a spiritual leader. I do not accept that role in life." I don't want the responsibility, and it embarrasses me, a little. Yet, at the same time, I know that I have gifts. One of the reasons I can weave the elements of a ritual together is because it is like creating a show, but more spiritual. I don't say during the ritual, "This is right. This is wrong. No, you can't do that; that's not part of it."

Is a connection between theatre and ritual? Did theatre begin out of ritual?

Yes. So much of our ritual has been stripped away from us. Rituals that we used to have to do—like squatting to pee, that became a sort of ritual—we don't have to do anymore. Now we just go and sit on the toilet. Picking our food out of the garden—gardeners are like magicians, the way they can bring food out of the earth. It is a kind of magic.

Creating a ceremony is a similar thing to growing a garden. You shape it, plant the seeds, and then what comes up, comes up. The gardener doesn't really know what is going to happen. Same thing with the ceremony. I just write the words, thinking, "This would work, that would work." And then it works or it doesn't work, and it usually does work.

It emerges as people's feelings expand into another place, a higher spiritual place. I was teaching a yoga class at the YMCA recently. A woman was there looking for spiritual guidance. I thought, "You're coming to the YMCA for spiritual guidance? Please! You are in the wrong building. Ashram—over there." If you come to the YMCA, this is for exercise, and community, even though it has "Christian" in the title.

She asked me after class one day, "When are you going to talk about the spiritual benefits of the yoga positions?"

"Well," I answered, "it is my consideration, here, that those will come to you if you do the physical postures. It is not mine to tell you what your spiritual relationship is going to be." We are breathing in different cycles; we have different bodies and memories. The way to teach yoga is to teach the physical aspect and let the spiritual aspect come, rather than the other way around. I am not here to be a minister or spiritual guru. I am here to teach these yoga positions and how to breathe correctly in them, so that you can find your own spiritual development through them.

How does one sustain a yoga practice?

Do the sun salutation always, and then pick your four favorites, the ones that make you feel best, and do them three or four times a week. That's all! Twenty minutes of centering in. You will feel better, and you will feel less blocked spiritually, and things will occur.

painting by Ted Keller

PEGGY HAMILL

"Four o'clock was a little early to be in camp, because it was a long evening ahead. I didn't really expect anybody else to come into camp. I'd been alone all day. You know, after the first two or three days on the trail, all the worries of your life leave you. Your daily life is the trail: whether you are going to become cold, or hot, or hungry, or sore, or tired, or safe, or wet. You're not thinking any more about what you forgot to do at work or if the house needs to be painted, or what you should wear to the wedding next week. It's very immediate: your needs, and you're looking for animals, you're looking for wildlife, you're watching the flowers and the plants, you're living outside."

PEGGY HAMILL

Peggy Hamill was born in Washington, D.C. in October 1951. At the time, her father was a diplomat and her mother was making home wherever they went by hanging curtains and planting a few geraniums in pots at the window. As the birth pangs began on that crisp, late-autumn day, Peggy's mother called her father to see if he could give mother and soon-to-be-born baby a lift to the hospital. Since he had a lot of meetings scheduled, Peggy's father advised her mother to take a taxi, which her mother did. Mother and baby did just fine, Dad showed up to lend support in the ways fathers were allowed in those days, which was at a distance, and baby was welcomed as the third born.

I know all of this because it is family lore. Peggy is my sister, older than me by two years. She was a somewhat forlorn child, following on my mother's heels everywhere, but she also harbored an innate, intense connection with the natural world. She sought it like a second mother. During Hurricane Donna in 1960, when my parents had the worrisome (for them) luck to be in Mexico and my fifteen-year-old brother was babysitting, Peggy ran into the back yard and, in a truly howling wind, put her arms around the willow tree, which was beginning to lean toward the house. She was not afraid for the house, for us or even for her own well-being. Her concern—her passionate, foolhardy love—was for the tree.

It was with Peggy that I roamed all over the fields behind the house, playing King of the Mountain on Big Rock (long since disappeared under a stream of steady development) and picking up caterpillars and snakes. It was with Peggy that I swam in the Atlantic, body surfing until we were both blue and reckless with cold. During the teen years, Peggy was the "wild" one, driving the family car without brakes and, once, after a rainstorm, all over my father's showcase New Jersey lawn.

As we grew into adulthood, she showed me wilderness vistas I might never have seen. We took several trips into the White Mountains in New Hampshire when my daughter was an infant. I can recall stepping gingerly over a rope bridge high above a chasm in a strong gale with my daughter strapped into a pack on my belly, wondering if the wind was strong enough to send us both into the drink. We hiked the Appalachian Mountain Club's hut system, cresting peaks with my oldest sister Jennifer and my mother (a stubborn trooper in her own right, disdaining hiking shoes for little tennis flats without socks).

My sister's paradox is that she is often tired, and she spends more time than most of us in stillness, whether meditating, or on her porch watching the birds, or upstairs in her bed, watching the trees. And yet, her remedy when exhaustion sets in is to take a long bike ride or a hike up the mountain, at the end of which she feels refreshed and full of vigor. Although she claims a sense of disconnection from her body, her body is a portal through which she accesses energy, insight and spiritual enlightenment.

Loquacious and deeply thoughtful, intuitive and sometimes bitingly sure of her point of view, Peggy is still passionate about what she believes. Fueled by the tea she drinks, her thoughts tumble over one another like pebbles in a stream bed. I am blessed to include the voice of this fierce and fragile woman who has not stopped looking for meaning on the tops of mountains and in minute rock cracks of wildflowers. She moved to Taos, New Mexico in 2009 with her companion, Ted, where they live in a house that they designed and built.

CROSSING THE VOID:
Interview with Peggy Hamill

Mahls Pond Road, Beaver Brook, New York
March

Peggy, when and where were you born?

I was born in Washington, D.C. in 1951, but I grew up at the New Jersey shore. My earliest memories are of being in the backyard, with the willow tree as my very best friend. There were some little hiding places in the backyard—one was under the forsythia bush—which were safe and sacred places to me as a little girl.

We grew up near the ocean. I graduated from high school in 1969, and the class of 1969 dedicated our yearbook to the ocean. It was our greatest teacher, really. I feel like the ocean saved me, from what, I'm not sure, but—I had an incredible connection to the wildness of the ocean.

What did the ocean teach you?

Connectedness to the wild. Life was crazy, meaningless, empty, full of materialism and greed, and the place that I felt happy and content was at the ocean.

We swam in the ocean for hours and hours as kids, but that's not what I remember. I remember being by the ocean, the power of it, the beauty of it and the sense of calm that it gave me. The sense of the sacred.

Do you live near the ocean now?

I do.

And do you still feel that way about it?

Yes. I have other ways of making that connection now, too. But I go kayaking on the ocean and get that same feeling.

When my partner Ted and I took our trip across the country, we hiked out through the Rockies and we went to most of the national parks in the Northwest. We went to California;

we were in Glacier National Park; we went to Yellowstone and the Tetons and the Cascades in Oregon.

At the end of that summer, we came back to Maine, and I went with a friend kayaking one afternoon, around the islands off the coast. We came back in as the sun was setting, and there was nothing any more glorious than that. I had been to all of the glorious spots in the country, and Maine was just as glorious.

Can you talk about the role that being out in nature plays in your life now?

Getting out to the woods is the most important thing in terms of my staying sane. If I have a problem, or I'm upset, or there is something that I'm trying to work through, I take a seven-hour hike, or even a four-hour hike, and the problem is solved, the feeling is gone. I get back a sense of serenity.

And if I haven't got a problem, I usually get into some sort of an ecstatic state during the day. My heart opens to the point where it almost feels like it's going to burst. And—it'll be just a moment. One I remember, from last summer. I was biking along, minding my own business, isn't this pretty, and then all of a sudden there was this patch of goldenrod. I got off my bike and just—worshipped.

There is another phenomenon: I'm out hiking, or biking, and I see a field or a meadow or a mountain. And my heart just yearns. It wants to become one with the field or the mountain or the rock. It's just an aching longing. Somewhere deep in my being I know that that connection is a possibility. And that's where I'm trying to go—to not feel the separation. To not be separate.

I've had that feeling since I was a little girl. I didn't know, until recently, that that separation was, in fact, not real. That the separation is the ego, and the reality is we're not separate. But it's hard for us to remember that. The veils are in place and we miss the connection.

You have studied Buddhism and meditated quite a bit. Does that relate to this feeling?

Well, I think that's where I got the idea. I've always had the feeling. It's not really a good feeling; it's loneliness, and a longing. I only get that feeling when I'm outside, and in some place that's wild.

So, being in a roomful of people or being with ones you love doesn't give you the same feeling of connection as being alone in nature does?

Right. There's no comparison. Which isn't to say that I would give up one or the other. I value them both. I need family and the connectedness with humanity and friendship and love. If I could get by without friends and family, I'd be up in the Himalayas.

When you are experiencing this open feeling, or longing, can you describe it? Can you translate it into physical terms?

When I get the ecstasy feeling, it's an open-heartedness. It's like the heart is just flowering open. Everything is full of love and joy.

And you feel that opening and flowering inside your body?

In my heart center. It only happens when it's warm.

It doesn't happen in the winter?

No. In the winter I just have to wait.

You feel like you are just waiting?

I make plans to escape.

Do you ever think about moving to a warmer place?

I do. I live in New England, so I do get out. I ski, I snowshoe, I go for a walk. It's just that for that open-hearted feeling to happen, I have to be more relaxed than I am in the winter. It has something to do with the sun and being warm and comfortable. It might have something to do with the nurturing of the earth, of Mother Earth taking care of me.

What about autumn?

Well, it happens in the fall if it's a nice warm day.

If you were to move to a tropical climate, or even the southern United States, do you think you would miss the cycle of the seasons?

I don't think so. It doesn't feel like I'd miss a thing. When I've hiked and traveled in the tropics, one thing I do notice is—without the cold weather, things get really putrid. The cold is a purifying thing. When you don't have that, and you have all the pollution that we have, things get really disgusting. I've hiked some places that are all, like, green slime. And there's no winter to ever clean that up.

If you were going to design your dream spot in the tropics, what would it be?

Mountains. A lot of trails. Very quiet. Very few people. No pollution. Maybe a river, or a roaring brook.

Talk a little bit about mountains. Where have you hiked?

Well, I can tell you my best hike.

It was at Glacier National Park, in 1999. Ted didn't want to go because it was an eighteen-mile hike. He thought it was going to be too far. He said, "I don't know if we can do it. I don't know if we're strong enough."

And I said, "We'll have to be. If we start, we'll have to get home."

It was a day hike, over the Continental Divide in Montana, around the edge of the most spectacular mountains I've ever seen. We had to get up at five o'clock and make our lunch and make our breakfast and start about six, 'cause it was such a long hike.

We started out along the trail. We weren't half a mile out of camp and Ted saw a mountain lion. I was like, "Oh, well, if there're mountain lions, you know, stalking us, I guess we'd better go back."

But Ted picked up a stick, and said, "I'll take care of them," and he carried the stick for the next ten miles, until we were out of range of the mountain lions. We walked out through this incredible valley. We were all alone; there were no other people. There were grizzly bears around, mountain lions around, and the scenery was exotic and gorgeous, with the high mountains. We walked all morning out through that valley, and across creeks. It was wide-open country; you could see for miles in all directions.

We started climbing up the mountain. We climbed way up and it was all perfect—beautiful and fun. Up top, the wind was picking up pretty high.

Ted didn't want to go on because there were snowfields. They'd just opened the trail the week before, because they were afraid people would get hurt in the snowfields. The danger was that you'd lose your footing and go sliding off the mountain, which was a true and definite danger.

We came to our first snowfield. There'd been a little trail packed down, so we made our way across. It was half a mile across this snowfield, no missteps allowed. It was starting to get really windy. It was getting to be lunchtime. We found a place out of the wind, and looked out over this unbelievable wilderness for as far as you could see in any direction. By this time, we'd met a few people, but not many.

This is when it got really exciting. The trail turned into a little narrow path, about two feet wide, right on the edge of a cliff. It went up one side and down the other. And the wind was, like, hurricane force. It looked like there was maybe a mile of this.

I'm terrified of heights, so I was just terrified the whole mile. But, I could do this; I'd done this before. It's the price of being in the mountains. We got to the end of what we could see of that, around the first mile.

Were you just walking forward or were you sort of hugging the cliff? Did you have a hand on the cliff? How were you keeping your balance?

It was just wide enough to stay on. It was windy. We came around this corner and for as far as I could see—it must have been five miles—the trail was just like that. This was a circle trail, an eighteen-mile loop. And the wind was coming even stronger, directly at us. I said to Ted, "Well, I can't do that; I'm going back."

He said, "No, you're not," because he knew I wanted to do it. And he was gone. And I was like, "Shit!" I could either go back alone, or I could go forward. You couldn't even talk, it was blowing so loud. For the next five miles, we were up on the side of the mountain, near the top, looking down on this magical valley, over sharp, snow-covered, wild peaks. Peak after peak after peak. They were an emerald green below. The sky was an incredible summer blue, the white fluffy clouds and the howling wind, and this cliff. And that was my reality for five miles.

We made it; I don't really know how. By the end I thought, "Whatever. I'm not afraid of heights. I'm just going to walk." And I wasn't afraid. I went from absolute terror to just, whatever.

You moved through something to a Zen state.

Exactly. There was nothing but the most beautiful scenery, one misstep and I'm dead, and the howling wind. And that was it.

We came around the next corner. We were out of the wind, we were back on safe ground, and we just lay down in the sun and took a nice nap.

And then we heard a little bell. It was so cute, coming up the trail from the other side of the mountain. "Ting-a-ling-ling…" It was such a wonderful moment, because we had conquered the Great Divide, so to speak, and here comes this little "ting-a-ling-ling."

Pretty soon, up comes this woman, hiking by herself. Out in the West, in grizzly country, people are told to wear bells to scare away the grizzlies. So she was wearing her bells. It was just another magic little moment. You could hear her coming a long way before you could see her, and she was in a sort of Swiss Alps outfit, as I remember. She was a costumed person, heading out into the Divide.

Then, we had some more snowfields to cross. The problem was that you might get lost. It was hard to follow the trail, because it was covered with snow. Everybody that had gone before us had gone in all different directions, because they couldn't find the trail either. So we weren't sure which trail to go. We spent quite a while, getting down the snowfields, but it wasn't dangerous anymore.

We had a water purifier, and we stopped at a lake and got some water; we were thirsty so the water tasted really good. We walked down and came into the valley on the other side. We took another long nap in the sun. Somehow this eighteen miles passed right away.

We were coming back into camp and Ted saw a lynx!

Then there were these Indians, Indian kids. They came out of the woods, right after this lynx.

They were hunting the lynx?

They were drunk, is what they were. They were kids. They said, "This is our land, this has always been our land. We know how to talk to the lynx; we're tracking the lynx, man." I mean, they were so drunk, they couldn't have tracked a dog. It was sad. They were right, but they were drunk.

One of the women in my drumming circle said the sacred drink for the Christians is alcohol, with the communion. And the sacred plant for the Indians is tobacco. They are obviously powerful substances, but powerful for both good and bad.

Was it still light when you got back?

It was still early. Four o'clock. It was the end of the summer, and it was our final hike. We were really strong—I have never been that strong—because we were hiking all summer. When I'm with Ted, I see a lot more than when I am by myself. He draws animals in, somehow. Ted has a very spiritual soul but he doesn't talk about it. He doesn't really even know it, or think about it. It's just him.

Last summer, you hiked the Appalachian Trail by yourself. Can you talk about that?

It's something I've wanted to do ever since I can remember, just hike for days and days, live outside by my wits. When I was young, I was too busy being productive. I had babies so soon, and then a job, and house, so I didn't get time. It didn't really cross my mind, although the ache and the longing was there.

Finally, the kids were grown and I realized I could take ten days off from work and just do it.

Where did you hike?

I hiked the last section of the Appalachian Trail before it heads into Baxter State Park in Maine. It's called the Hundred Mile Wilderness, but it isn't a wilderness anymore. Now you can buy beer, hamburgers... get a taxi out, probably.

How was the experience compared to how you thought it was going to be?

Well, I wouldn't call it a wilderness, but it was wild enough to suit me, hiking by myself. I went in September. In the summer, it's too crowded. There's no place to camp and the lean-tos are all full, and every time you try to set up your tent there are thirty other people setting up their tent, too. I missed that, by choice. After September, the kids are back in school and the big groups don't come anymore.

It was, truthfully, physically harder than I thought it would be to hike a hundred miles.

How many days did it take you?

Nine. It should have taken longer. I don't know what I was in a rush about.

The interesting thing about being out in the woods is that there's no television, no computer, no telephone, no coffee shop, no library, no books: nothing to distract you from yourself. Which is why I go. But, I'll tell you, nine days with nothing to distract you can be pretty intense in terms of the emptiness that comes up.

At home, the emptiness comes up but you turn on the TV, get a cup of tea, it goes away. You get a good book, you go to work, something happens. And you don't let the emptiness in.

I did some backpacking alone, and this feeling always comes up. I call it "the void."

The void is what rises up when you are away from all of our normal distractions?

It does. There was one night when it came up the strongest. It was my last night out. I was at Rainbow Springs campsite. I pulled in to camp about four o'clock. It was just a campsite; there was no lean-to. If you have a lean-to, there is a little book that people write notes to each other in. It's like the telephone out there on the trail. They call it the trail log.

So, if there are lean-tos, at least you've got the trail log to read. But there were no lean-tos, so there was no place to put the log.

Four o'clock was a little early to be in camp, because it was a long evening ahead. I didn't really expect anybody else to come into camp. I'd been alone all day. You know, after the first two or three days on the trail, all the worries of your life leave you. Your daily life is the trail: whether you are going to become cold, or hot, or hungry, or sore, or tired, or safe, or wet. You're not thinking any more about what you forgot to do at work or if the house needs to be painted, or what you should wear to the wedding next week. It's very immediate: your needs, and you're looking for animals, you're looking for wildlife, you're watching the flowers and the plants, you're living outside.

So I was fully into that. I'd seen a moose earlier that day, and spent quite a while just watching the moose. I don't think I'd talked to anybody that day that I remember.

I got into camp. There was this beautiful lake, and this beautiful, great big spring—three feet across, bubbling out of the ground. It was too cold to sit by the lake, and there wasn't a good rock to sit on. I couldn't get comfortable; I couldn't even just rest. So, I was left with myself and this great big wilderness—this big woods.

I could feel how little and vulnerable I was. All I had was a little tiny tent. That was my protection from the world, and there were bears and God knows what all. I'd had my supper, a cup of black bean soup and some rice crackers. I didn't have much left.

I was—oh, I wish I could think of how to describe this feeling. You just feel how very, very insignificant we are. It's a lonely feeling, sad, with a little boredom to it. There's a boy-I-wish-someone-would-come-into-camp feeling. There's the I-wish-I-was-home-in-my-own-bed feeling. But at the same time, underneath all of that, there's a sacredness to it, and the sacredness is: this is how it feels without all the distractions.

My faith is that if you stayed with that feeling long enough, that little lonely sad self would dissolve into the grandeur of the spot. But it's not an easy thing to do.

Is that connected to ego or is it really just self, soul self?

I don't know what it is. I don't like it when it's going on, but when it's over I cherish it endlessly. I think back on it and just deeply cherish that I got there.

Would you describe it as an other-than-human feeling?

No. I think it's very human. Maybe essentially human. You have to feel the essential vulnerability of our humanity to transcend it.

You have to be comfortable with that—there's absolutely nothing comfortable here for me—feeling. There's not one comfort here, except that it's gorgeous, and I'm at one with this beauty.

Is it frightening?

I don't get frightened. But I feel vulnerable. I have no protection, and I think that's essentially our human condition. We buy insurance, and drink caffeine, and ride in fast cars and it all makes us feel powerful, but we're not powerful.

If you were in outer space, is that what outer space is? Just the void?

It's more like a void in our psyche. Empty of distraction and diversion, it becomes our essential nature. I think our essential nature is more than empty, sad, lonely and bored, but you have to get there before you drop through to another world, or rise up, I don't know.

And when you transcend the human condition, what does that mean?

I don't know. I've never done it.

But do you think that's what people meditate to do? And what the great yogis are able to do? Is that enlightenment?

Maybe.

How do you connect "making friends with the void" to this new interest that you have in shamanism and ritual?

Intuitively I have this idea that the condition that I experienced out there at Rainbow Springs campground is a doorway into a deeper, more profound understanding of what this world is about. I also intuitively believe that there's much more to this world than is apparent on the surface. That there are undercurrents and other worlds happening at the same time, and magic happening. That's where I'd like to get to. I think the rituals and the shamanism also are doorways. I'm looking for the truth underneath the apparent, underneath what's obvious in this world.

When I started looking into shamanism, I realized that part of me feels intuitively so connected to the natural world. And then to find there is actually a tradition that also uses that—I think, "Well that's it!" I'm home, or I'm going to start home.

It's comforting to me to meditate, and read Buddhist scriptures, but the traditions of Buddhism where you sit in a room and listen to bells, all day every day for years and years, doesn't appeal to me. I need to be outside.

I went to the Insight Meditation Society in Barr, Massachusetts and did a ten-day silent meditation retreat, where we alternated periods of meditation with periods of walking meditation from five in the morning to eleven at night. I found it very powerful, and I think that it is a doorway, too. But I don't feel drawn to doing it on an intensive level, because it works too well for me to be outside. That's where it happens the most often, and most intensely, for me.

The funny image that I have of you is when you say, "Oh, I'm so tired. I think I'll go and bike for thirty miles."

I know.

Not everyone has the store of physical energy that you have. Yours is quite phenomenal. You are driven to find connection through your body.

I get this charge of ecstasy, so who wouldn't?

Well, if it motivates you, it's got to be a strong charge.

It's a huge charge. It's a blissful, ecstatic charge. You know how people are talking about ecstatic dancing, now?

Yup.

I can understand that, except it happens to me biking or hiking.

As part of your attraction to the wilderness, is there an edge that happens, a sense that there is some danger, that you don't know what's going to happen next?

Oh, absolutely.

Why is that attractive?

It forces us to be more attentive. And when we become more attentive, it takes us more into the moment. You have to be watchful for signs of bear, or to put your foot in the right place, because if not, you're off the cliff. When there's danger, you have to be fully present and be watching, and be very aware, and I think most people find that feels good.
As I've done some Buddhist studying and have understood what they're saying, being present is bliss. That's the goal.

Have you read **Into Thin Air***, by Jon Krakauer, about the 1996 Mount Everest climb?*

Ted read it to me, in pieces.

And how did that book affect you?

I hated it because the climbers on the Everest expeditions were trashing the place, leaving their oxygen tanks, and bodies, and my feeling is, if you can't carry in and carry out, you have no business being there.

Krakauer's reasons for being on Everest were the same as yours, as best as he can describe his reasons.

Being on the edge?

Yes.

Well, but it's not fair to take the planet down with you. They aren't being responsible up there. I understand that when you're up there you're fighting for your life, and if I were up there I'd do the same thing. I'd leave my oxygen tanks to get down safe. But I wouldn't go there! I don't think it's right to take the grandest mountain on the planet and trash it.

My feeling is if you were really and truly connected, you wouldn't dream of trashing a big mountain like that. I'm not sure what they're doing is any different than riding motorcycles fast. It doesn't feel like a sacred activity to me.

Do you think there is such a thing as evil in the world?

I think that there is a supreme laziness that sometimes manifests in what we look at as evil. People are so lazy that they just take the easiest route to try to feel better.

This fellow wakes up one morning and he's had a horrible life, and a horrible childhood, and his father pounded on him; he gets up in the morning, starts drinking early and by the end of the day he's killed his wife.

He's choosing to go a route that seems easiest to him. Which is: dull the pain with the drink and then the pain is dulled, and he's working from buttons that are being pushed, that he hasn't ever looked at, never paid attention to, spent all his life avoiding, and he becomes a violent man.

I don't really think that's evil; I somehow think of it as laziness. I suspect that somewhere along the line that gentleman had moments of grace when he could have made other choices, but he was too lazy. And that's what I see in lesser forms in people around me. They know better, but they choose to take the easier road, which leads to both their and other people's pain.

Is there an evil force in nature?

I don't think so. Nature is just indifferent. Nature doesn't care if you live or die. Nature is the life force. Individuals would matter not at all to nature.

My sense of nature is truth and beauty. I don't sense a lot of love in nature. I don't know what the love is. I don't understand the love.

But isn't this love? Look at this palette of colors, the trees, the field, the sky?

Well, it's beautiful, but is it love? I don't know. This tree could fall on you; it wouldn't care. When I look out here, I see a great grand beauty that maybe loves me deeply on some level, but this particular, unique existence it cares about not at all.

I'm not thinking so much of a personal love. But it seems to me beauty is a form of love, or an expression of love. It's not directed love, it's just the embodiment—beauty and truth, both—of the expression of a spirit that is loving.

The creator spirit...

On my Hundred Mile Wilderness hike, I stayed at a little hotel, sort of a hostel, and the woman was telling me how they had this family of loons out on the lake. One day the eagle came and ate all the babies. She said, "Well, the eagle has to eat." She was heartsick, but she said, "It's just the way it is."

When you look at a tree in the forest, and another tree falls over onto it, it'll subsist there for a very long time, as long as is nessecary, holding up the fallen tree. It has no choice—it can't stand up and walk away—but that is its nature, to hold up that tree as long as it has to. I mean, it can't be very comfortable. Is that love? I don't know.

When I was a little girl, I fell out of one of the higher branches of a willow tree onto one of the lower ones, and I believe the willow tree caught me. It didn't let me fall all the way to the ground.

If that's true, I guess the willow tree loved me. Enough to at least catch me.

Can you talk a little bit about your relationship to wild plants?

I had this idea, and for many years I did so religiously, that you should eat a wild plant every day when they're around and growing. I used to go out and gather wild herbs and leaves and nuts and seeds. The idea is to bring the wild into your own being.

When I'm out hiking, living in the woods especially, I always find a little wood sorrel and eat those from the special places, and I'm sure to take a little sip of water from all the little special springs that I find. And if I find a spring on top of the mountain I fill my water jars and bring that home for dinner, because I feel the energy of the place is in the plants and the springs.

I used to go out for the first little shoots of dandelions, get the little dandelion leaves and bring them home and eat them. Now, even though I am not so good at bringing it in for dinner, if I see a little dandelion leaf I just pick it and eat it. A little tonic.

For years, I worked in a nursing home. There were these dear old souls living in this concrete building that, you know, felt dead. There was a difficult energy in the building; there wasn't a lot of life put into the building itself. These old people had been gardeners and hikers and bird watchers, and they were stuck in this building, day and night, for the last years of their lives.

So when I hiked up in the wilderness, I gathered in some wildness and brought it back to the nursing home. It was in my being, and these people could enjoy it.

What about people who live in urban areas and cities? Do you think everybody has a need for wild nature and if so, how are these people coping or not coping, or what is that doing to them and to the human race as a whole?

I have no idea because I have never lived in a city.

Do you think the system of parks and trails that we have developed in this country are a good thing?

Yes. And I'm not sure but what they are fairly unique. It seems to be a cultural, Western mind kind of thing.

I don't know enough about the world. I know whenever I've traveled I've had a terrible time getting out of the towns and cities. But part of that is because of the desperate poverty, and we're Americans, so that makes us vulnerable.

Living off the land in Mexico is hard-scrabble living. It's hand-to-mouth: starving, hungry people. It's interesting that in Mexico, Nicaragua, Honduras, anywhere I've been where it's tropical, I don't see people raising gardens. I saw almost no gardens. I've talked to a few people about it, and they say people have lost the knowledge of raising gardens. I met some NGO [non-governmental organizations] people trying to instill a tradition of gardening in the people. I can't imagine that they didn't used to have gardens.

This lack of gardens is astonishing, because it's such a primal thing. And the people are hungry.

photo by Mary Olmsted Greene

DOROTHY HARTZ

"I have a little trouble with the word *divine*, just as I did with *evil*. But *order*, yes, for sure. I mean, look—why don't acorns become pine trees? When you pick up a leaf of any kind of tree, the web work, the veins—that's DNA. That's not order? Even this, where we're walking, where it seems some trees are dying and rotting, and other trees are growing, and underneath every tree there are little saplings taking their crack at it, and it seems so random which ones make it and which ones don't—I don't know how I reconcile what seems to be random destruction with the random abundance, but I know that there's an order there."

DOROTHY HARTZ

Dorothy Hartz is a woman at home with beauty. She herself is beautiful, with a face straight out of a Greek myth: fine sculpted bones, silver hair and merry eyes. Her home is beautiful, with no corner lacking in meaning, usefulness and art. Her flower gardens flourish under her careful and dedicated hand. Her mind is equal to her looks, holding a vast canon of mythology, history, science, poetry and playfulness.

I first met Dorothy and her husband, Ron Pollero, soon after they returned to the Upper Delaware River valley after many years in various locations in Orange County, New York, where Dorothy served her time as a high school English teacher. She taught English in the valley too but opted for early retirement so she could pursue her greater interests of writing, history, dream work, genealogy and astrology. For Dorothy, the woods, ponds, rivers, forests and valleys of her homeland, along with its lore of adventuresome and sometimes eccentric people, define the landscape of her spirit and her intellect. A lover of ritual and magic, coming home was no casual convenience; it was a soul journey, and every day she celebrates her connection to the towns and rivers of that region.

Her interest in her own ancestry took her on a solo voyage to Newfoundland, Canada not long ago, to research and experience her maternal grandfather's roots. There, she found a new connection to vast ocean and harsh weather, and she brought me back a pair of rainbow-colored hand-knit woolen socks, the warmest socks in my drawer.

Dorothy confessed to me the unusual habit of trapping mice that attempt to escape the cold through the walls of her house in the wintertime. Lured by cheese and fruit, the mice climb into the have-a-heart trap and are discovered by this big-hearted woman in the morning. Most folks would simply drive a mile or two and let the mice go, but Dorothy keeps and feeds her mice in a cage until the warm weather returns, when she sets them free. "I like mice," she explains, although she also likes cats and dogs, eagles and coyotes, and the fawns that she sometimes sights in the springtime around her home.

For a few years, Dorothy and her husband spend the worst of the winter months in Florida, but she longed for the Upper Delaware valley, no matter its storms and howling winds. Like the North Star, she has one home, and she celebrates it continually in her thoughts, her poetry and her generosity with family and friends that co-inhabit the neighborhood.

Dorothy is an independent thinker, put off by polarization from both the right and left. She is a passionate loner who relishes her solitude. She is also a good and loyal friend, a down-home kind of gal who can put on a good supper and bang out a tune on the piano or guitar. She is welcoming and gracious, and will go out on the proverbial limb to state her point of view, even if it is not the most popular one in the room. Most of all she is beautiful, and sometimes mysterious, donning her gardening gloves and capes and velvet hats to set about her chores. She journeys through every day to meet her past and her dreams, and all of us along the way.

MUD PIES AND THE ORDER BENEATH CHAOS:
Interview with Dorothy Hartz

Dirt road, Kellams, New York
March

Where and when were you born?

I was born March 18, 1947, in Jersey City, New Jersey. However, I was raised in Callicoon, New York, in Sullivan County.

The topic is wildness, and you asked us to prepare—to think about it, to have some responses. That's an analytical process; that's a left-brain kind of thing. I had to do it twice: in a left-brain way, and then in a right-brain way. Because I incline toward analysis and dissection and thinking about things, I was getting into real intellectual conversations with myself about human nature, and the nature of wildness, and the seeming dichotomy between body and spirit, and I was having wonderful head games with myself. Then, I decided: think about the images, and the sense impressions of what we actually feel, when we feel most wild. And that gets closer to the heart of it.

Can you talk about your childhood and your connection to Callicoon, where you grew up? What did it mean to be living in such a rural setting?

I always enjoyed it. I took a lot of it for granted until I became older.

I used to take walks by myself in the woods. My parents always sent me outside to play, because that was the healthy thing to do. I guess I made mud pies and got dirty enough, but doing outdoor activities—that never got me. But taking walks in the woods, enjoying nature for its own sake—brooks and trees and paths—I liked that a lot.

Can you talk a little bit about the mud pies you made as a girl?

It was a hoot to be using regular household utensils. I would borrow spoons and measuring cups from my mother, and it was so incongruous that it was fun. It was a minor thing, but it seemed almost forbidden, to be getting them dirty with mud.

Talking about sensuality—and Proust knew this, with the madelines—smell. I don't remember making the mudpies, or squishing them, but I remember the smell of the earth.

Can you talk a little more about what moved you as a child?

My religious upbringing was very important while I was young and, naturally, St. Joseph's Seraphic Seminary, in Callicoon, staffed with Franciscans, had a lot to say about Saint Francis. He was offered as a role model, and he was someone who was very much in tune with nature. I responded to that.

The chapel itself at St. Joseph's seemed a less spiritual place than the paths and the outdoor grottos, dedicated to Saint Francis and some of the other saints. I had a friend who lived behind the seminary, and the walk to her house was a journey. I'd walk from the seminary itself to the outdoor grottos, to cultivated hayfields, to cool woods, and then to her house. That progression became a metaphor for my appreciation of nature because the more wild it got, the more different and special it felt, the more I felt like I was in touch with something invisible. It was a mystery, and I enjoyed it.

It never really threatened me, although I think there is an aspect of wilderness that can be threatening.

How did you experience the invisible?

As a heightening of senses, especially walking from an open area into cool woods. There was a period where your consciousness was basically the same, and then all of a sudden things looked, smelled, felt different. There was a heightened awareness, and maybe I was open to subtler levels of energy, or maybe it was just the cleaner air in the forest.

Can you describe the grotto?

It was a winding path through the woods. It followed a very small brook, and on either side of the brook there were little niches with statues, and larger rounded stone alcoves with life-sized statues. There were three or four of them, but they were screened from each other; it wasn't set up in any precise way. You'd be in one section of woods, with shrubbery or tall bushes around you, and that was one little experience, and then you'd follow the path and you'd have another. There were a few benches, and there was an old tin drinking cup by a section of the brook that was dammed. It was very sweet, clear, wonderful water. I used to drink it whether I was thirsty or not.

They had outdoor Stations of the Cross there—a series of fourteen icons that represent different moments of Christ carrying the cross and the crucifixion. It was very moribund—the punitive, sorrowful, "Let's all wallow in guilt and beat ourselves up" aspect of Catholicism and Christianity that I find least useful for living a purposeful life.

But the Stations of the Cross seemed less oppressive in that outdoor setting.

Do Catholics pray at each station and ask for forgiveness?

It's a meditation, I guess, and an acknowledgement of the suffering of Jesus… reminders of the debt that we owe to Christ for offering himself and dying for our sins.

When you are getting close to nature, and wilderness, ethical and judgmental tones on life and death are different. Wilderness is amoral. Ordinary human morality and a sense of ethics do not apply there, because nature is about evolution and survival of the fittest. I don't think Darwin was right about everything he said, but that certainly is going on, seemingly random selection and all that, it's happening out there.

It's a hallmark of wilderness—a combination of the grotesque and the beautiful. Things are grotesquely beautiful, or beautifully grotesque.

This summer, we've had two little fox cubs living very near to our house. We've had a few little sightings of them, here and there. The other morning, I saw them across the road. It was dawn, and quite dark yet. I couldn't really see what was going on, but I heard them playing very energetically, playing mouth to mouth, fighting over what I knew was some sort of creature—a large squirrel, maybe, or a bird. It ended up being a piece of a newborn fawn. And there you've got the adorableness of these little foxes, and you've got the grotesque nature of this fawn's head, which didn't even look real because it was so small.

If you try to bring a sense of rightness or wrongness to nature—they don't go together, do they?

Do you feel there is an evil force in nature?

No. Nature can manifest in such excessive forms that people experience it as evil, like cyclones and hurricanes and floods and blizzards. The effect could be called evil, but I think for evil to exist there has to be an intention, a consciousness of doing harm.

Do you think there is an evil force, an evil intent, in the world, whether manifesting through nature or through people?

No. I don't—not as a separate force. I can comprehend evil as emanating from someone with malicious intention, but not coming through someone from some discrete dark cloud.

We are walking on a dirt road, almost a path, near Kellam's Bridge. Does this road have special meaning for you?

This used to be a real road although I have never taken it to the end.

I chose this place for our walk because my boyfriend and I would come here, often, when we first became sexually active, as the saying goes. Even though it is not that remote from civilization, it is where I first felt, through the instinctive activity of sex, a direct participation in wildness, rather than as a visitor.

And, right now, there is something very sweet—

Sweet fern.

Oh! It's wonderful. Smell. It's the first sense that comes when I think of participating in the sensuality of wildness.

You mentioned earlier that when you think about wilderness, what comes up first is rational discourse, an intellectual direction that your mind goes in. You said you wanted to stop that process and participate in a less intellectual, more organic way. Can you talk about the division that you see there, between experiencing wildness and talking about it?

It's a level of awareness, a level of consciousness. As human beings, we are always taking motion either toward or away from greater consciousness. That's what we are doing, in every moment, getting either closer or further away from total awareness. More mind, more understanding.

That's the nature of being human?

I do think there is a dichotomy between body and spirit. Maybe it has been ingrained in us to think so; so many thinkers through the ages have presented it that way. But, for me, it seems to be that I can't even walk, let alone chew gum at the same time, if I'm more focused on *understanding* the spiritual significance of an experience than on spontaneously *having* it. You can't experience, and understand, completely, simultaneously. You've got to do one and then the other.

I think when the two are out of balance, doing and thinking, and that's to differing degrees for different people, you get illness, and mental illness, and lack of understanding instead of increased understanding. And people who aren't balanced contribute to the imbalance out there and around us.

What else in your life has brought you close to wilderness, or wildness?

I don't think you necessarily have to be in a natural setting to experience wilderness. It helps a lot, and no doubt most of what we call wilderness encounters do take place in a natural setting. But, as part of preparing for this, I had to define for myself: what is a state of wilderness? What is wild?

To me, wilderness is a state of harmony based on an absence of ego-consciousness. It belongs to the organic world, to the world of instinct, whether in or out of doors. We are in the wild whenever we are at peace with that. We're innocent.

When we are being ethical, moral, self-conscious, striving, doing this, going there… we're caught up. But in wilderness, there is a sense of participation with the natural world, and a recognition of it.

As a human being, anything instinctive that you are allowing to happen and feeling okay about can give you that state. It's a form of grace, actually—no matter what setting you are in, whether you're alone, with one person or with a group of people—whenever you feel that you are giving full expression to your instinctive energy, or as much as is appropriate in the moment, and it's working in that you feel a sense of harmony, that's a positive wilderness encounter.

Can you tell me of an instance or two when you have experienced that?

Again, sex at its best. When you are with someone and there are no emotional politics going on. Pure lovemaking does that, because the physical parts of a person, the systems, the respiration and all of that, suddenly become attuned to their most natural rhythm. And you become aware, with breathing, with the gyrations of sex, that you are taking part in something that is so primitive, and the pulsations of creatures and plants around you feel like they are in the same energy pattern, almost. And that's a direct experience of the wild.

During sex, I have sometimes experienced a sense of dissolving boundaries.

Absolutely. And that's the absence of ego-consciousness. You are participating in something larger than yourself, but you are not feeling diminished. You are feeling celebrated.

Do you have another type of experience in your life that gives you the sense of participating in wilderness?

There are many places on Cape Cod where I have approached it, and places around here: the Delaware River, in particular. All up and down the river corridor, there are places where I have spent time where there has been a sense of relaxation, where there has almost been a transporting. A sense of, "Oh, it's happening."

Do you seek out these experiences?

It's more that I put myself into a certain setting. To "seek them out"—then you are doing ritual, and that's another thing.

Can you talk a little more about ritual?

If you go through some sort of effort to make the connection happen, if you're invoking the setting in some way, to create a state of mind, to me that's a form of ritual. If it works, that's good. My problem with ritual is that I don't always trust that it's working. I hope for spontaneity.

I feel as though you have an affinity with spatial beauty. You consciously create a sense of space and harmony in your surroundings. And, you study astrology, and you do practice some ritual. What is beauty, and how does beauty relate to wildness? There is beauty order and chaos in nature, as we can see, just looking around. So what is the process, what is going on, why do we try to recreate it? What does that mean for you?

What is beauty? I guess beauty is a glimpse of the order behind the chaos. There is so much about wilderness that people attribute, savagery and chaos and excess, you know, the lushness of something, and the balance can so easily tip to that being harmful. Beauty is an occasion to experience, to perceive, the order that informs nature and wilderness without feeling any of the harmful excesses.

My husband Ron loves to watch those tornado shows on the weather channel. He's so impressed, he's awed by what nature can do. I don't experience that so much as beauty because they usually show it funneling down on a building or a town, and it's too overwhelming.

But, a lot of people see beauty even in the savage aspects.

For me, the beauty of nature is more the soothing, the healing aspects. Again, it means you are tuning in to it, you are tapping into the order behind it.

Is there a divine consciousness, a divine order behind the physicality of this world?

I have a little trouble with the word "divine," just as I did with "evil." But "order," yes, for sure. I mean, look—why don't acorns become pine trees? When you pick up a leaf of any kind of tree, the web work, the veins—that's DNA. That's not order? Even this, where we're walking, where it seems some trees are dying and rotting, and other trees are growing, and underneath every tree there are little saplings taking their crack at it, and it seems so random which ones make it and which ones don't—I don't know how I reconcile what seems to be random destruction with the random abundance, but I know that there's an order there.

Order doesn't mean pre-destiny either, but there is an order.

How does poetry and writing poetry work into all this for you?

Sound and abstract meaning—the combination of the two pierce that veil to the invisible. It makes me feel and think about that order without the physical experience. Poetry takes me there. It's a way to share what's worked for me, to anticipate what I want to find. It's a tapping into that order through sound and meaning, the sometimes arbitrary meaning of words.

Robert Graves, who wrote *The White Goddess*, said there is only one subject for poetry. And that is the constant cycle of vegetation: the death of the corn king, hail to the new king, and the earth goddess who is both the mother and the consort, and death again. The life of every organism from the simplest to the most complex is a repetition or a variation of that theme. And when you think about it, even in modern disguise, the poetic metaphors that work best are nature metaphors, not metaphors based on what's man-made. When you deal with metaphors relating to machinery, and industry, a lot of the heart and soul goes out of poetry.

What about your interest in mythology and history?

Well, they are collective versions of individual experience. A lot of people seem to experience nature in the same way during the same time. And their collective understanding, their efforts at expressing it creatively become mythology, and epics, and sagas, and so forth.

Do you think the land has power?

Some land does. I think more of the land used to. But as humans have become more complicated, as we have developed functions for ourselves other than a kind of collective participation in nature, we've become immune to some of the power that is there. And I guess because the land isn't cultivated as it traditionally was, it isn't paid attention to. And some of the places where there is magnetic energy and that sort of thing—we are not as attuned to it.

The people that I spend most of my time with—the people who think most like me in my generation—we have a very romantic approach toward nature. "Save the earth," and there is great fear for what we've already damaged. I'm not completely well informed, but I have an instinct that tells me the earth is not in as bad shape as a lot of us fear. I don't know if that is wishful thinking, but I have enormous respect for the earth's ability to self-correct. If we get to the point where we are really screwing things up, the earth will shrug us off. Like it is said in the Edgar Cayce prophecies and by everybody else with the gloom and doom. It's easy to talk about that in a very dispassionate way. I acknowledge that if it's my house going over the cliff, that's something else.

But nature is constant flux. And if, in the process of taking care of ourselves, some things change, I don't think that automatically spells gloom and doom. It sounds like I'm endorsing drilling for oil in Alaska, or something. I'm not, but I also don't think that if it happens it's going to be the last straw on the camel's back. Nature is, in most respects, very self-correcting. I'd rather see energy created and utilized in a less aggressive way. What we really need is to put our attention into creating the next energy paradigm, whether it be solar, or even atomic. We let that genie out of the bottle. We can't put it back. It makes me nervous, but I think we have to deal with it.

I'm getting away from wilderness right now . . . My moon is in Aquarius, it's very dispassionate and airy. I pride myself in seeing both the strengths and foibles of any side of an issue—I'm registered independent, and now I'm resorting to that comfort zone instead of talking about wilderness.

What about your connection to the river?

I lived many years in close proximity to the Hudson River. I lived in Cornwall and drove along the river going in and out of Newburgh, and it's beautiful, and it's lovely and impressive and it has history, but it never moved me in the way that the Delaware does.

Why is that?

I don't know, I guess maybe because the beauty, the psychic attunement that you feel—you can assimilate it with the Delaware. The Hudson is too big for me. I came to that conclusion about the ocean, too. For twenty-five years, I spent part of every summer on Cape Cod. Sometimes it was three days, sometimes it was three weeks. I loved it. A lot of it was social, a relief from my everyday reality. It was vacation time. I was seeing people I liked, I was spending money, and all that fun was there. But I realized over time that, for me, the nature of the Cape was just plain overwhelming. The ocean diminishes me. The river rejuvenates me.

The Delaware is special in that it's so accessible. It is majestic in a way, and yet you can plop yourself right down in the middle of it and spend the afternoon there, if you want to. On the Cape there are some Sunday mornings when you load up the car, and you sit in a long line in the heat waiting to get into a parking lot so you can shlep all your crap back out so you can build your camp, and it's like, wait a minute! This is way too removed.

In your notes, you write: "Become wild. We already are. We uncover it." Could you talk about that?

Well, the energy. We're batteries; we're electromagnetic fields. Our physical bodies are containments of an energy field. We're illusions; we are more space than we are solid matter, if you look into us. And that "yes, yes, yes," the pulsations of energy that lead us to eat and digest and defecate and move and relate to each other—all the energy exchanges that propel us through life!—they're all the big "yes, yes, yes." The people who don't trust wildness, who don't feel wild, they've got their fear shawls on. They're just trying to get through life without noticing too much that upsets them.

So you think that wildness sometimes has to do with shaking ourselves up off of our moorings?

Absolutely. And if we don't choose to do it for ourselves with awareness, the body does have its own wisdom. Those energy patterns will have their way. They will turn into illness, or will create a synchronicity, where you have this "accident," when you're trying to avoid something or when some kind of wisdom inside knows that if you have these accidents it'll lead to something that you won't get to in a more direct way.

So, in a way, it gets back to this order of the universe that you were talking about before. That, in the midst of all this chaos, there are lessons that we are meant to explore.

Right. And if you do explore whole-heartedly, if you really master a lesson and do something for yourself that's really proper and healthy, you're benefiting others as well, in a ripple effect of responsibility. To revisit the beginning of the interview, this principle is behind the Christian faith—the idea of Christ sacrificing himself to take away the sins of others. But it seems that in the traditional denominations, the faith gets stuck in guilt and a gratitude that's never enough, instead of taking the example to become one's own light. Whatever else they may have been, the resurrection and the re-opening of the gates of paradise are metaphors. For me, Christ represents the attainment of a state of consciousness that wasn't available before to humans. Because he attained it, we can, too, probably through a combination of emulation and morphic resonance.

It goes back to what you were saying: "Is there a consciousness above and beyond what you and I can sense right now?" Yeah! But how to tap into it, how to control it, how does it work?

Do you think there are different realms of being?

I want to, and so I say I do. When I am on my death bed, I want to feel "yes" instead of fear. I want to say, "Consciousness continues. One energy pattern is fading and so another will emerge, so yes."

That's how I hope it will be.

If I'm fearful on my death bed, I don't know if I am going to believe anything that I've wanted to believe through my life. That's why the Tibetans call it "the art of dying"—to bring your consciousness, to live your life in such a way that you can feel okay when you are dying. Risky business!

Do I believe that there are levels of beings—hierarchies of intelligence out there in the ether? Yes, I do. I have no proof and I don't know why I want to believe it, but I do. I think it's part of the order. Call them what you will.

There is a lot of folklore about that. Some people might call them angels, other people might call them aliens. Maybe it's just intelligent energy taking a form that will make us notice it. Maybe that is what we are, too.

During Penguin Camp [a summer arts day camp for elementary-age children], we did several units on fairies. The boys didn't want to participate until they saw pictures of goblins and gnomes, and the like. The campers transformed the woods behind my house into little fairy houses. It was magical to see. It was fun to watch these little fairy houses, long after the kids were gone, sort of sink down into the forest. I have always wondered whether they drew any kind of manifestation of spirits, or energies, or fairies. Once my brother visited us when the houses were about. He wanted to put some food out, which he did with my daughter Cassie, who was seven or eight at the time. I think they put some blueberries out there. We planned to sneak back out later and steal the food, so Cassie would think fairies had visited. Well, we forgot and in the morning the berries that we had set out there were all gone. It could so easily have been animals, and it probably was. But, it gets back to what you were saying about a belief system. Who is to say what is true?

There are a lot of different ways in which it could work. "Fairies" could be other souls on their way in or out of manifestation. They could be our own electro-magnetic projections, coming back. I don't even care about the explanation! I don't know how a friggin' radio works; I believe it does, though. I can turn it on.

What if we had never discovered physics? What if there are other things, other systems, which we have just never stumbled upon? Maybe there are. Maybe not.

That sort of answers your question, doesn't it? A lot of the discoveries of physics in this past century have validated the ancient Asian belief systems. Gary Zukav, the physicist who wrote *The Dancing Wu Li Masters*, and Fritjof Capra in *The Tao of Physics,* pointed out that the Vedic scriptures are really consistent with quantum physics.

Hey, Einstein believed in God. That's good enough for me. My own working definition of the Indefinable is that God is the perpetual process of all there is waking up to at-one-ment. And wilderness is one of the alarm clocks.

Driving into Town

Kristin Barron

The man just appears
Limping, dirty
at the edge of the road
How could it be
our eyes meet
at 60 mph
Are you ok? my mouth moves
Yes he grins
throws an arm
toward the woods
broken brush
the gape of a new logging road
My heart pounds
at our sudden connection
gone, small
in the midst of our vast movement
our living
I feel relief
me the able bodied
as if I were the able bodied
driving us to town
my passengers
the old woman and the baby
stay asleep.

The Mimosa Tree

Karen MacIntyre

The child looked up into the vast blue, declaring out loud: *I want to do something grand. I want to make something that is larger than life. I want to praise that soft place called sky.*

The child lay on her back. She could feel the cool dark massage of moist earth and the silken tickle of feathery grass. What to give? What would the sky like best? The child rolled over and searched the sea of green around her. Eye level with Earth's gentle curve, she spied a crisp brown pod. Pulling it apart, she picked out one small dark seed. When she placed it close to her heart, it revealed ancient secrets to her, saying: *I want to go home. I want to be held by my mother.*

So the child planted the seed, digging small eager hands into brown dirt. She placed the seed with care, patting it flat with warm palms. Next day, the child rushed outside and in amazement viewed the mighty tree that stood right in the place she had been. She knew she had worked magic.

The child lay on her back, looking up into broad limbs above her. She could see sunlight peeking through the delicate leaves and thin pink flowers. She could feel the sky smiling down at her. And she kept this to herself, whispering gently: *Praise to that soft place called sky.*

Jimson Weed

Dorothy Hartz

Just when the garden was good
and dry and love hurt the most,
Jimson forced itself under the fence.

Knotty root to start,
then—elegant in its dark splayed fingers—
pale girl bloom whirling skirts, seducing yet
twisting away
from its hundred maddening little pricks.

I kept it, awed, outraged
by its self-trumpeting
hermaphrodite beauty
its thousand terrible womb-mouths
that green to brown
to spit black bits that
hit the dust,
bit in, grew sullen
and choked
the slow ground growers.

Only a climbing thing
survived Jimson for a while,
clinging to its strong legs,
stringing along,
tender and tempting
to the million harsh barbs
that pierce the reason to be
for no reason at all.

Happy as clams,
drunk on Jimson,
the mad still will take
to the air
to inherit the earth.
Raped,
they burn back
to the ground,
dirty work for the nurse
who loves first
her changelings.

Dusk

Sandy Long

There is only a short time
when it is perfect—
you and I, the golden light
the dip and glide as our paddles
drive the hulls like whispers
over this water.

Enter merganser
trailed by duckling trio.
Slash a vast sky across
the slow buzz of backlit bugs
zigging like drunken fairies
over the bog mats,
steaming and sunken.

Nudge the noses of these plastic crafts
into channels carved through the stiff grasses,
into places of dead ends, where we are
over our heads in the wild climb of
the marsh's succulence.

In this place, I remember the dream:
        water's edge, the piled rise of
        river's riffraff, the broken and abandoned,
        accumulated by effort and chance,
        this dance of water and wood.

        There is something that compels me
        to place my foot, and then
        my weight onto the base of this
        ponderous thing.

The instant the shift occurs, the
        moment the mass begins moving,
        I understand.

        In my rubber boots,
        the tumbling logs
        push me into the water
        trap my means of mobility
        place me swiftly under,
        still me.

As we carry the kayaks down the trail
something in the grass snares my eye—

a gnarled paw near the path's entrance—

this portal where land and water clasp
while failing to define,
where entwinement
confuses perception,
and perfection
wears the jagged claw of decline.

October Nocturne
Mary Olmsted Greene

       All through the month, I swim laps
in my neighbor's deserted evening pool, taking
the path Hans has mowed between our two houses,
wearing sweats and rubber boots, my dark hands
floating across old milkweed curling in the twilight.

       The coppered pool is cold and hard to enter.
I knock against it, spin. Return. The low moon
is a trail of ash on the water. My ash hair
a tangled map on the water. Laps pile up.
The dog shifts her yellow light against the fence.

       Apples drop with ripe readiness. Late wasps
grab sweetness, low and buzzing. Katydids croon *she did,
she did. She did her forty laps.* Hunter moon rises,
silky and full. The arrows of the night
turn toward winter. I am walking the trail

       vibrating in the dusk, a husk of happiness.
The lights of my house ignite like glow-worms.
It's the last of the light, the last of the season.
I'm turning the white blank page again. And Hans
is a hymn on his red tractor, out mowing down his field.

Coast Guard Beach

Mary Olmsted Greene

If you love me as you say,
present the willing self, the green king
spreading the purple robe
of desire. Or let the wild birds
fly over the sea, white

birds with loss in the straight hollow
passage of their bones. Love,
you have caught me at the brink,
a woman risking every wave,
every dark shark spilling teeth.

I sing with the body of the moon,
take the round wheels
of the woods into balance, stand
like a queen in the surf's cold thirst.
I am the silver ribbon of flesh

swimming back to the Sargasso,
the gull's savage dive,
the hard tumbled speech
of the wave. I am the turquoise
circle of windy air,

the red cliff's indifferent eye
casting a glance
over sky, over sand, over bird,
over storm, over the dark
and restless hairline of the sea.

answering

THE CALL

ELIZABETH KAYE KAMINSKI, when this book was compiled, lived outside Narrowsburg, New York in the woods, with a husband, a dog and a pond, along with itinerant bears and deer. Her paintings, reflecting a meditative practice, were shown in area galleries, having previously been exhibited in Santa Barbara, Seattle and New York. During this time, her day jobs included program coordinator at the Delaware Valley Arts Alliance, facilitator in a recuperative arts therapy program, and clerk in a health food store. Friends and clients benefited from the healing she offered as a Reiki Master. Kaminski now lives and paints among the redwoods above Santa Cruz, California. Her favorite wild place is among trees.

DRUIS ANN IYA OSHUN KOYA BEASLEY is an artist, educator, poet, musician and storyteller who has lived and worked in the New York State capital district for over twenty-five years. She is a founding member of the Sisters of Color Collective and the New African Music Collective. As an initiate in a number of African mystery systems, Beasley uses mythology and praise poetry as a working metaphor for today's world. Her relationship with nature informs her ceremonial, performance and literary work, as well as her spiritual counseling. Beasley is director of Afterschool & Literacy Education for an agency in Troy, New York, and is a Woodhull Fellow with the Woodhull Institute for Ethical Leadership. She has several favorite wild places from both her childhood and her Orisha in adulthood: the mountains and woods (Obatala), the banks of rivers and lakes (Oshun), around a camp fire, under trees, with turtles (Shango).

MOTHER JOAN LALIBERTE was born in Texas in 1938. Her father was career military and the family moved a lot, which, says Mother Joan, was a great education. She received a BS in psychology from Portland State University in Portland, Oregon and a Master of Divinity from the Church Divinity School of the Pacific in Berkeley, California. Her work experience over the years ranged from picking crops in the Pacific Northwest to driving a cab, working for the Census, teaching guitar, journalism and, finally, the ordained ministry. She is currently pastor at St. James Episcopal Church in Callicoon, New York. Favorite wild place? "I used to get away to Craters of the Moon, a national monument near Arco, Idaho," says Mother Joan. "It's high desert, stark and beautiful. I'd stay there between seasons when there were few visitors. I liked Yellowstone before or after the summer season, too, but Craters was closer and gave me a great sense of peace."

answering **THE CALL**

What does it mean to answer a calling? How does it happen, exactly? Is it brought on by a sudden awakening or is it the result of years of living in which faith gradually accrues? Are periods of loss, sorrow, alienation and self-doubt helpful or harmful—or perhaps even essential—to acquiring a faith-based and/or mystical life? Each of the three women in this section has lived a life defined by spiritual seeking, by a yearning and a stretching toward connection with our essential human nature and with the divine. Each has lived full secular lives, studded with messy relationships, turbulent dilemmas, missteps and gambles. And for each, a relationship with landscape, animals and nature was essential to the journey.

In the words of one contributor, "I did some heavy-duty naughty things," but such things—along with a career in painting—led her into the arduous inner journey of a Sufi master. For another, a rough-and-tumble childhood, laced with stories passed down by a tough and loving grandmother, led her to her Afro-Caribbean roots, her matrilineal soul-knowledge and ordainment as a priestess in the nature-based Orisha religion. And finally, an Episcopal priest found her calling on a late-night bus in South America in the midst of a career as an international journalist.

In lingering over these conversations, I am struck by the similarities, as well as the differences, between each set of beliefs. Only "beliefs" is not the right word, nor is "faith" or "religion" in every case. "Knowledge" might come closer, but it is a subjective knowledge based in experience rather than books. Each of these woman was sparked—driven—by something internal, reinforced again and again by actions and events, leading them deeper into a path.

A wave is perfect. Every wave cast toward the beach from the sea is perfect. A rock is perfect. A tree. We do not feel the need to judge the elements, to judge the four directions, the sun, the fields, the stars as they implode over our heads. Yet we do judge ourselves, and others—harshly, at times. Humans, it seems, are imperfect and must constantly strive to do better—to achieve enlightenment, connection with God, right thinking, whatever we wish to call it. As the world continues to erupt in racial divisiveness and wars fought over faith, we ignore at our peril the call to find a pathway into acceptance, joy, forgiveness and service to others. To divide the spaces between us—between the all—and achieve the one—unity—could perhaps be a common thread here. At any rate, it is my hope that the stories and poetry in Answering the Call will lend inspiration and comfort. They are all adventure stories, within the "soul" if I dare to use the word, and without.

photo by Mary Olmsted Greene

ELIZABETH KAYE KAMINSKI

"I have to start by saying that there is no distinction between anything. We are, right this minute, rock and trees and birds and plants and earth and everything. As we separate ourselves from different things, what's left over there that we perceive as rock is just, in a sense, the distillation of that part of everything. We are more complex than a rock, because we can move, and think, but we also have the rock in us. There is that rockness, there is the treeness, there is the airness."

ELIZABETH KAYE KAMINSKI

I first met Elizabeth Kaminski (who in those years called herself Sofia Singher) in the 1990s when she was a coordinator at the Delaware Valley Arts Alliance in Narrowsburg, New York. An artist herself, she was gifted at supporting other artists in the community, and she extended her healing nature to many others, including terminal cancer patients, through her Reiki practice. We became friends, and I also got to know her husband, a quiet and generously spirited musician. I visited often at their cottage in the woods and before our formal interview, Elizabeth and I had many informal conversations about her art, her experiences and her Sufi practice. We walked along the circular paths she had built through her small woods, complete with chairs for rest and contemplation.

Elizabeth's paintings were geometric wonders of form and color, based, as she explains in her interview, on the four elements. She helped me try to find my own "artist within," although it was a struggle. I tried to copy the little booklets she made—beautiful, contained representations of her spiritual practice and her artistic expression. Hers would contain a simple piece of thread connected to a splotch of vibrant blue paint that somehow spoke—to her and others—of deep feeling and connection to spirit. My own little artist's journal was an awkward hodgepodge of things pasted up, like a match I used to light a special candle or a sea shell I tried to glue in. It was too bulky and did not lie right. And yet I have kept it as a reminder that—as Elizabeth taught me—this sort of expression has no right and wrong. It is available to everyone and simply *is*.

Elizabeth often gave forth a sense of fragile vulnerability that was soon disbanded by her competence at most everything. Once she asked me to help her plant a garden. I arrived at her house prepared to take the lead, my car filled with gardening tools and my head with helpful hints and advice, only to find that she had marked out her plot with kitchen string, planned her arrangements and bought bags of humus and peat moss. We enjoyed the time together and her flowers thrived.

In 2002, Elizabeth moved to the West Coast to be nearer to her sons. She has a nomad's heart, and she has moved many times in her unconventional life. She has also changed her name more than once. Although we do not see each other much any more, her soft voice, her courageous frankness and articulate spirit continue to guide me through times of hardship and joy. If souls are meant to return to one another, then certainly she is a soul I have met up with before, and will do so again. She is a complex gift, a contradictory mix of the most troublesome and uplifting parts of ourselves. Due to a recent injury, she paints with her fingers now. Her paintings are still small boxes packed with color and geometric shape, power and beauty. She plans to take up watercolor soon. Earth and water, wind and fire will continue their expression through the hands and heart of this extraordinary, gentle and profound woman.

ELEMENTAL NATURE:
Interview with Elizabeth Kaye Kaminski

Lackawaxen Road, Narrowsburg, New York
June

Where and when were you born?

I was born in Milwaukee in 1949. I lived there until I was in the second grade. We lived in a house, in Wawatosa. I had very little relationship with nature there, except snow in the winter. Then I moved to Chillicothe, Ohio. I was there from the third to the seventh grade. And there I had a very strong relationship with nature. We lived in a really nice house—small, but wonderful, which backed up against the far end of a country club, which we couldn't belong to, but I got to use a part of it.

There was a rich house on a hill. They had a swimming pool on the top and a creek that ran down the side of the hill. I would walk through the flat part and go up and play by the creek. I was an Indian.

How did you learn about Indians?

Probably in school. They made us do booklets, little writings—they had covers with little strings attached. I imagine we did one on Indians. Chillicothe is an Indian name—it's right near the Indian burial mounds in Ohio.

How did it feel to "become" an Indian?

I would lose myself, in a sense. Of course, you don't think in those terms when you're a child. Looking back, I just think of a place, sitting there on a rock, looking at the grasses move and feeling very much a part of it. Not that I was a scientist, looking; I was not an observer, or critical, or even thinking "how beautiful." It wasn't a sense of beauty. It was just a sense of being. Watching the water.

It was always very private. I didn't go in a band of kids. I didn't speak to anybody about it. It was not part of my verbal life.

Do you remember entering that state? Do you remember how you did it, and how you

stopped doing it? What happened during those transition moments?

I'd leave our backyard, which was all trimmed and nice, and walk into the flat mowed place, and that was like a transition, and when I walked into the woods, I was there. Just a sort of walk, you know, that made one go deeper.

And leaving was always when I heard the whistle, which meant that I had to come home. It was a rude awakening; no sense of completion or finishing. It was just that the whistle blew, and I had to get home.

Do you remember if you made up stories, or if there were images or words, or music that went to any of this?

I was aware of finding things, and making things. I would not do anything grand, but there'd be a rock, and there'd be a place that I'd sit in next to it, and then I'd find twigs, and act out that kind of thing. Feeling and touching, maybe arranging. It was tactile and visual.

It wasn't to make an object; it was just as I think most people do—they just take some twigs, and start to tear the bark off maybe, and see what's inside, and how it could bend.

There were never any real story lines. There were never any people hunting me and I didn't hunt or anything like that. It was just the story of being there.

And as you got older, what happened in terms of this area of your life?

I was still very young when I left Chillicothe. There, I lived with my grandparents. My mother was a nurse and she was out of the house most of the time, either teaching, or away. I was raised by my grandparents.

Then, my mother remarried and I went with her to Albuquerque. In Albuquerque we lived in a housing tract on the very edge of the city, right below the Sandia Mountains. Our house was on the edge of the desert, between civilization and these mountains. I would often walk out there and have a relationship with the desert. But it was not as intense, not as rewarding or full, because I'd become a teenager, and my mind turned.

And since you've become a grownup? How do you see it manifesting?

I am very conscious, very aware of having lived out the stages of my life—like, when you're in junior high, then you have to be a junior high person, and high school, and then a young adult, and then a parent. I've lived out lives that have taken a lot of attention and time and focus. I feel now, in the last five or six years, that I'm in the stage where one looks back, or relaxes, doesn't have to succeed in all these different ways. So I can allow, somehow, that inner constant—the "Indian"—to surface again.

Where did you live before coming to the Upper Delaware River valley?

In Manhattan, for ten years. For six years we lived in Washington Heights, right on the edge of Fort Triumph Park, which is a huge, big, green, wild area.

I'd wait for the bus or the subway there, and I'd go out five minutes early, just stand and breathe at the trees, while "whiz, whiz, whiz, whiz, whiz!" traffic would go by. Coming home, I'd get off the bus and just stand there, meditating on nature as fire engines were going by, and the Dominicans were boogying across the street, and salsa music was coming out of the corner store. I didn't care; I would just stand there and meditate on the trees, and all the seasons. It was wonderful.

Then, I moved to a little place where I actually had one small tree in the window, in the courtyard, a paved courtyard. My chair was facing the window and I would sit, and that was the focus for my life, really. You can get so much from a little tree in the middle of a courtyard.

What did it give you?

Well. Everything. Sustenance.

It gave me the passage of time, in the cyclical sense. I was reminded of how beautiful all the seasons were, with that tree. It kept me conscious of non-judgment of beauty or time—that no matter what time of day it was, what season, that tree was absolutely perfect. As we all are, but we forget, because we are not trees. Trees are there, no matter what: roots in the earth and arms spread out to the wind and the sun and the rain and birds.

Do you think trees have consciousness?

I think everything has consciousness.

Is it, for instance, the nature of a rock is to sit in one place, and be very heavy and dense, and we can learn aspects of our own being, and how to be certain ways, from watching how things are in the environment?

I have to start by saying that there is no distinction between anything. We are, right this minute, rock and trees and birds and plants and earth and everything. As we separate ourselves from different things, what's left over there that we perceive as rock is just, in a sense, the distillation of that part of everything. We are more complex than a rock, because we can move, and think, but we also have the rock in us. There is that rockness, there is the treeness, there is the airness.

Fire has very impressive energy. As a child I would not look at a fireplace. I got scared by the fireplace. Whether it's fire inside or fire outside, fire's very hard to control.

I know that you have a strong relationship, in your meditation practice and in your life, with the four elements. Could you talk about that?

Breath and the elements are, for me, the window, the opening, to everything. Everybody has something that allows them to reach where they want to go.

If you are searching for something, you can find a key that's yours—that you recognize. For me, the elements are a really important key. I came to them when I started studying Sufism. When I turned fifty, I was initiated into the Sufi order. One of the first practices is the purification breath, a very simple practice of purifying with the breath, with the elements. You breathe in and breathe out, in a certain way. But at that time I was dissatisfied. I wanted the heavy duty practices. I didn't want this "breath, air, fire, water" business. I wanted Zikr.

What is Zikr?

Well, Zikr in Sufism is a practice—a phrase that you repeat over and over again, along with a head movement. You just do it and do it and do it. It's praise, and it's really heavy practice. You can use it to go deeply within as a way of finding your heart, making your heart bigger; you can work with it with light, defining your body as light; you can work with it in many ways.

It was esoteric-sounding, in a foreign language—Arabic—and I wanted to do that!

But, okay, I'll do this little breath practice with air, bla bla.

Then, you start really paying attention, and you realize that you are made up of those elements. Everything you see is those elements. Then, the elements begin to grow, and you can see them from different points of view, and you see the emotional content of these elements. And then your relationships tend to be these elements. It continues to grow, and God is these elements. So, it goes from being a simple little practice to the foundation of—what would you call that?—existence. Foundation of being. It *is* being.

Some people think that Sufism is an esoteric part of Islam, based in Islam, which, in fact, the words are. Early on, Mohammed embraced Sufis and made them his own. Sufis are usually considered Muslims, but they are and they aren't. It's very complicated.

In my Sufi order, everything is God, and in Islam, that's heresy. In most religions, that's heresy. Sufism separates itself from other religions in that everything is God. I am God. You are God.

It's based on experience, also. It's not based on learning things, or belief. Christianity is based on the belief that Jesus died for our sins. Islam is based on how you act. It's a code of action. Sufism is not based on how you act or a belief system; it's based on your own personal experience. It's completely experientially based. And the point of it all is to experience God. Which is you.

The four elements are, for me, the fundamental key to doing that.

In a relationship, are there are aspects or characteristics of the elements that run through the relationship? And do you find that the elements as associated with astrology signs—water, earth, air and fire—are related to this?

I see the elements working more in the interaction, the dynamic of a relationship. For instance, fire is loosely translated as anger. Or if you are in a conflict with someone, you bring out the water so that you can go around the conflict, do what you want to do but not burn the other person.

I'm a Virgo, and Virgo is very earth-oriented, and I do acknowledge that. I think people have an affinity, a preponderance of one element or another.

In doing these practices, I have a strong affinity for the earth part of the practice, because I have a very earthy nature. Say, if you have a lot of fire, you have to be careful and maybe do more water practices. They become more intense. You start doing the fire practice and you can get physically hot, and emotionally hot, and mentally hot, and morally hot, and sometimes that's good. To have a lot of heat morally, you can go in there and say, "This is not right. We have to change this," getting that fire behind a moral issue.

On the other hand, you have what Jung called the shadow side of all that, so if you are a very heavy earth person and you do a lot of earth practices, you can become sluggish. It can be overdone that way. I concentrate on becoming the most pure aspect of each element, and am therefore able to interact with the most pure elements in all the other parts of the world and the universe. There's a thing, it says "toward the one." And that's why I do these practices, is to go toward the one. And the one, of course, is everything.

Has art been an opening for you as well? Or a doorway into anything?

Art has saved my life!

I did naughty things, often. Heavy-duty naughty things that hurt other people. Painting allowed me to forgive myself for that. I spent many, many years pounding paper against the wall with paint. Many years dealing with my emotional life, my pain. There came a point when I got tired of it. I said, "Okay, okay already! There has to be something more. Like, who cares, anymore!"

I started to look deeper into a more specific spiritual life. As I did, I remembered that, for instance, being at the pond behind my house is an incredibly spiritual practice.

As a child, I did that, but it was non-verbal. At Sunday school, I'd sit and wait for Jesus to come into my heart. They would say, "Jesus is this, and Jesus is that," and it was the same as sitting by the pond. Waiting for that kind of thing to happen with Jesus. Waiting for union.

Do you still paint?

Oh, I've always painted, yes, right.

When I turned more toward the spiritual life, it was as if my heart opened up. I paint directly from there. That's one reason I paint small. As I paint, I am doing spiritual practice. The majority of my paintings are about the elements. I just keep doing series of four—four paintings about the elements—or eight, because you do the breath in and breath out. The practice grows, and the paintings grow. As I paint it's a continuation of the practice. Like sitting at the pond.

What are the heavy-duty ways in which you hurt people?

Well. I gave back my boys.

I left my husband in 1972. We had been childhood sweethearts, and we became different people. When I first left him, I took the children with me. We went first to this little house in the woods below our house, the mountains behind Santa Barbara. Later I got a little tacky apartment in Santa Barbara. But I was young for my age and I've always been very emotional, vaguely depressive. I had never lived by myself. I couldn't get a job. I cried all the time.

I asked my husband to take Blue back. Then I asked him to take Little Stevey.

How long did you keep the boys?

Maybe six months.

What about your own father? Did you have a relationship with him?

I never met him. I was never allowed to ask abut him. I knew nothing about him until I went to college in the early '60s.

Growing up, there was a covert message not to ask about dad. I'm still dealing with that in my life right now—how repressed everything was. I'd hear my mother and my grandma arguing about it. I had to be a really good girl—living with grandparents. I knew if I said anything it would cause trouble, and I could not cause trouble.

Where did you enroll at college?

University of California at Santa Barbara. I was supposed to name my father on a college form, and I got curious. I found out he was a doctor living in Philadelphia.

Did you try to find him then?

No. Not then. Not for a long while. When I had my first child, when I had my second child, I thought of telling my father that he was a grandfather. But I couldn't do it.

Then, as I said, I left my husband and my children in 1972.

Around that time, I got involved with a man named Larry who I met at a poetry class. He was into religious studies, a free spirit. He picked up hitchhikers. One night he picked up a couple from Philaelphia. They said if we ever came to Philly we could stay with them.

So, a plan began. Larry and I decided to go to Philadephia.

We drove out to Philadelphia. I went to a library and looked up my father's address and telephone number. His name was Walter Stanley Kaminski.

First I drove by his residence. I was afraid it would be a house with a picket fence, grandchildren in the yard. If that had been true, I wouldn't have approached him—couldn't have. But where he lived turned out to be this huge apartment complex and I thought—well, that's okay, that's not too homey.

We went to use a phone at the Bluebird Café. I called the number. A man answered with a strange, fake-sounding voice. Scratchy, flat, no intonation. Like a cartoon. I said, "May I speak to Dr. Walter Kaminsky?" The voice responded: "This is he."

I told him my name was Kaye Kaminsky. He did not react or say anything, so I knew he knew who I was.

I asked if I could come see him. He said, "No. I'm very sick." I kept asking and he kept saying no. Finally I just had to say okay and hang up. As it turns out, he had cancer and was speaking through a voice box.

Did you continue to try and see him?

I wrote him a letter but never received a reply.

By this time, Larry and I were living in Philly, with jobs. Unbeknownst to me, Larry was watching the obituaries. A month after we had arrived, he showed me the obit for my father.

I wanted to attend his funeral. We got lost trying to find the Polish area of the city. When we finally got to the funeral home, they were carrying the casket out. So, I never got to see my father's face.

We followed everyone to the church, a beautiful old Polish Catholic church. It was about 11:00 in the morning, foggy; everyone seemed to be short and old, wearing black. We were tall, light-haired—out of place. The service, which was beautiful, was all in Polish and Latin. As they carried the coffin out, I was sitting by the aisle in the back of the church. I could have reached out my hand and touched the coffin. That was the closest I ever got to him.

Next was a slow procession down the street to the graveyard. The bells were tolling, the incense was burning. There was a service at the graveyard and everyone dropped a carnation in, and I dropped my carnation in.

Later I received some pictures of him and learned he was a good man, a dedicated doctor; he'd taken care of the people in his neighborhood for years.

Why did he leave you and your mother?

My mother was a nurse; he was a doctor at a hospital in the South someplace. She was madly, madly in love with him. Everyone told her: "Oh, don't think about Walt, he won't marry anybody who's not Polish." She got pregnant. He wanted her to have an abortion but she refused. So, I think because he was a good man, he married her to give me a name. But they divorced right away.

Do you see a thread between your parents' behavior and your own?

Well, it's more complex than just: "I was abandoned, so I abandoned my boys." I don't like the word "abandoned." It's more like a door that was open. My mother was mostly raised by her grandmother because she and her mother did not get along. So even though they lived together, it was her grandmother who raised her. Then I was raised by my grandmother.
It's not an excuse, it's just what happened. I had no mother connection.

When you moved to California in 2002, was it to be nearer to your boys?

Yes. I thought I could make it come full circle.

Did it come full circle?

Well… in some ways, maybe. They are busy and they have their own lives. They find time, though. It makes me feel really good when my son turns up at an opening.

How would you say the story of your father still affects you?

Well, it's only recently that I can say the word "father" without my lower lip trembling. That's progress, I guess.
I leave people all the time. I have realized about myself how easy it is for me to leave—anything. I never really developed a sense of home.
I counted recently: I have lived in forty-two different places in my life.

I would like to return to the subject of your art. I'm fascinated by the little books that you make, and I'm wondering if you can talk about them?

The little books are about seeing things. I pick up little things all over the place that remind me of states, or places I have been in meditation. They are little self portraits, physical reminders of particular states.

Creativity has gotten so far away from the individual, co-opted by capital letter words—like "Art, Poetry, Collage"—not that there's not a place for that, but it disallows an individual to find anything within herself to do. To take up any little scrap you have and do something with it, or any few words you put together, and put them down, have them recognized as something. Maybe there should be a word that's not art.

Expression, or something—

Yes.

I gave up talking to artists years ago. I can't make a blanket statement; I'm sure there are a lot of artists that do talk about process, but I just wasn't involved with them. The whole thing was: "How many paintings did you do this month? What's new? Did you go to your studio? Did you finish anything?"

I went to a beautiful Albert Pinkham Ryder show at the Brooklyn Museum with some artist friends who came out from LA, and we got in the car, and they began asking, "Which was your favorite?" You know, judging, judging, judging, judging.

I don't understand judgment, although I use it all the time, of course, because one deals in the world. But what makes one thing better than another?

I want to ask you about your reiki practice, and how it fits in with what we have been talking about. The idea of healing, having a healing gift, and the intuitive nature of it.

Well, reiki is perfect for me. I don't know.

I never made a connection between the reiki and that little Indian girl before. But there is an amazing connection in terms of the power of nature, or the power of something. The word "power" is just really clear. There is so much power every place. I knew that then, the magic of it and the unknown randomness of it. And yet, as a child you wouldn't know how to take it and make it into something.

Doing reiki is not about *me having* that power, it's that the reiki is *tapping into* a power. As a reiki practitioner you don't do anything. You don't know anything. If someone is coming in for a reiki treatment with a certain ache or condition, then you know positions that are better, but you could put your hands on somebody's cheeks for half an hour, and that would be fine, even if they had a broken toe. It's the power of it that comes through.

How do you tap into the power?

How one does it is by getting out of the way.

There are symbols, positions, there is breath—there are certain methods, but the most important thing I do is remind myself to get out of the way.

There is a beautiful prayer by a 15th century Sufi: "Adorn me with thy unity/ clothe me with thy I-ness/ lift me up into thy oneness/ so that when thy creatures see me, they may say/ 'I have seen thee, and thou are that'/ but I will not be there at all."

With reiki, that is the practice. Reiki is a practice, a meditation, an experience, too. Which is, "and I will not be there at all." Whether you call the power God, or energy, or oneness, it's there; you just have to get out of the way of it.

"Getting out of the way" does not sound simple.

It isn't. Because aren't we just egos.

Although I never knew my father, he was Catholic, and a doctor. Catholicism always had interest for me. It was this forbidden thing, you know.

At one point, I got interested in the Stations of the Cross. They are fourteen different stages, or places where you go and pray, usually in a church, sometimes outside. You follow Christ from when Pontius Pilate said, "You are going to die," to when Jesus was put in the tomb. I did several series of paintings on them, but more importantly, I did a series of poems. Instead of viewing the stations as negative—a lot of people see them as negative, as death—for me, they represented growth.

It was a practice of getting the ego out of the way. Your ego is condemned to death, and you accept that—Christ accepted it. Condemning your ego to death is step number one. I walked through all the Stations of the Cross until the final station, when the ego died.

It was an incredible experience to get rid of the ego—to put it into different situations and see how, in those situations, your life is controlled by that. Not that it's gone, of course. We always have to have our ego, but the difference is whether it rules us, or we rule it.

Language is a tool we use to talk about stuff that really has nothing to do with language. Language is a barrier, in some ways. It's both a tool and a barrier. It's turned us abstract. When we began making sentences and language, we stopped connecting directly with this world. We try and use language to talk about the ineffable.

Sometimes it's silly. We could just hold hands.

Yes, or swim to the middle of the pond...

Sufis are really big on that. There are a lot of Sufi stories where they start a conversation and they say, "Well, let's eat."

As a painter, I base my painting on either what I write or on words, you know, even like the word "fire." It's a conscious process of getting beyond the word—getting into the image.

Everything I paint comes from either a poem or a word.

Also, the mantras, using words that are so deep that you can't just say, "Oh, I see, that means that. Good."

Have you ever participated in extreme nature experiences, like hiking or climbing?

No. I'm not a very physical person. I test myself the other way, of how *unphysical* I can be. Instead of pitting or confronting nature and seeing how much I can do, how far I can push it, I do absolutely the opposite: push against myself, get rid of myself into nature. I can sit down here at the pond, without moving a muscle, and I can get sort of afraid. Because psychically you can just keep going.

So, someone who heads out into a raging blizzard on snowshoes in the woods, looking for the edge, is really actualizing something that you are doing with your mind?

Yes. She is doing it physically, whereas I am doing it on a spiritual level.

What about that fear of bears you had, before you got the dog?

Fear of bears? Well, they're big. They've come right up on my deck, eating seeds. I can't lose myself if I don't have a body. One day I was sitting right over there and two bears came by. I was far away from my house and the bears were right there. It was a push and a pull. My mouth dropped open—they were so beautiful—and I just started going with them, while every muscle in my body knew exactly how close it was to the door. Bears are awesome, in the true sense of the world.

What do you think about the existence of an evil force in the world?

I don't think there is any evil. It's just a covering. Evil is a covering. It's a veil that mostly people have. Wrongdoing, or not-right doing, is a veil. There is no intention in a rock, or a storm. With people there is intention. If I can get beyond getting upset at the news in any regular way, I see it as a veil to be lifted. People are not evil, it's just their goodness, their perfection is obscured. And that can happen in many ways. By having someone who has really a lot of veils mess with them. That's what some receive, and that's what they perceive as what activity should be.

What about the idea of karma or an afterlife? The idea that what you do will come back to you in one form or another?

Cause and effect? When my first husband, Big Stevey, died of alcoholism, I took a year, a strange year. I studied Buddhism very strongly over the year. His death was really much more shocking than I thought it was going to be.

I had to think of karma a lot because it's right up front with Buddhism. And, as with all Buddhism, I find the concept helpful in terms of dealing with one's life, and one's mind.

What I have studied in Sufism is that cause and effect depends on linear time. You have a cause, you have an effect—and it keeps you on a low plane, a low level of consciousness. As you start raising or altering your consciousness to different planes, or different ways of experiencing things, there is no time. Time is silly, really. There is no time; there's now.

You can experience what the future does to the past; what the future is doing to the present, the now. You can see time manifesting on the earth plane, the physical plane. If I spill my drink, I am going to get a wet shirt. On that level, cause and effect works. If you go to other dimensions of consciousness, there is no cause and effect, because there is no time.

What is memory, then? Why do we have memory?

Again, memory is something that we have on different conscious levels. I think that it's useful, because without memory, you wouldn't know how to get home. It's also destructive, because a lot of people keep memories that are harmful to them. And it becomes hard to forgive people. I mean, we all have experiences that have formed us. And yet, if we could have been able to not keep certain memories so fresh, we could have been formed in a different way.

So, memory can be useful, but it can also be very destructive. As I well know.

photo by Bolade Miles-Beasley

DRUIS ANN IYA OSHUN KOYA BEASLEY

"By third grade, I gave up the wild woman in myself and started trying to be the socially accepted individual. It mattered that people liked me. I had to deal with the nuns and some were absolutely and totally abusive. Most of them were Irish and racist, but in this odd way, because who were the Irish? ... Sister Regina was my favorite. She was a red-headed nun with freckles. She used to fight with us the most, loved us the most. She read out loud to us. She introduced us to Madeline L'Engle's *A Wrinkle in Time*. She said, 'I have a treat. At two o'clock, if you finish all your work, the treat starts.' And she opened the book, told us to relax. We closed our eyes and she started reading this book."

DRUIS ANN IYA OSHUN KOYA BEASLEY

I met with Druis Beasley in her apartment in Albany, New York on a quiet, cold day in February. I had arranged the meeting after a mutual friend thought that Druis could add another rich dimension to the book I was trying to write. Although she had never met me, and although I was about to pry into the deeper corners of her life, she was unhesitatingly kind, warm and welcoming. We talked through the morning, fueled by herbal tea and sliced banana bread. Druis explained that she comes from a long line of story tellers, which I had no trouble believing. These pages have room for only about a fifth of the wonderful tales she told that day, stories about stubborn grandmothers and tender distant fathers, Island oppression and need for deception. She told me about attending Catholic school in an age of integration, of field trips to art museums and lessons about poise. She related how her family and friends relished nature through trips to the parks and beaches. She told me a number of interesting things about astronomy, astrology and signs and portents. At the heart of our conversation were her insights about coming of age as a black woman in New York City in the 1960s, during the birth of black pride and black rage, Harlem jazz and street poetry. During these turbulent but thrilling times, Druis found her head, her dance moves, her voice and, eventually, her spiritual path.

The Orisha order, in which Druis is an ordained priestess, is a complex system of nature spirits that, like Sufism, is too complex to be grasped within the confines of this book. The real story here is Druis the woman, Druis the student, Druis the priestess, Druis the mother, Druis the artist, Druis outside, Druis the urban dweller who finds a bee hive wherever she lives. This, she would tell you, is no accident. This, she would tell you, is just as it should be. It is because, in Orisha, she is aligned with the mothers, and bees and birds are the "thorn" of the mothers. Hence, where Druis goes, they appear, physical manifestations of energy and power.

During our visit, Druis introduced me to her daughter (she has two daughters and two grandsons) and showed me her art pieces and Batik that decorate the walls and tables of her apartment. Long after I left, driving south on the thruway and into the days beyond, I thought about her complex stories, her enthusiasm and her quick laugh, her sometimes wry, always canny insight. She does indeed enrich this book, as she enriches the places she inhabits and the people lucky enough to inhabit her sphere, if only, like me, for a little while.

ANCESTOR WORK:
Interview with Druis Ann Iya Oshun Koya Beasley

Albany, New York
February

Where and when were you born?

I was born in Kings County Hospital in Brooklyn, New York, August 19, 1955.

My mother is second-generation Carribean. My grandmother came from the island of Trinidad just before the stock market crash in 1929. There is some issue about how old she was, but she came from a very strict Carribean family. I identify with that immigrant piece in a lot of ways.

My grandmother had a relationship with a man she knew on the island. He came here and then she came here and he wound up being married. They had a relationship, and she got pregnant.

My mother was born in Harlem Hospital. She is the first child of that union. So, she is first-generation American.

My grandmother was raised by very petty bourgeois Caribbean Negroes—Creoles. The family has lots of mythology. Trying to get to the real story through the mythology is an interesting experience.

My grandmother was profoundly abused because she stood up for her rights and the rights of the family—not allowing the family to lie too much. She took the brunt of it, physically, psychologically and emotionally. That really affected how we grew up. I was very matriarchal identified, matrimonial in my focus.

My grandmother was a seamstress by training. She had been trained by the best seamstress on the island of Trinidad. But there was so much abuse and trauma that when she came to this country she never used her sewing abilities. She did office cleaning and that kind of work. My mother experienced the brunt of all that family history. What I experienced from my mother was a certain amount of aloofness. She was very philosophical about things. I was identified with her, but it was less about her and more about my grandmother, who lived with us.

My father comes from southern stock. He was born in Virginia or West Virginia. But whenever he told a story, it was always about Alabama, Georgia and Kentucky. So apparently, they traveled around a lot.

He was a Native American and he was always telling us, "You're Indian. You're Indian."

My father was a very smart man, an industrious guy. But he started drinking when he was twelve. Life was real hard with his mother. She hurt him so bad that we had to live with that hurt until he died. He died at forty-seven.

He was the kind of man a lot of women would like now (minus the drinking), because he was a tender, sensitive, caring individual who got stomped on for being that way.

He was the one who taught me to cook. He's the one who named me.

Does your name have a meaning?

Yes, it means "the one who knows prophesy." It's an anglicized Gaelic name. It belongs not only to the village, but also to that part of the clan that are the bards, so it makes sense that I'm a storyteller.

To whom do you credit your story-telling abilities?

My grandmother was always telling stories when we were growing up, stories about the island. They were a way of passing on genealogy, and it gave her an opportunity to create a reality that worked for her. Her ideas about family and what family should be made a real big difference. The kind of abuse that my grandmother experienced is a part of the Caribbean culture that still holds facets of slavery in it—especially the corporal punishment. How is it possible to experience that kind of abuse and still transmit the amount of love and caring and generosity that she did?

My grandmother used stories as a way to teach us how to negotiate life when it got tough. She told stories to make us laugh and to lift the tension, because life wasn't easy. She told us one story about Emmett Till. When Emmett Till was killed, *Look Magazine* had a picture of his mutilated body on the cover. My grandmother was in downtown Brooklyn, on Fulton Street. It was crowded. It was a summer day. She got angry. She bought the magazine and she rolled it up. She rolled up the magazine and she decided, "I'm whooping some white person's head up today. Okay? Because I'm pissed."

So she's standing at the bus stop in front of our favorite frankfurter stand. The bus is coming; it's crowded and there's this big fat white woman making nasty comments about "that" Emmett Till, and he was "this" and, you know, it's 1935. That poor woman didn't know she was a target. My grandmother rolled up that magazine and started reaching up and reaching up, getting herself ready. She got up close; the bus pulled up; this woman is talking and the next thing you know, my grandmother said, "Don't step on my foot!" That was always her favorite line. She started whooping that woman, taunting and hitting at the same time. My grandmother got on the bus and the bus took off. She said, "I got her that day." She said, "I whooped her good. I was whooping her for that boy!"

That's what a lot of our ancestors did. One person would become the repository.

My grandmother told that story over and over. We never got tired of it. For me, she was the one. If she went to the door, I'd have my coat and I'd be ready. She created a lot of confusion but I loved it. I learned how to stand up for myself observing her.

What was your grandmother's name?

Her name was Idalia Hyacinthe Cumberbatch. How she got that name, I don't really know. Something about a German slave or a slave captor who had a plantation. We come from a line of people who were on the plantation in Barbados because our island was originally the island of Barbados. Then our people moved to Trinidad.

Are children being raised differently these days—for instance, your own two daughters?

Well, I think we've evolved and it's different. Less the fear factor. But we still try and teach our children how to negotiate the world, and the world is still hostile.

Alongside of this, you were raised in the Catholic Church. You went to parochial school. Can you talk about that a little bit?

Ah, yes, the nuns, the Irish nuns.

I went to Our Lady of Lords in Brooklyn, the second largest cathedral church in New York (second to Saint Patrick's), on Aberdeen Street in Bedford Stuyvesant. It was in a small Polish and Irish neighborhood until more color started moving in. Polish, Irish, Italian, Puerto Ricans, African Americans and African Caribbeans as well. I make the distinction between African American, which is more the southern experience, and African Caribbean, which is more the island experience.

I started off in public school, but I got pneumonia because I used to love to be Superman. I would, on my way to school, fly down the street with my coat open and I caught pneumonia. Grandma got permission to take me to Trinidad so I could heal.

How old were you?

I was six. I turned seven when I was in Trinidad. When I returned after nine months, I went into our Lady of Lords second grade.

By third grade, I gave up the wild woman in myself and started trying to be the socially accepted individual. It mattered that people liked me. I had to deal with the nuns and some were absolutely and totally abusive. Most of them were Irish and racist, but in this odd way, because who were the Irish?

They're interesting women, these Irish nuns, because they are, I know now, sacred and yet practical. "I'm a teacher. I'm here to teach; you're going to learn." There was an interesting tension there.

Sister Regina was my favorite. She was a red-headed nun with freckles. She used to fight with us the most, loved us the most. She read out loud to us. She introduced us to Madeline L'Engle's *A Wrinkle in Time*. She said, "I have a treat. At two o'clock, if you finish all your work, the treat starts." And she opened the book, told us to relax. We closed our eyes and she started reading this book.

It changed our lives. I ran to the library, took out the book. Smart woman. It bonded us in this really interesting way.

She took us to museums. We learned how to carry ourselves on the train. We took field trips. She took us to the art museum. We'd have a tour and then she'd say, "All right, you're on your way to becoming young women. So you now have ninety minutes to be on your own." We were, like, eleven and twelve years old, proving we could explore the museum on our own, pay attention, don't talk to strangers, know where all the exits are. And she'd tell us, "Find a spot that's your spot, that you can use to reflect on."

Years later, when I went to Hunter College, I would go back to that museum. Monet's Garden was my "spot." Whenever I wanted to reflect, to write, I'd go there. It's still one of my favorite spots.

The nuns made sure we learned and told us we're not animals. You know what I mean? A lot of us went from that grammar school to a diocese high school. Desegregation happened and we wound up going to Christ the King High School, a whole group of us, to desegregate this all-white school within the village of Queens. In 1969, that was freedom.

I was a radical. People respected me, but I didn't know how to negotiate. Martin Luther King didn't work for me. Malcolm X was my man, the Black Panthers.

How was your high school experience?

I had a wonderful experience at Christ the King. It was the next part of my training. I had some of the best English teachers ever, who turned me on to everybody: James Joyce, Virginia Woolf, Sylvia Plath, James Baldwin. I mean, there was all this juxtapositioning. The nuns there were split between the old-school women who wanted to treat us like children and the new group of nuns who changed their habit or didn't wear a habit.

Mrs. Tuchi was this platinum-blond Italian, liberated English teacher who took the seniors up into the convent that was there; it was like a secret society. She'd take us and have conversations with us about our sexuality. I was the happiest ever because she took us to museums and to plays. I was blossoming. It was wonderful. And it was also when I realized that being a Catholic was something I was not going to do.

How did you come to realize that?

Well, partly because of my grandfather, who used to talk to me about the Vatican, the house of the church and how Catholicism was started. He was a self-taught man, like my father. When I made Holy Communion, he'd say, "Come here, let me tell you about this ritual." I learned about ritual, ceremony and questioning from him. I was raised a heretical Catholic, in the sense that I followed the more Gnostic path. I believed that Christ was a prophet, but also a human being, that he married Mary Magdalene and they had a child.

Can you tell me about your dance background?

Because mommy couldn't afford to pay for an instrument and dance, the girls got dance and my brother got classical guitar. We went to the Brooklyn Music School, which is an internationally renowned school. I worked with a teacher that we called "Madam" from the time I was nine until I was fourteen. She had a French name and had been a principal dancer with the American Ballet.

She encouraged me to audition for the High School of Performing Arts, which I did. I choreographed my own piece in my mother's narrow apartment. I knew how to use space. Don't ask me how; in my mind I had all the space in the world.

At the audition they lined us up and I looked lovely in the front. Then they told us to turn around and, of course, I had more to lose than anyone else. I was rejected.

You felt that was strictly on your physical appearance?

Yes. I was told. At the time, ballet was really a two dimensional dance—all about being flat. A year later, Arthur Mitchell would create the Dance Theatre of Harlem and more brown people would start getting into the High School of Performing Arts.

But, I had a way of processing it and somehow bringing myself out of it. I went to auditions, danced at the Apollo, took African dance. I told myself, "I don't have to be like them. I can be more independent."

I started studying modern dance and African dance. I never really had the full desire. But I didn't want to give up the arts, so I taught dance. That's how I made a living and got though college. I started reading poets, writing poetry. I found other ways to express myself.

What poets did you study?

Harlem Renaissance poets, writers in general. Baldwin was my favorite. He's a storyteller that uses the language.

For me, there's always a connection between art and activism. So at fifteen, I'm right in New York City where it's happening. LeRoi Jones, Sonja Sanchez, Nikki Giovanni. There's music happening everywhere, poetry happening everywhere. I saw Malcolm X on the corner of Nostrand Avenue and Fulton Street. He was a storyteller. He was a spoken-word artist. I'm in Harlem and it's popping in the '60s and it's popping in Brooklyn.

I was on the elevator train, the J train, going from Brooklyn to Queens when I opened up my first marble notebook—I still have that notebook—and wrote down my thoughts. For me, my thoughts were precious and I didn't want to change them. I was a purist for a long time. I continue to practice my journaling and writing my poetry. It's a part of who I am.

Do you have early memories, aside from becoming Superman and running down the street, of being in nature, connecting with nature?

Yes. In New York City there was Prospect Park and Central Park. Because we lived in the city didn't mean that we couldn't have access to the green. We planned picnics, barbeque, being outside. Grandma was always about being outside. "Get out. Get air. You need the wind to your brain."

We'd go to Prospect Park, which is so beautiful. There are parts that are like wetlands.

I remember climbing trees and running, rolling down the hills and the grass. I loved that. Twirling around and falling on the ground.

As a teenager, Central Park was what was happening. In the summer, we went into that green, to know that there was more than just concrete. Drummers were in the park, roller skaters, concerts, Shakespeare in the Park.

As teenagers, we used to plan trips. We'd be on the train traveling to the park. Sometimes people would bring their bikes.

Or, we'd plan picnics and go up to Bear Mountain. You'd get all your stuff organized the night before, get up real early in the morning. Everybody lugging coolers to get on the train, to get to the pier, to get on the boat, to get on the water. You see, because we're island people, we still had to be connected to that dirt. My aunt would be drinking beer on the boat, going up those steps once you get to Bear Mountain.

There were trips to the beach and that was a whole other feeling, associated with the water, the sand, the discomfort of stuff all up in your pants. Then you'd have to get on the train and go home with sand all over you.

Can you talk about when your spiritual practice began?

My spiritual practice? A lot happened to me at fifteen. I was aware in my being that the natural world influenced me. I was attracted to the orisha, which is what we call the energy. It's the nature and the spirits.

In '55, we had African spiritual practitioners coming from the island of Cuba to the Bronx. By 1965, they let certain African Americans in to be initiated into the practice. And so, now we're starting to practice African religion as part of a political practice.

I started studying and reading. I had people around me who were practitioners. I went to dance class and the drummers who worked with us would play and I would dance; they could see the presence of the orisha in my dance.

What are the orisha?

Orisha are manifestations of the one source, Olodumare in the Yoruba spiritual system. The Yoruba people were the largest ethnic group, among many others, to be shipped to the Americas during the Maafa (or African Holocaust). The many faces of this spiritual system are the result of a cross-fertilization of many indigenous African religious systems. In addition to the veneration of God manifested in nature, the Orisha system includes ancestor reverence, and consultation through Ifa, which is a geomantic system of divination.

A core belief in the Orisha system is the practice of Iwa-Pele—good and gentle character—which is attained through the proper alignment and knowledge of one's Ori, which in Western terms means the higher self, or soul's code. Spiritually what this means is that when you are aligned with your destiny and expressing that through personal power, known as Ase, you are living a fulfilled and happy life because you are in sync with the life force of the universe, accessible to you through natural spiritual forces, your ancestors and your own head.

Is it the same as what we know as Santeria?

Well, Santeria/Lucumi is the masked face of traditional Yoruba beliefs. In order to continue practicing their religion, which was forbidden by the masters in Cuba, African slaves disguised Orisha with Catholic Saints.

Thank you. You were talking about your earlier development?

Yes. In those days, I was making my own spiritual objects. I made my own clothes. I'm saying prayers on my own. I go to a crossroad and I'm interacting on my own. I'm a little afraid because I'm on my own and I also have this thing about having a teacher. So there's this tension, but I stay on my own a long time.

I became a Buddhist in the winter of 1987, which is an interesting path that people take. You come out of Christianity and go to Buddhism. Buddhism brings us right to nature and gives us access to the energy in a whole other way. It feeds me philosophically, intellectually, and feeds my spirit. I see what happens when I send sound out in a mantra and what comes back. I see the protection. I'm putting three and three together.

What I mean by the work—it's just we're always connected. Growing plants, studying herbalism, wanting to live a more organic life. The work is always there.

Then, in the early '80s, with my second husband, I started learning drumming, percussion. When you play African percussion, there's no way that you're not connected to nature. The drumming itself is a process of bringing spirit closer.

Can you talk a little more about nature being in our bodies and what that means for you?

We're just one more physical manifestation of the diversity that exists out there. I may not look like a polar bear but I'm connected to the polar bear. We have a circulatory system, we have a brain, we have consciousness; we have ways in which we function in the natural world. Your body is a manifestation. We're taught to be afraid of it, so we don't see it as the temple that it is. I see the body as a reflection of the natural world.

When did you become initiated into the orisha?

I had my formal initiation in 1992. It's a real complex initiation. I'm initiated into the archetype that we know as Oshun, the goddess of creativity. She is created energy; she owns the circulatory system—meaning that she represents that part of the body. She's very complex, independent. Her generosity can also be her downfall. She has a tendency to give it away and people never give it back. So she has to learn how to control herself.

I have two other orisha who are with me. Chango, sometimes called Shango, the organizer, is one of the few that were human first and then elevated to a force of nature. Fire is his primary force, and then thunder and lightning.

Chango is courageous. He teaches through experience and he wants those who are initiated to have balls.

Then I also have Babalu Aye, who is the spirit of illness and disease. He is a very complex character. He is the owner of the DNA.

The orisha tradition has science. It's not primitive; it's spirituality and science together. One actually confirms the existence of the other. You can't have one without the other. Babalu Aye, he calls all that is dark in the light. He's the "Owner of the White Cloth" and represents illumination. For me, to get there, sometimes I have to go through the underworld.

What does "Owner of the White Cloth" mean?

Obatala is the "Owner of the White Cloth," which means being the divinity of light, illumination, purity, keeper of the light within the dark and moral turpitude.

Babalu is in lots of different stories. He has a close relationship to the dark phase of the goddess. In my practice, it is what you would call the theology of the mother.

The mothers are under everything, but neutral, so they can go either way. Sometimes it means working the dark side. They represent Mother Nature and birds are their thorns. So, birds are very important to me.

Everywhere I've ever lived there has always been a bee's hive or a wasp's hive—because bees and wasps belong to her, too—in the walls, up above a doorway.

How do you "work the dark side," as you put it?

The mothers are about acceptance. Light is not always pretty in others, or in yourself, but you have to accept. Sometimes you have to be your ugly face to negotiate the world. The truth is what the truth is. You have to appease them, though, because what happens when you let the dark phase of the mother out? You have to have a coolant. Babalu is the coolant. So in some ways, philosophically, you can't have one without the other. You can't have yin without yang. You can't have male without female. It's all about that balance and the mothers are under everything. And it's all in nature. Learning to recognize it and allowing it to inform how you live, now, that is the biggest challenge.

Does Orisha include a concept of evil, whether in people or in nature?

In the Ifa/Orisha cosmology, as in all Eastern practices, it is the fundamental idea of balance. The multiverse exists in a state of energetic balance that is manifested in the forms we perceive in this third-dimensional reality, and those we don't see. There are symbols and names within the spiritual system that enable one to recognize the many states of imbalance, and balance that exist within one's self, community, environment, and so on.

Divination enables one to most appropriately assess the nature of the energy: is it hot or cool, is it chaotic or ordered, and so on. You are then given prescriptions that can include all kinds of sacrifices to restore a state of balance, including sacrificing favorites foods, drinks, clothing, tools and the like. From a quantum perspective, this is a practice that acknowledges we are co-creators in our reality, that we are aspects of the divine and connected to it in all its manifestations.

It is important, however, to actively and consistently develop Iwa Pele—good, gentle character—which involves stalking yourself, becoming the ultimate observer and expanding your consciousness to recognize being connected. So good versus evil is too simplistic a concept, because it leaves space for superstition which is grounded in fear.

When you interact with nature, for which the orisha are manifestations, you live in the knowledge that balance is a paradox in and of itself. The Orisha become pathways, keys to the active partnership we have with earth and sky. Good and evil represent the choices we make based on our character and personality. Prayer, sacrifice and Iwa Pele become the tools used daily to support your manifestation of all that you have come to offer the world.

What happens after initiation?

After initiation you're called Iyawo. You're in this Iyawo state for a year in the West. But in Africa, you're Iyawo for seven days; you're in what is like a womb. Then you come out and go on with your work. But you're new, so you still have elders that are taking care of you. Here, you wear white for a year. A lot of the way we do our initiative process is grounded in slavery, and it's got certain Christian elements for survival purposes. I wore white for a year. That was when I made my formal initiation.

When I made my initiation to the mothers, I had to wear hunter green. I thought it would kill me. I wore green everything. I ate off green plates. I wore hunter green underwear, I had hunter green shoes.

Elders will tell you, you can leave a house but you never leave orisha. Anything that we create "out here" is just a symbol of what's "in here." The river is Oshun, the crossroad is Eshu, the mountains are Obatala, Ochosi is in the woods.

Do you see this working on a concrete level and also a symbolic level?

The post office is, to me, orisha operating on the concrete level. I can see Eshu at the crossroads keeping communication, making sure that the mail gets to where it's going. And Ogun is about clearing the pathway. So Ogun makes sure that the mail will get there in a clear way, but he also represents technology. Look at all the technology that you have to have in order to get that letter flowing. And Ochosi is the address. It's going from this place to that. So, there's a direction, a certain direction.

I see it all the time, everywhere. We give acknowledgement to the tools. Your car, for example. We'll take alcohol, which is a form of disinfectant, and put it in our mouths but we also spray it on our cars. We want to make sure that there's no accident. We need to get to where we're going.

So it's like physical crossroads, physical car, and yet it's also working on a symbolic and spiritual level?

Yes.

How many spirits are there?

Four hundred, at least. In the West, we have about fifteen primaries. Everything else is just an expression.

Like an aspect?

Yes, an aspect of an archetype. That's why the old archetypal system works with my ability to communicate what it is that I do. There are these archetypal structures. This thing that is larger than you, that is a higher power, is what you call God. Or a god. Then there are all these different aspects, which are the ways you express or experience it.

What is your take on global climate change and extreme weather events in relation to the orishas?

Well, the weather: that's one place where you really get to see them and their work, because they're forces of nature.

The wind belongs to Oya. Hurricanes are formed on the west coast of Africa. Those are her children and when Oya comes, she doesn't play. She clears everything, okay? Oya sent her daughter, Katrina, to clear everything up. To bring the message: "You all are living in a dream world; time to bring you into reality."

Voodoo is a part of the African spirituality, the system that I practice. The people in New Orleans should know better. Yet, they're having a hard time with it.

New Orleans cannot build a city shield. It's below sea level. The depths of the ocean belong to Olokun. Whatever's deep at some point will have to come to the surface.

You can't have the water without the wind—they're always together. So Mayana, who's the top of the water, and Oya, the wind, are always together, because the wind is always over the water. Oya forms this hurricane and it gains strength given the moisture that's in the water—condensation. Oya says, "I'm slamming New Orleans. Taking the coastline back. It's mine."

Hurricanes and tornadoes, both belong to her. Again, there's a scientific relationship. When it's an F5, I'm in heaven. It's terrible. I'm almost thinking of becoming a tornado chaser, I swear. I get glued to the television.

That technology—television—belongs to Ogun. He gives you the spark to change your tools. What's happening from a spiritual perspective is that with technology, we're starting to act like we are God. What's technology? It's simply an extension of brains, hands, feet and all the senses. Tools could be created to make our lives in harmony with nature better. But that's not what we're doing.

As Marshall McLuhan said, our nervous system is on the outside of us now, which gives everybody access to us.

What do you mean?

Our nervous system is our electrical system. There's a way in which television has programmed us to want everything. Fifth Avenue, getting us to buy certain products. A lot of our lives are informed by television. Here's a wonderful tool that could inform and inspire, yet it's being used to manipulate. So, you always have the dark and the light side. Do you see what I mean?

There will still be hurricanes. There'll still be an ice age. There'll still be flooding. There'll still be all those things, but how we deal with them will be different if we are more in sync with the flow of things. We have to take our mammalian selves back. We're in denial about the fact that we're natural animals. We've created this false tension between the natural world and this other artificial thing.

The first thing we have to do is put the electrical system back inside ourselves. We're overstimulated. Electricity is important because it helps things to flow in unison. This fire thing, this spark thing, it's another form of energy, right? But when you're using it all of the time, you're overstimulating yourself. So the very thing that's a positive becomes a negative. For those of us who do spiritual work, we know energetically that the phallic centric way is not working. So, we have to bring the goddess back. To create balance in the world, you need both the male and female aspect.

Do you see this manifesting? A balance being created?

When the planet Sedna was discovered and identified and acknowledged, the astronomers, who are also astrologers, chose the name.

Sedna is an Innuit goddess who owns the depths of the ocean. The seals and the whales belong to her. The shamans that work that energy among the Innuit, in transpossession, descend into that cold ocean, that underworld and they comb her hair to cool her.

In the mythology of Sedna, she was a woman who was abused by her father. She was sold to the raven that was in the skies.

The tsunami came because she was not happy with what was happening with the children in that part of the world. They were being abused. People were forgetting themselves. So she shook and brought that energy, that water up, and she took the children back.
In Greek mythology that energy is called Poseidon.

The people in Sumatra knew what they're looking at because they've got an equivalent Indian goddess. They knew exactly. People were… you saw thousands of people that went to the shrine and they wound up getting sucked away.

There's always a sacrifice. Mother Nature will always balance itself.

The naming of the planet Sedna awakened that energy?

The naming, the acknowledgment, the fact that she made herself known. When the scientists recognized or saw that planet, she made herself known. Like, the dwarf planet that was discovered and named Xena, renamed Eris. The presence of these planets is quickening us, but our quickening has also brought these planets present.

Do you think about this stuff every day?

I see meanings everywhere and I laugh to myself. It could be burdensome. It could drive you crazy. You have to relax and accept the gift. What you choose to do with it is up to you. We don't have to whack a thing. We don't have to kill a bird. We don't really have to kill animals. We don't have to do any of it. Mother Nature will always take whatever is necessary. That's what I trust.

photo courtesy of the Archives of the Episcopal Diocese of New York

MOTHER JOAN LALIBERTE

"One Sunday, I think it was Palm Sunday, or some terribly inconvenient time, I got a phone call: the wolf; was I ready to take it? 'Okay,' I said, 'let me see him.' Up came this station wagon and out came this emaciated black dog, who was terrified of everything; he was shaking with fear. The breeder took him back because the first owner kept him on a chain, fed him a diet of raw meat and named him 'Howler' because he howled. He was smeared with excrement. You could count his ribs. She brought him out, told him to sit and he sat. I talked to him a while, he calmed down. Then I knelt down and talked to him; he put his head against my chest and leaned into it."

MOTHER JOAN LALIBERTE

I was first introduced to Mother Joan LaLiberte and her church, St. James Episcopal of Callicoon, New York, when I began a series of articles about women in the ministry for *The River Reporter* newspaper. I attended service at St. James and was impressed with the inclusive spirit of the church and the quiet, intelligent charisma I felt emanating from the woman in robes. St. James is situated on a steep hill above a country highway, and I noticed several large dogs in an enclosure in the yard, which intrigued me further. During my first formal conversation with Mother Joan, I learned that she was a Westerner, having lived most of her adult life in Oregon, Utah and Idaho. She'd owned horses, and she'd also sustained a rather intense career as a journalist. How, I wondered, does one go from horses and newspapers out West to serving God and community in a small parish in upstate New York? I asked Mother Joan if I might interview her for *Women Outside*.

Mother Joan graciously agreed to participate, and we spoke several more times. She is a woman who comes from diversity and celebrates diversity. Each time we spoke, I was more impressed with her knowledge about wildlife, wolves, Arabian horses and the different populations and cultures she has served. Her no-nonsense manner, born of the West and of a roaming, roguish Army childhood, masks a deep tenderness and insight toward her parish, toward landscape and its wild creatures, and punctuates the deep, if at first reluctant, dedication Mother Joan feels toward her calling. She did not plan to become a priest, but Mother Joan is a woman of some experience and savvy who does not ultimately second-guess what life has to offer. Her deep, resonant voice, sometimes witty, sometimes wry, unfailingly perceptive and honest, is a fitting conclusion for all the voices of *Women Outside*.

A HARD CALLING:
Interview with Mother Joan LaLiberte

Callicoon, New York
March, October

Mother Joan, can you tell me a little bit about your background and childhood, where you were raised?

My father was career military. I was born at Fort Sam Houston army hospital, in Texas, which later became Brooke Army Medical Center. Shortly after I was born we moved, so some part of my infancy was spent in West Palm Beach, Florida; and we were in Albuquerque and Las Vegas. I guess I got the desert imprinted on me.

How long did you spend in each place?

From a few months to two and a half years.

And did your father see any combat?

He wanted to but, thank heavens, he didn't. He had a family and he was in the medical corps. So he was a hospital administrator at the time; he started out before I was born in the Army Air Corps. I'm grateful he didn't go over. But I do remember overhearing my parents arguing about it, because he wanted to enlist.

And how did your mother cope with all the moving?

She loved history. She loved learning about new places. She'd immerse herself in finding out all about the place.

Did you have siblings?

No, I was an only child. I had an older brother who died at birth.

How was it for you when you became school-age, to have this wandering life style?

I'd usually miss a month or six weeks of school in a given year, but I had a low boredom threshold, so I'd read the textbooks ahead and then sit back and coast, daydream and stay just connected enough to make good grades. I'd have been a holy terror if I had spent too much time in one place through the whole school year.

I was always the odd child, the outsider, never one of the inner circle with a clique, and that makes a difference, too, I think.

Meaning?

Well, meaning that I never got in with the popular students, that kind of thing, because I was an outsider. I'd make friends; some of them were other Air Force brats, so we would continue writing for a while.

Since you were the outsider, coming and going so quickly from places, were you able to observe things in a deeper way than the average child?

I had to because I had to blend in. It came in handy when I was a reporter. I could walk into a meeting and be invisible.

But, I was just trying to fit in as well as I could. Usually, I pulled it off. Again, I was not one of the popular students, but, so what? At age thirteen, I was interested in horses, training horses and the like, so I didn't care about being popular.

Did you go to college?

Oh yes. I'd have to have a college degree to get into the seminary.

What did you major in?

Psychology. Started out in pre-med, but I didn't have the passion for it. So I went with a psychology major, but my first love is Spanish and Spanish literature.

Do you still read and speak Spanish?

I'm very rusty, but I still treasure it.

Do you have any Spanish in your heritage?

Not that I know of, except by proxy. My mother had an interesting life. She was Pennsylvania-Dutch, raised initially by her grandparents, and when they died she ended up with her mother and step-father in San Antonio. My step-grandfather was a raging alcoholic at the time. He drank himself south and west down there. So, my mother worked after school in a dime store supporting her family. And the other girls in the school were all Latinas, Mexican-Americans. So she spoke Spanish, she sang with them, she danced with them and she learned to make Spanish and Mexican food, Tex-Mex food, which I dearly love. I was reared on it.

So there was some cultural immersion as you were growing up.

I didn't realize it at the time.

You mentioned that you joined the Peace Corps. Where were you sent?

Peru. I was fluent in Spanish and it was a beautiful language and culture. It was funny, though; we took our Peace Corps training in Puerto Rico, and Puerto Rican Spanish is machine-gun fast: you aspirate the double Rs, you swallow the ends of words. So there I went into the mountains of Southern Peru, into a village where everyone spoke Castilian—very nice, Don Quixote-type Spanish. I was rattling off, and they were looking at me like, "Where did you come from?" So I got into the Castilian, which was spoken beautifully and mixed with Quechua.

Anyway, I got married in the Peace Corps, and when I returned from Peru, I did different things: taught English and Spanish at a junior high school in Lebanon, Oregon. Worked with vocational rehabilitation and was offered a full scholarship to get a Masters in vocational rehab counseling in the state of Oregon. Went down and after one year, realized if I went through and got the degree I'd be working for the state of Oregon. I didn't want to work for the state of Oregon, and I was arrogant enough to think that the person who taught mental retardation didn't know what he was talking about because I worked with people with various disabilities on various jobs and I hadn't worked in the same world he knew. So, I bagged the second year. Looking back, it was a stupid move.

How did you become a reporter?

By accident. I did some freelancing for the Associated Press, which bought some of my pictures.

Next, I started with the Sweet Home, Oregon bureau of the *Albany Democrat Herald*. I did proofreading and got into journalism there, just at the end of the time when they still had the linotype machines, the wood block floors; you could hear the roar of the presses. It was a great place to be. Everybody must have been dying of lead poisoning, actually, but it was a great place to be.

Then I got the job with the *Lincoln City News Guard* in a rapidly developing area. I did community outreach and put out *Coast Tidings*, a monthly tourist magazine. Did all my own photography. Then a former competitor called and offered us a job, my husband and I, in Pocatello, Idaho.

Here I was, getting paid slave wages. I said, "Why am I getting paid so poorly and my husband's getting paid so well?"

"Well, you're a woman." That was the answer, and I didn't want to stay there.

So, we went to Pocatello.

In Pocatello—this was the 1970s—I started out on the county beat. The paper was a small daily, so it allowed me to generate features and all kinds of things that you get into as a reporter.

Pocatello was founded when the railroads came through. It had the Native American population. It had, of course, the Anglos, including a lot of Latter Day Saints. It had Mexican-Americans, who came and built the railroads. At that time it was the only town in Idaho that had a black population and had the first black mayor in the state of Idaho.

This was just coming out of the era when store windows had signs that said "No dogs or Indians allowed." It was an interesting place, with all of the minority people and also sheep herders and the like.

During that time, did you ride horses, go hiking?

I did go hiking, but the horses, I didn't have access to that. But back before bicycling was popular, I got on my ten-speed and did a story about bicycling the Grand Teton Park. Got there a little ahead of the season, no people, nothing. I got these wonderful shots, out in the wild, biking. I did a lot of things like that. Just head out to the hills and go up on government land.

And as for the winter, cross-country skiing hadn't been discovered as a sport yet. The outdoor program at Idaho State had good workshops; they taught you cross-country skiing, rented you those old, wide, heavy planks. It was neat there because of the powder snow. You'd go out to a wheat field, take off and just go skiing; blaze your own trail, sink into the powder, and it was fun.

Tell me more about your journalism fellowship in South America.

Let's see, I was in South America in '74. I returned to Peru, to see it again. I had an opportunity to take this fellowship with the Inter-American Press Association. I did, and all I had to do was generate one feature article a month. It was a piece of cake. While I was there, the military government nationalized the newspaper, nationalized the magazines and pretty much wrecked everything for independent journalism. I was interviewing people in hiding; there were riots in the streets.

Wasn't Peru on the verge of nationalizing everything at that time?

Yes, they were. They had a leftist military as opposed to a far right, which was in Chile.
 But if you're in a repressive government, it doesn't matter if it's left or right. And the nationalizing meant that the press from the government got prime place. It just shuffled the deck; it didn't really change anything.
 Chile was bad. But it was an education. I was on an overnight bus. In the far back of the bus there was a kind of middling-looking guy and a U.S. teenager talking. The teenager was on a trip through South America, tooling around. It was night, so everyone was sleeping—I don't think they realized that anyone else on the bus spoke English. I heard their conversation. The man explained that he was a Roman Catholic priest who'd been kicked out of Chile; he was smuggling himself back in. I knew what that meant. I knew—I was a journalist.

Extremely dangerous?

Yeah, torture, death, dropped from an airplane into the ocean—whatever.
 The kid said, "Well, why did they kick you out of Chile?" The priest said, "For preaching the Gospel."

I thought: "What is there, getting him to go back, when any person in his right mind would stay away?"

When I got back to Lima, where I was based, I picked up the Bible and started reading the gospel. It didn't sink in at that point, but I started going to church.

Were you raised up in a church?

No. My father was Roman Catholic and had broken with it. My mother was Pennsylvania-Dutch, but she'd go to any church that had a choir she could sing with.

She had a nice voice?

Yes, an alto.

I didn't have much of a religious education, although I was into Zen Buddhism in high school, and then later I got interested in meditating and all that sort of thing, but not with a religious focus. When I was in Trinidad, as a child, it was a wonderful island culture. We had Muslim friends and we'd visit their temples and things like that, so I got a good cross-section of religion. My mother was interested in all of them.

Was the priest on the bus the first big inkling you had that there could be such a thing as a calling?

Yes. I didn't know how to think of it then, but it hooked me.

Did you begin thinking that point about the existence of evil, given what was going on with the governments of these countries?

Evil? That takes a while to talk about. I do believe there's a personalized force of evil, but I think our human failings are the cause of most wickedness: greed, self-centeredness, sociopathy, and so on. That's a major topic, which deserves more space.

Anyway—I got back from Peru and, professionally, I was doing well. But in my personal life, I was miserable.

I was working on a feature about a motorcycle gang in Pocatello. Kind of "Heck's Angels;" they weren't real hard core, but they were Pocatello's motorcycle gang. I had won their trust because they knew I wasn't going to write something that would mess them up. I was going to be fair; I had a good reputation.

I planned to go with them on a motorcycle trip up to Virginia City, Montana over Labor Day weekend, but my bike wasn't doing very well. At that time, I had a little Yamaha, which was totally unreliable. I decided it didn't look good. There was a chance to make a Cursillo through some people at the church. I thought: "Three-day retreat, I'll just kick back and get some rest."

What is a Cursillo?

It's "short course" in Spanish. It's a three-day course in Christianity, led mostly by lay people.

What year was this?

It was 1975. The first night they had a Stations of the Cross, and then a silent retreat. As I say, my personal life stunk. I was really miserable, so I went to sleep praying, "God, if you're there, help." The only prayer I had was "help," and I was crying myself to sleep, off in my corner, being alone.

I woke up the next morning and I knew real joy. I knew I was totally loved, totally forgiven, the whole nine yards. I don't know what happened. It was an incredible experience. Then, I was hungry to keep going deeper and deeper into the Bible.

Meanwhile I ended up, at some point, on the magazine section of the newspaper. There were church pages that I expanded, because there were so many different beliefs. Basically learning more, deepening my relationship with God.

I was a lay leader, which meant I first started out reading the Old Testament, New Testament lessons in church, assisting the priest, serving the chalice. I was the first woman in the diocese licensed to preach sermons. I worked hard on it because I didn't want to commit heresy, or something, but I was all right. Everything I did made me feel good.

I was thinking, "I don't want to be a priest, but it feels like that's what I'm called to do."

I went to a Roman Catholic priest friend and said, "I want you to talk me out of something. I think I'm supposed to be a priest." He said, "Go for it!" Well, that was disappointing!

I hadn't told anyone about this calling. People at work knew I was very involved in the church. So—it was 1976, and the wire editor came out of the room with the wire machines—it was so noisy and the bells went off—he came out holding a piece of paper and said, "Joan, you're going to be so happy! The Episcopal Church just voted to ordain women."

I said, "Oh, shit!" Because I didn't want to do it! This is not what I had planned! I wanted to go on in journalism.

Anyway, then, I hit dead ends at seminary because there was no money to go. Then, on a fluke, my husband's mother flew us out to California and I visited the seminary at Berkeley, and everything fell into place. Like that! Took a typewriter in the library, filled out the forms, the admissions committee was all on campus at that particular point in space and time. It was incredible. They offered me financial aid. Went back to the paper and said, "I'm leaving in August."

It was total insecurity from then on. We ended up with a basement apartment for $75 a month, one thing after another, but with a certain kind of timing so you couldn't see any security. You just kept stepping.

My second year at seminary, the bishop of Wyoming came to visit the campus, and at our community dinner on a Thursday night, he stood up and said, "The diocese of Wyoming is looking for a few good men… " and then with the hisses and the cat calls…"and women!" I was accepted by the diocese of Wyoming.

I went, after graduation, on a long retreat to the Jesuits in Kansas. I admired the Jesuits' spirituality, like Marine Corps spirituality; I wanted that kind of tough relationship with God.

I was ready to be ordained, and I ended up back in Idaho as a deacon with no place to go, trying to eke out a living. I was ordained a priest in my first parish in western Idaho. The idea of women priests was new, and I was the first woman to be ordained a priest in that diocese. I spent time as a deacon, half-time, in the priesthood at Fort Hall Reservation. That was where I was based for the rest of my ministry in Idaho. I had various other churches.

And you were there for how long?

Oh, what, June '85 to October '99.

On the reservation, was there any blending in the church of other traditions, such as Native American?

Of course.

Some of the older people didn't like to be too "Indian." Fort Hall had an interesting assortment. They had an Assembly of God, a Southern Baptist Church and a Catholic Church, so you had a few different Christian traditions. But you also had what you would call simply traditional people, with traditional ways; you had a lot of people who danced the Sun Dance, which is a huge tradition up there, and some of my church members also were Sun Dancers.

The Sun Dance arbor has 12 poles surrounding the circle. In the center is one pole—usually it's a buffalo skull or some such—and they pray to the Creator. Now, if you have a central pole with 12 poles around it, and you're coming from a Christian church and you can't preach on that, you're in trouble.

Also, Fort Hall had the "peyote" (or Native American) church. I did respect all of that—I wanted to learn about it. I didn't have a problem with the peyote church; they put an altar there and they prayed to Grandfather, to the Creator, and also to Brother Jesus.

Do you believe that different religions and cultures actually share a lot of the same symbolisms and beliefs around one god?

Yes, in general, although I am not familiar with all kinds of religions. Among the Indian population, there are many religions and traditions because each tribe is a nation of its own. You have as much difference between tribes as you have between Scandinavians and Italians. With spiritual matters, one is well advised to be careful. But Christianity would be a great religion if everyone practiced it.

We can look at instances where Christianity has been damaging but, overall, where would we be without certain concerns that come out of the church? There's always been a concern for the individual, even though different cultures could get very messed up, like the many churches that supported slavery. But there were many other churches that were smuggling people to freedom.

How did you come to be the pastor of St. James Episcopal Church in Callicoon, New York?

This was among many calls I was exploring. The diocese kept saying Callicoon was so remote. I don't know how they get "so remote" when you're two hours from New York City. But to New Yorkers, it's remote.

Anyway, I was flown out here to interview and things fell into place. I said, "Okay, God, the touchstone will be if they accept the wolf."

The wolf?

Yes. At that time I had a wolf—a sweetheart. The big bad wolf was a big friendly black love of a thing who was trained to basic commands. I had two other dogs.

How did you come to have a wolf?

My wolf was a rescue.

I was out on the res and I had my Arabian mares; I still miss them terribly.

And, let's see, I decided I would need to get a watch dog, because the place kept getting broken into. On the reservation, dogs are real deterrents; res dogs are something else.

I went to the pound, fell in love with a blue-eyed Siberian, who looked wolf-like, of course, as Siberians do. She was wonderful, very loyal, and she did indeed deter. There was only one break-in after I got her, and they didn't stay. She was there in the hall, wanted to greet them, because she's not a watchdog. She went "woo-woo-woo" at them—

And they took off.

Took one look at those ice-blue eyes, yeah. But she was a friendly animal. Then I got a husky-cross with some Australian shepherd or cattle dog in her, named Ptchee. Pretty soon I got a phone call from a gal who had a neighbor who raised wolf-dogs. The neighbor moved to Salt Lake and was inquiring whether there was anyone who might take a year-old wolf.

She asked me, "Would you be interested?"

One Sunday, I think it was Palm Sunday, or some terribly inconvenient time, I got a phone call: the wolf; was I ready to take it? "Okay," I said, "let me see him." Up came this station wagon and out came this emaciated black dog, who was terrified of everything; he was shaking with fear. The breeder took him back because the first owner kept him on a chain, fed him a diet of raw meat and named him "Howler" because he howled. He was smeared with excrement. You could count his ribs. She brought him out, told him to sit and he sat. I talked to him a while, he calmed down. Then I knelt down and talked to him; he put his head against my chest and leaned into it. There was no aggressive behavior.

I asked, "What happens if I don't take him?" She said, "We'll have to shoot him tomorrow." A responsible breeder isn't going to turn an animal loose or allow it to be treated cruelly.

So, I took him. My little female, Ptchee, fell in love with Singer at first sight, which was good, because then he needed another dog to keep him calm. If friends came in, he'd climb the cabinets, he was so frightened.

She fell in love with Singer; Singer fell in love with her. She bossed him around, you know, this big male wolf; she could just look at him and he'd do anything. She'd grab him by the muzzle. They were funny.

Did you feed dog food to Singer, like your other dogs?

Yeah, high-protein, good quality. He had special dietary needs.

Was that because he was a wolf?

Well, partly. The other part was the pancreatic insufficiency. It took some time, but he did become very, very trusting. He had these gorgeous eyes, a white patch on his chest.

Around here, you don't hear of wolves much as pets. Is it more common in the West?

In Idaho, at the time I lived there, all you need is a fish and game license, renewable every year. Laws have probably changed. Idaho is now very anti-wolf and is trying to kill off all the government-introduced wolves and their offspring.

When I was on the res, having a wolf was not a big deal. A lot of the dogs around that area had some wolf in them. And they were good dogs.

When Singer was a baby, he nursed with the mother, but was also bottle-fed, so he knew he was a canine, but he also thought he was also human. It was a kind of bonding that worked very well.

I took Singer into schools and he loved it. Wolves are timid. Things that they don't know, they don't trust. But he loved the children. The first school I took him in, we were lecturing the children—they were sitting on the floor—"Don't try to pet him or anything." I heard laughter and looked down and Singer was on his back, back-stroking across the floor to get to the nearest child to be petted.

Is it hard for you living in upstate New York?

I get claustrophobic. I didn't realize I was claustrophobic but I felt closed in by all of the trees. Then in autumn the leaves fell and I thought, "Oh, this is what goes on." It's like the Willamette Valley in Oregon used to be before California moved north, with little streams, two-lane winding roads, farm stands, rolling country.

How has your experience been here in general?

I look at people as a pastor does, which doesn't put the labels on things. My idea of a community, my model of so-called leadership, is not hierarchical. I am the priest-in-charge, the spiritual light, but I want people to be involved; I get joy out of encouraging people to discover what they can do. I love to see people stretch themselves, get excited about something. I don't want to be the boss.

You said the lay person is important to the ministry. Can you talk about that a little?

Every lay person, by virtue of baptism, is a minister. Our catechism is, "Who are the ministers of our church? The ministers of the church are bishops, lay people, priests and deacons." A church doesn't grow because a priest goes out and tells people to come in, it grows when people invite other people, when they reach out into the community. I'm the visible part, if you wish, but I'm not the community. I'm the quarter-master; I feed the troops. Lay people are the foot soldiers, out on the front lines doing it.

When I first came to St. James, it was not a comfortable mix. But, I see the congregation deepen with a developing spirit and good enthusiasm.

Used to be, after the service, people would come around to have tea or instant coffee and there were some cookies and all; it was nice. And people visited. It wasn't cold, like some frozen-chosen churches, but it wasn't a place where people really lingered. Now, we have wonderful coffee hours with freshly brewed coffee, water for tea, sometimes pot luck. People spend time; they visit with each other; they have a sense of the community. This is something I prayed for, wanted to encourage. But you can't force it to happen, you have to allow opportunities for it to happen.

Since it's almost Easter, could you talk a bit about the Easter service and what it means?

It's what everything else revolves around. Holy Week for me starts with Palm Sunday, the sense of joy and betrayal of loss and everything that sets the tone for the week. And then we have the Maundy Thursday services to commemorate the last supper, the institution of the Eucharist and the commandment to love one another. At the end, we take all the decorations out of the sanctuary and we leave in silence.

Good Friday, of course, the Stations of the Cross, remembering the sacrifice. Saturday, a day of fasting, special devotion, polishing the brass for the service. And then, Easter vigil, which is the high point of the church year as far as I'm concerned.

We kindle a fire outside in the parking lot. It's a symbolic thing. "This is the new fire." We light the Easter candle and bring it into the darkened church. This is a service that the Episcopal Church has rediscovered. It goes to the roots of the old church when people spent the whole night in prayer, fasting, scripture reading and then baptism at daybreak.

Now, we don't go all night, and we don't wait until late into the night to start, because that just doesn't work here. But we kindle the new fire, we bring the Easter candle inside chanting, "The light of Christ," and the response is, "Thanks be to God." Then, there's a special ancient hymn that is chanted or recited at the Paschal candle. Then we have the Eucharist and all the flowers, the lights, go on the altar. It is a celebration. Christ is risen.

What is the wolf population out in the West, now?

At last count there were two thousand five hundred in Montana, Idaho and Wyoming. And they want to get it down to about three hundred.

So will they allow hunting from airplanes?

That is one of the things being discussed.

The wild wolf has been federally protected as endangered. The reintroduced wolves don't have quite that much protection; they are an experimental population and, since you have big game there, they thrived. Even the buffalo—they will take down bison. The wolves created an ecological balance out in Yellowstone. One of the things wolves have done is to make prey animals wary. So hunters have to work harder. And who wants to work harder?

But, the wolves also cull out the sick. The saying goes: "The wolf depends on the elk and the elk depends on the wolf," because wolves make the herd stronger. Populations, in all of the species, will vary up and down. But what you want is diversity.

What do you think of the coyote hunts here in upstate New York?

I think it's barbaric. But people like to kill. They like to kill things smarter than them.

People worry around here that coyotes will kill pets, and maybe worse.

And they might! But pets should be in the house. Coyotes are a timid animal, but smart. Anything that can survive in Manhattan in the wild is pretty darn smart. There is not as much known about coyotes as wolves. Wolves are timid enough, but coyotes are even more so. So people call them sneaky... but they're smart. And if you've ever sat out on a cold night in the desert and heard the coyotes—oh! It's marvelous.

We have put so much out of balance. Once upon a time, we had all these animals, including the Southwestern wolf, which is more than endangered. The red wolf. But predators? Most of them are not going to come and eat your family. Mountain lions might—they're cats. When I see the way my cat looks at me sometimes, I'm glad she's not that big.

I would happily camp out in the wilderness with wolves and coyotes around, but I wouldn't do it with that many mountain lions.

How many Arabian mares did you own?

I had three. I had gotten two young ones that were seven-eighths Egyptian. One had been abused. She was really afraid—explosive. I put up a fence and had them grazing in the yard, so that my sounds and my presence would become familiar. I'd look out the kitchen window sometimes, and there'd be this grey mare's head, looking in at me. And she'd be lying down in the corral and I'd go out and handle her, put my weight on her back, so she got used to me. She became the easiest one of all.

Never had to tie her. I'd drop the reins; she was grounded.

Then I got the old mare, Sugar. She was a retired brood mare. She was a grandma horse. She loved small children.

How did you learn so much about handling animals?

I don't know. Just kind of watching, I guess.

For me, being with the horses was like being with my therapist. Riding through the sage brush. Going along the ditch banks and seeing the little fox cubs peeking out of holes there. Flushing a pheasant going straight up in front of the horse, there. The horse was solid as can be. But he'd spook at a puddle!

The grey horse taught me you have to stay focused. If I weren't focused, the next thing I knew, she'd play some little game and I'd be on the ground looking up at her. She'd have a smile on her face!

In your earlier life, did you have what we might refer to as a risky lifestyle in terms of drinking, burning the candle at both ends...

Well, I was a journalist.

Yes.

But I had an automatic brake on, too. I had a compass. I don't know what it was—by the grace of God I'd go just so far and no further. With drinking, I had a balance that I kept. Call it an ego formation before I got into journalism, what have you. I mean, I did drugs. I liked parties. But I knew where the line was.

After my divorce, I ended up in AlAnon and got a lot of training in addictions. After the Crusillo, I just didn't have the desire to get drunk or stoned, not that I did that much of it before. The psychedelic drugs scared me.

Were you a feminist?

I would not have used that word, but I certainly treasured fairness, for all populations. And women are a part of that.

It sounds as though you had passion for your work.

Yes.

And later, a passion for keeping your horses and other animals.

Yes.

I'm wondering if you think it is part of the same thread that led you to the priesthood—if there is a spiritual connection between what went before and what you are doing now, as well as your connection to landscape, the landscape of the West.

Well, probably there is. To use an overused word, there is a mystical connection between all these things. It ties together. I can't imagine living without passion.

I have been fortunate—graced—blessed—to have been able to do it my way, by and large. That's not the total picture, obviously. I have been in dead-end jobs. I have done everything from pick berries to driving a cab. I know what it is to work hard and get paid pennies. I've been unemployed. I've been without a place to lay my head, living on the grace of friends. But I have been able, through all of that, to end up doing things I didn't expect or plan, but greatly enjoy.

Do you plan that someday you'll go back out West?

My heart is in the West; I'm a westerner. I love looking out at the mountains, smelling sage brush after a spring rain.

But, do I plan? I have no idea, really, what will happen.

Adrift

Mary Olmsted Greene

I set my boat upon the water
The tongue of the wind lapped at the sails
Until I turned the corner of the sound
And reached the fierce horizon of an open sea.

The greedy gulls came near as I set my sails about
But I had no food—no voice for singing, only the vast and hungry silence.
Always, I have longed for a numb forest, deadened by winter
White space with no edges. A blue void.

Alone upon the ocean, there are only the systems
Of my own body, the aching joints of my wrists
Unwashed grit of my groin, the salt beneath my lashes.
Emptied of thought, of theory, I circle the sun of my own being

Circling and circling, ravenous as any shark
For something as soft and true as laughter.

How Far Two Birds Flew to Carry Good News
Lori Anderson Moseman

1.

the distance oarsmen covered
before changing out crew

a measure as variable as the sea
go ahead, count syllables

the runic inscription constant:
"often I was tired when I pulled you"

vika at vatne = rost at lande
the distance between resting

parch earth a pit to trap what drags us
snowmelt a torrent against humble bow

what the gulls said: a secret still
a gruel of vocabulary held high

2.

mourning dove nestlings within dog's reach
I was disassembled by their fall

I hardly knew what to do
tube the bruised one, flush its sour crop

"they need structure"
orphan opossums to an empty pouch

a shoe-sized skunk tries to pull its mother
(road kill) from the center line

stroking the epileptic squirrel
a human meditates on the evolution of brains

refusing to map synapse
a kestrel kept covered so it doesn't imprint

Casting Lots

Druis Ann Iya Oshun Koya Beasley

I

Dreams of pots
Streaming salt water
In to and out of
Blue cauldrons

Algae covered water

Forced
In
 To
  The
Sacrificial
Throat Willing

"let us suppose...
that the little girl drowning
in the peat pit"

Saw the mud covered womyn
Beckoning her to slip through
The cut in the veil

A brown hand motioning

Her coat of sea shells
& moss twinkling
Undulating

Her serendipitous
Smile shining in
The mud and murky
Water

II

Sacred sticks marked
Divine symbols
A way to speak with
The gods
See the road markers

A prayer of supplication
Sticks thrown up in the

Air of time

Free falling out of
Human Control
Becoming
A divine communiqué
Rested on the cut
White cloth

A portal

Stations of the Wind

Elizabeth Kaye Kaminski

We enter the river splay-hearted and turning.
Look now! Our nature surrounds us, our yearning's within.
Look now! And notice our dear fragile wrappings
sustaining the indwelling longing we tend.

What is the river?
Breath is its mother, she offers her bosom,
the rising, the falling, working the bellows of our hearts.
The body its cradle, a furrow of earth to carry the wind.
Its chant thunders and sings and pierces our souls.

What is the river?
Speak with your life.

Why is the river?
Our shrouds snag and we're naked.
Only wind can support us.
The river devours us.
Weep!
And rejoice!

Biomimicry: A Blessing, A Binaural Beat

Lori Anderson Moseman

A currach is simple nest
in the history of exile:

hazel & hind's hide float
stones to trap light.

Come solstice, ask Newgrange
why Moses is hissing

from the genre of voluntary
voyages. In need of twin tablets

for immrama, I paddle wicker
tarred with a skin of (c)odes

to add wings to my rib cage
to glide on regenerative pitch.

An echo is a simple test
in the exile of history:

heron & hardcover flap
water records in waves.

Come sundown, ask Big Ben
why Al Khidr is missing

in the vocabulary of genes.
Theta state of neural knocks.

Gunwale at a dock. Bows
in another hemisphere

rise up in as Rishi Ki dragon
or Basara Taishō at your door.

White Bed, April Moon

Mary Olmsted Greene

Never despair, but if you do, work on in despair.   -Chinese fortune

Among the swimmers, I am the breath.
Between the waves, I am the salt.
Between the lovers, I am the knife.
Inside the well, I am the rope.

> *I never loved you, she said, petting the dog.*
> *I would have thrown myself off a building*
> *for you, he said, petting the dog.*

Between the mountains, I am the sky.
Among the birds, I am the note.
Outside the wall, I am the gate.
Inside forgiveness, I am the truth.

> *god came to her through her feet*
> *after a hotel luau when the secret*
> *of surfing was revealed*

> *she left her father after that*
> *although he never knew it*
> *and she still cooked for him.*

Inside the child, I am the mother.
Inside this earth, I hold my way.
Colors blend the sky to earth.
Horses call the thunder down.

horses call the thunder down

Among the pine, I am the woman.
Inside the woman, I am the child.
Inside the child, I am the wind.
Inside the wind, I am the prayer.

Hands too stiff
to hold the shovel
Wind blows all the seed away

Among the mountains, I am the lion.
Among the lion, I am the fear.
Among the fear, I am the muddy gnome.
Beneath the stair, my eyes are brightest blue.

rain falls on the roof
moon has disappeared
first peeper calls from shallow pond

I stand still until you, world, open your arms.

photo by Carrie Coil

LORI ANDERSON MOSEMAN

"That is what I love about this book: I nod in recognition and agreement, and then a word or phrase triggers resistance. I am back in a discussion I thought I had finished.... I fast forward through old reading lists, leaping from Susan Griffin's *Woman and Nature* to Rachel Blau DuPlessis' *The Pink Guitar: Writing as Feminist Practice* to Varela, Thompson and Rosch's *The Embodied Mind* to Temple Grandin's *Animals in Translation*. Before I know it, I have new eco-poets in-hand.... These interviews push me into a thicket, into the thick of it; they drive me to the desk to write. I hope *Women Outside* does the same for you: pushes you into a creative exploration."

publisher's AFTERWORD

Lori Anderson Moseman

Simply put, this book invites readers to reconnect—to nature and to spirit. How? Through our bodies and our art. Mary Olmsted Greene believes we all need to intensify our contact with the outdoors, with other species, with spiritual practices. As associate editor of *The River Reporter* and as facilitator/founder of The Upper Delaware Writers Collective, Mary cultivates aware individuals active in their ecosystem. This book is an extension of her daily work. She hopes the insights of women from her bioregion will encourage you to learn more about your own. Perhaps you will rekindle your childhood awe. Perhaps you will lobby for sustainable land use policies. Perhaps you will pray with your neighbor. Maybe you will even befriend a skunk.

In 2004, Mary interviewed me about my work as a forester, outdoor guide and farm reporter. I was delighted to be a part of this project, but I had no inkling I would one day publish this book. But three one-hundred-year floods in twenty-one months forced me to refashion my relationship to the flood plain where I live. My dwelling and its maintenance grew paramount, then irrelevant; I had an urgency to support creative endeavors of those who lived along the Upper Delaware. When my husband and I started Stockport Flats press, I knew Mary's *Women Outside: Conversations about Nature, Art & Spirit* should be a part of our Witness Post Series—books in that series are dedicated to visionaries working locally for sustainable living. The community that supports Stockport Flats press is a community that Mary helped build. Mary and I decide it politic to pull my interview, but she invited me to write this afterword.

No doubt as you read *Women Outside*, you interrogated yourself, continually refining your answers as you cycled through the twelve interviews. For me, answering Mary's questions on the spot in a single conversation was a very different experience than carefully reading the multiple replies that pulse through this book. Being interviewed was like a walk in the woods: one question was my favorite rock; the next was a rattlesnake in my path. Some questions made me conjure landscapes I love; some questions bored me. One question—her inquiry about evil—still haunts me. The slow cut-n-paste of bookmaking intensified this range of reactions as did the multiple, conflicting voices. Is a consensus possible or desirable? None of us has a fully formed relationship with nature, so each woman's ongoing discoveries render her answers incomplete. This is both aggravating and exciting. If these thirteen women ever achieved unison, it was in a chorus chanting: "Go outside, engage, and then think some more."

These women's preoccupations and passions are as varied as their speech patterns. One knows how to feed a falcon, and another knows how to appease an Orisha. Such complexities, relatively unmediated by our interviewer, can be unsettling, but I came to love their collisions—sonic and ideological. Ruptures are the beauty of oral communication. One woman's assertion can leap laterally or even counter her next. Then, when we layer on the concrete particulars of another woman's life, we have to revisit our understanding of, say, body knowledge or interspecies communication. By including poems, Mary immerses readers in recurring images, allows them to fixate on moments of shared awareness. Likewise, stark juxtaposition can recharge an overused image. Because poetry tends to refuse closure, it does become a way to suture together the experiences of so many women. In fact, one of Mary's original intentions for this project was to generate poems in response to the interviews. "Doorways" and " Four" are such poems; Mary built them borrowing words and insights from her interviewees. That is why these are the wildest poems in the book. They embody the alchemy of exchange. These are my favorite wild places.

Before Mary came to interview me, she warned me she would ask me to define "wild" and "wilderness." To be honest, I dreaded the question. I had a bookcase full of work by ecofeminists who had been playing with these words for decades. I was ready to dissolve distinctions between the wild and non-wild; ideally, I want to be equally present with both. Codifying difference would be counterproductive. Nonetheless, Mary sequenced her questions to push me: *Is it possible to encounter wilderness in a city? What about a wilderness experience that depends on urban terms? Is there such a thing? Do you consider those kinds of boundaries to be polarizing?* I tried to equate the ecosystem in a Manhattan sidewalk crack with that of a High Sierra watershed, but I had to admit I had "physical and psychological preferences"—what I thought about (memories, ideas) and what I felt (sensations, experiences) did differ. As do the images and cadences I then bring to the page as a poet.

This explains the numinous in Karen MacIntyre's poem "Mimosa Tree." Matter matters. Readers fall into Kristin Barron's intricate description of "The Snail" the way Jenna Snow encounters a water spider: simple and spontaneous wonder cultivates attentiveness. Internal self-discovery is honed by the sensory data we encounter externally. Elizabeth Kaye Kaminski's ability to experience tranquil transport sitting in a chair at home is informed, I believe, by her walks among redwoods. As Krista Gromalski says, "I think that we have those experiences where you see crisp stars in the sky, or the moon, or the crowns of trees that you love on the hill. And something happens inside that allows you to get to that wilderness place, some sort of magic, or, mystic, place. It's not human." Landscape dwarfs us. Awe born of an encounter with the non-human need not be as dramatic as Peggy Hamill's dangerous traverse across glacial scree. Just look at the hands of these women: Amy Gillingham cradling a plantain poultice around a shorthorn's udder, Stephanie Streeter cleaning maggots out of an owl's wound, Sandy Long pulling her shirt over her head so she can look directly at a dead bear. Images in one interview resonate in another: I cannot hear the coyotes howling in Eileen Pagan's interview without replaying the moment when a wolf first nuzzles Mother Joan LaLiberte.

The book's accumulation gets luminous when you add these women's encounters with/ as risk-takers: hover over Mother Joan's eavesdropping on a priest smuggling himself back into Chile or reread Druis Beasley's listening to Malcolm X on a street corner. These women's lives are inspiring. Oddly enough, the image that crystallizes all this for me is a jimson weed Dorothy Hartz once placed in a fine porcelain bud vase. For a gathering of women poets, she did not offer a perfect peony as centerpiece; she gave us *Datura wrightii*—a disinfectant, an analgesic, an antidote, an antirheumatic and a hallucinogen: "Happy as clams/ drunk on Jimson/ the mad will still take to the air/ to inherit the earth./ Raped they turn back/ to the ground/ dirty work for the nurse/ who loves first/ her changelings." Her words, a tonic, offer transport and a task. That's why I hover again and again over a provocative claim Hartz made:

> "I don't think you necessarily have to be in a natural setting to experience wilderness. It helps a lot, and no doubt most of what we call wilderness encounters do take place in a natural setting.... To me, wilderness is a state of harmony based on an absence of ego-consciousness. It belongs to the organic world, to the world of instinct, whether in or out of doors. We are in the wild whenever we are at peace with that. We're innocent. When we are being ethical, moral, self-conscious, striving, doing this, going there... we're caught up. But in wilderness, there is a sense of participation with the natural world, and a recognition of it."

Yes. *Yes.* I agree. But when I reread it, I stumble on the words "harmony" and "innocence." Really? That is what I love about this book; I nod in recognition and agreement, and then a word or phrase triggers resistance. I am back in a discussion I thought I had finished. Is not *harmony* as much of a conscious construct as *ego*? Are you looking for the Chora—Kristeva's, not Plato's—that pre-lingual space that most resembles animal thinking? I fast forward through old reading lists, leaping from Susan Griffin's *Woman and Nature* to Rachel Blau DuPlessis' *The Pink Guitar: Writing as Feminist Practice* to Varela, Thompson and Rosch's *The Embodied Mind* to Temple Grandin's *Animals in Translation*. Then, I have new ecopoets in hand: Juliana Spahr's *things of each possible relation hashing against one another* and Debra Poe's *Elements*. Soon, I am online, ordering Frohoff and Peterson's *Between Species: Celebrating the Dolphin-Human*

Bond. These interviews push me into a thicket, into the thick of it: they drive me to the desk to write (e.g. the poems in this book). I hope *Women Outside* does the same for you: pushes you into a creative exploration.

Shortly after pasting up Stephanie Streeter's interview, I met a wildlife rehabilator (I brought her two mourning dove nestlings). My conversations with Victoria Campbell were richer because of the conversations in *Women Outside*. I found myself asking Campbell (as I did with other writers, artists and activists who crossed my path): "Do you believe in evil?" That question shocked me when Mary initially asked me in my interview. And the answers assembled here—no matter where they fall on the continuum—trouble me. My answer is: "No, there is no singular force called evil." I lived in NYC through 9/11, I still say: "No." I lived through Federal Disaster #1649, I still say: "No." That one could consider evil a matter of belief is exactly what troubles me. Terrorism is often violent acts committed when one belief system deems another "evil." I do not know what to do with this book's collection of comments on evil. Although I locate myself at one end of the continuum, I keep trying to use my response as a fulcrum on which to balance divergent responses: what if Eileen Pagan's sense of predation as evil was on one end of a seesaw and Druis Beasley's explanation of Katrina on another? How could I balance that? Does Elizabeth Kaminski's discussion of veils outweigh Krista Gromalski's articulation of greed? How does Mary synthesize these answers? I vow to ask her: **"How are these women's articulations of evil useful to you?"**

I came of age on the West Coast in the '60s and '70s, so I am conversant with the spiritual experiences of women featured here. I have sung hymns from mountain tops, memorized the bible in Spanish, studied liberation theology; I have performed with an Israeli folk dance troupe at Seders and county fairs; I have taken whirling dervish lessons and been transported through zikr; I have chanted with Hindu nuns in Sweden, prayed with Buddhist monks at Koyasan, and gathered with Yoruba priestesses at former stops on the Underground Railroad. A good citizen works to preserve ecological and ecumenical diversity. In the Midwest in the '80s, among Mayo Clinic medical students and the University of Iowa's cultural feminists, I experimented with alternative healing practices and participated in women's circles. So, I was not surprised that my age-mates in this book talk of such experiences. We are products of similar subcultures. "Answering the call" was part of attending to "the call of the wild." These interviews invite contemporary ecocrtitics and ecopoets who do not address spirituality in their work to revisit conversations ecofeminists embraced in the 1980s and 1990s. To intensify that invitation, I have asked Mary to answer another question: **"Why is spiritual practice still critical to our understanding of women's interaction with nature?"**

author's AFTERWORD

Mary Olmsted Greene

How are these women's articulations of evil useful to you? Why is spiritual practice still critical to our understanding of women's interaction with nature?

When I saw the questions posed by Lori in this afterword, my first response was: "You've got to be kidding." You want to know if I am satisfied with everybody's responses to the question of evil. You want to know my definition of evil. You want to know how I might synthesize the responses in this book and come to my own definitions of art, spirituality, creativity and relationship to wilderness in a threatened world. And immediately, I had to laugh at myself and feel chagrined, for my indignation bloomed over exactly the questions I posed without mercy to the thirteen women in *Women Outside*.

I began this book to try and find some resolution to these questions. The beginning point was wilderness, but that led with this particular grouping of women to ideas and queries about art, God and evil. Put on the spot, my contributors came up with theories. Good, solid theories with merit. Perhaps in some cases they are even beliefs, dependent on faith. And I, in the end, have no resolutions—no resolution. The questions remain. What we have are the questions, and some groping toward truth.

Truth, to my way of thinking, is defined by experience—as in the Sufi practice. And it is defined by culture. And our astrological makeup, our biological makeup and our intrinsic nature. As a child, confronted with the Christian notion of "doing unto others," I would try for whole days to be "good," to be "selfless." Yet I always came back to the conundrum—the compelling reality—of "self." Unfortunately, we were not taught that to be truly the self is the very best way to be good, and the only pathway to God. I found God in the ocean once, when I was twenty-six and in deep despair. I took a walk along the beach, and when I put my feet into the ocean, a feeling of complete acceptance and love came up through my feet and into my body. The message was: "You are loved just the way you are. You deserve life because you were born. You are perfect and you need not do a thing other than wake up each day and live." This message is the same one we could get on Oprah any day of the week, if only we could actually feel it as a physical force in our bodies. If we could, then we might believe, as I did that night on the beach, and indeed every day since, although sometimes I have to work at it.

If I had to define evil, I would say it is a complete lack of empathy, an alienation from our humanity and our connection to spirit so deep that it becomes a connection to the Devil.

The Devil is not a figure with horns and a tail anymore than God is a man with a white beard. Yet I would say that to find the Devil is to fall from grace. I would say that evil is as strong a force in our world—and as indefinable and unknowable, or every bit as definable and knowable—as goodness and love. Is it confined to the human world? I really am not sure. I don't think that a hurricane or any other force of nature is evil or has evil intent. And yet I wonder about the cruelty in nature and whether wrong-doing and evil might connect to it somehow—as a distant relation, or a primitive ancestor. In other words, could Darwin's survival of the fittest have morphed somehow into something with intent to hurt, to destroy, to maim and kill after causing great pain and suffering—for the *sake* of that pain and suffering?

I would say evil is a force that comes in—like wind, like gravity—when circumstances align, when hurt is so deep, when alternatives are not present. I would say it is a covering of veils, brought on by bad experience, burying our joy and essential goodness. And yet we all know stories of people subjected to unspeakable horror that come out on the other side—the side of goodness, compassion and forgiveness. Is it fate? Is it karma? Is it simply strength and belief? Is it because—as the psychologists say—there was someone, somewhere, who affirmed us? Is it truly the hand of God? And if so, why does God touch some of us and not others? I do not believe any of us are unworthy of finding the path. Where there is life, there is hope. Even beyond life, far beyond this veil of tears, no matter what horrors and wrongdoings have been manifested upon us or by us, there is hope of redemption.

If I could choose a belief system, it would be the pagan way—full of trees and magic. And yet, I, like so many in our troubled world, do not find enough time to spend on the contemplative moments, the ways of the body, the discipline of observing the insects and flowers and animals that populate our planet, to dare call myself a pagan. Instead I limp along, caught betwixt and between the worthy obligations of work, family and self, and the longing to become the other, the otherworldly. I wanted to know if others shared this division of time, of self. What I found is, yes—in this historical moment in time, all of us do. All of us hope for leisure and contemplation. All of us bury ourselves in worry and obligation. All of us hope that as we get older time will slow down. Time will change. And yet death finds some of us before this book is even finished. Is this a reason to stop the questioning? I have a feeling that Eileen Pagan would say—uh—no.

What I have found in the practice of this book is that the imperfect remains. With all of our striving, we all remain less than. And yet I believe that it is in our failings that we find our humanity. That in our sufferings and littlest moments, we can find grace.

Grace is my definition of God, grace in the sense of perfect, effortless communion—and the thoughts and actions that stem from that state, momentary as it may be—rather than the strict Christian notion of grace as the absence or erasing of sin. A covering of veils is my definition of evil. Deepest expression combined with freedom is my definition of art. The wonder of everything in its unbounded form is my definition of wilderness.

When I began this book in 2000, my daughter was thirteen. Bill Clinton was our President, but George W. Bush had won a controversial election and was coming into power. The World Trade Center was still standing. The United States economy had began its slide from grace as the dot-com bubble burst on Wall Street, foreshadowing the collapse that greed, corruption and deceit would bring on before decade's end. World population had passed six billion. The weather was relatively quiet after a horrific previous year, which saw tens of thousands of world citizens killed by earthquakes, cyclones, tsunamis, tornadoes and blizzards. Global warming was receiving increasing attention and debate, at the summit at The Hague in the Netherlands and among people in small towns and big cities. The United States refused to sign an international pact to combat global warming even as America's West was burning and Southern/Midwestern states suffering severe and prolonged drought.

At the start of 2010, our country is waging long wars against terrorism in Iraq and Afghanistan. The economy tanked into its worst period of recession and unemployment since the Great Depression. Barack Obama is serving as the nation's first African American President. World population is edging toward seven billion. Weather continues to be extreme and unpredictable. In January, an earthquake struck in Haiti, leveling the capitol of Port au Prince and leaving hundreds of thousands dead, injured, homeless and orphaned. The H_1N_1 virus—swine flu—threatened to become a worldwide epidemic. Climate change is a very real and dire threat, drowning polar bears in melting ice caps and soon, if predictions are correct, whole cities—nations even—will succumb to rising sea levels. Everyone is looking to go green and decrease their carbon footprint. We in the United States know, intellectually, that things need to change, but we don't *know* it, just yet.

My daughter is now twenty-three. Within the book's process, we celebrated her graduation from high school, then college. She is at this moment a Manhattan girl, fashionable and quick, living her inclusive values by working for an organization that promotes women's reproductive rights. Her relationships to wilderness and nature, art and spirit are still being shaped. But what we take as abstraction may be all too concrete for her and others in her generation, left to sort things out as best they can and endure the suffering and difficult choices of the planet's decline: severe weather, wars, famine, pollution, tremendous overcrowding, floods, droughts, global pandemics and refugee cultures. Or maybe miracles will be manifested and evolution will have unforeseen and more hopeful outcomes. The world could right itself. Who can really say?

Rebecca Solnit writes in her book *Hope in the Dark: Untold Histories, Wild Possibilities* that into the first six months of the First World War, Virginia Woolf recorded in her diary: "The future is dark, which is on the whole, the best thing a future can be, I think." Rebecca responds: "Dark, she seems to be saying, as in inscrutable, not terrible. We often mistake the one for the other. Or we transform the future's unknowability into something certain, the fulfillment of all our dread, the place beyond which there is no way forward. But again and again, far stranger things have happened than the end of the world."

Rebecca writes: "Cause and effect assumes history marches forward, but history is not an army. It is a crab scuttling sideways, a drip of soft water wearing away a stone, an earthquake breaking centuries of tension." Like the crab, my relationship to the issues raised in *Women Outside* continues to evolve, regress, digress and scuttle on. It is a conversation that can never be finished, only lived. It is my hope that you, dear reader, will carry the questions raised by this book along your journey for a little way. That they will defy definition and make you a bit freer in your inquiry. That you, in your ordinariness, will find the sacred, and the sacred will speak to you in its thousand tongues. In your musings along the beach, in a forest or an orchard, in your bed at nightfall, in your crowded kitchen, in a library, a hospital, a church, a school, a cemetery. In the gesture of a rock, a bird, a child, a dog, a sky about to storm. In the music of words— vowels, consonants, their roll along the tongue just before they find their meaning, and the vast, unformed realm of understanding that waits just beyond them, just beneath the sound.

Cape May, January

Mary Olmsted Greene

The earth will shrug us off—
but first, split the oak, tend the fire.

The earth will shrug us off—
but first, get your paints, render the sky.

Green surface of the earth
tugged down by the weight of monastery walls,

Green surface of the earth
obliterated by the white worms of blizzards.

The earth will crack at its polar edges
and we'll be as shells, smashed

to bits, hardening to glass. But first—
the fog is lifting. Waves break, shapely and silver.

A young girl holds a white cup.
She is about to begin.

Lori Anderson Moseman (left), Mary Olmsted Greene (right)   photo by Sandy Long

about the AUTHOR

MARY OLMSTED GREENE, a resident of Narrowsburg, New York, was born in Mexico City and raised at the New Jersey shore. She received her Masters of Fine Arts in Poetry from Brooklyn College. She is founder and director of the Upper Delaware Writers Collective [www.upperdelawarewriterscollective.com], which sponsors workshops, publications and events in the Upper Delaware River valley. She is also associate editor of *The River Reporter* newspaper in Narrowsburg. Mary's poetry has appeared in numerous national and local journals, and she has given readings and performances in venues all over the region. She has published two books of poetry, *Where You're Going in this Dream* and *A Painting With You Running Through It,* and her work has appeared in several anthologies. Her favorite wild place is the Atlantic Ocean.

about the PUBLISHER

LORI ANDERSON MOSEMAN founded Stockport Flats Press and the High Watermark Salo[o]n after Federal Disaster #1649, a Delaware River flood. Her poetry books are *Walking the Dead*, *Cultivating Excess*, *Persona* and *Temporary Bunk*. Her Doctorate of Arts in writing is from the University at Albany; her Masters in Fine Arts in poetry is from the University of Iowa. She has a Bachelors in Forestry from Oregon State University. She has been a forester, outdoor guide, farm reporter, educator and editor. Lori was born in Montana and raised in California; she now lives in Ithaca, New York and Equinunk, Pennsylvania with her husband and two mutts. Her favorite wild places are the rocks of the Adirondacks.

works CITED

Abram, David. *The Spell of the Sensuous*. New York: Vintage Books, 1997.
Alves, Rubem A. *The Poet, The Warrior, The Prophet*. London: Edward Cadbury Lectures, SCM Press, 2002.
Banks, Joanne Trautman, Ed. *Congenial Spirits: The Selected Letters of Virginia Woolf.* New York: Harcourt, 1990.
Berry, Wendell. *The Selected Poems of Wendell Berry*. Berkeley: Counterpoint, 1999.
Borland, Hal. *Beyond Your Doorstep: A Handbook to the Country*. New York: Alfred A. Knopf, 1962.
Capra, Fritjof. *The Tao of Physics: An Exploration of the Parallels between Modern Physics and Eastern Mysticism*. Boston: Shambhala Publications, 4th edition, 2000.
Carson, Rachel. *Silent Spring*. Boston: Houghton Mifflin Company, 1962.
Chase, David. *The Sopranos*, Season One, Episode One: "The Sopranos." HBO Original Series.
Childs, Craig. *The Animal Dialogues: Uncommon Encounters with Animals in the Wild*. New York: Little, Brown and Company, 2007.
---. *Soul of Nowhere*. Boston: Back Bay Books, 2003.
---. *The Secret Knowledge of Water: Discovering the Essence of the American Desert*. Boston: Back Bay Books, 2001.
Dillard, Annie. *Three by Annie Dillard,* New York: Harper Perennial, 1990.
Dreiser, Theodore, *An American Tragedy*. New York: Boni & Liveright, 1925.
DuPlessis, Rachel Blau. *The Pink Guitar: Writing as Feminist Practice*. London: Routledge, 1990.
Erdrich, Louise. *The Painted Drum*. New York: HarperCollins, 2005.
Frohoff, Toni and Brenda Petersen. *Between Species: Celebrating the Dolphin-Human Bond*. San Francisco: Sierra Club Books, 2003.
Frost, Robert. "Nothing Gold Can Stay," *The Poetry of Robert Frost*. Ed. Edward Connery Lathem. New York: An Owl Book, Henry Holt and Company, 1969.
Grandin, Temple and Catherine Johnson. *Animals in Translation*. New York: Simon & Schuster, 2005.
Graves, Robert. *The White Goddess: A Historical Grammar of Poetic Myth*. New York: Farrar, Straus and Giroux, 1966.
Griffin, Susan. *Women and Nature: The Roaring Inside Her*. San Francisco: Sierra Club Books, reissue, 2000.
Hayek, F.A. *The Road to Serfdom*. Chicago: University of Chicago, 50th Anniversary Edition, 1994.
Hogan, Linda. *Dwellings: The Spiritual History of the Living World*. New York: Simon & Schuster, 1995.

Johnson, Thomas H., editor. *The Complete Poems of Emily Dickinson*. Boston: Little Brown and Company, 1960.

Krakauer, Jon. *Into Thin Air: A Personal Account of the Mt. Everest Disaster.* New York: Anchor Books, Doubleday, 1999.

---. *Into The Wild*. New York: Anchor Books, Doubleday, 1997.

L'Engle, Madeleine. *A Wrinkle in Time.* New York: Macmillan, Square Fish, reissue, 2007.

Louv, Richard. *Last Child in the Woods: Saving Our Children From Nature-Deficit Disorder.* Chapel Hill: Algonquin Books of Chapel Hill/Workman Publishing, 2008.

McNeill, William. *The History of Western Civilization*. Chicago: University of Chicago, 1986.

Miller, Henry. *Tropic of Cancer*. New York: Grove Press, Inc, 1961.

Milne, Lorus and Margery. *The Senses of Animal and Men*. New York: New York, 1962.

Peacock, Doug. *Grizzly Years: In Search of the American Wilderness*. New York: Holt Paperbacks, 1996.

---. *Walking It Off: A Vetran's Chronicle of War and Wilderness.* Spokane, WA: Eastern Washington Press, 2005.

Poe, Debra. *Elements*. Forthcoming. Ithaca, NY: Stockport Flats, 2010.

Pollan, Michael. *The Botany of Desire: A Plant's-Eye View of the World*. New York: Random House, 2001.

Rezendez, Paul, Bill McKibben and Kenneth Wapner. *The Wild Within: Adventures in Nature and Animal Teachings*. New York: Berkeley Publishing Group, 1998.

---. *Tracking and the Art of Seeing: How to Read Animal Tracks and Signs*. New York: Quill, 1999.

Solnit, Rachel. *Hope in the Dark: Untold Histories, Wild Possibilities.* New York: Nation Books, 2004.

Snyder, Gary. *The Practice of the Wild*. San Francisco: North Point Press, 1990.

Spahr, Juliana. *things of each possible relation hashing against one another*. Newfield, NY: Palm Press, 2003.

Thoreau, Henry David. *Walden*. New York: Konemann, 1966.

Turner, Jack. *The Abstract Wild*. Tucson: The University of Arizona Press, 1996.

Williams, Terry Tempest. *An Unspoken Hunger: Stories from the Field*. New York: Vintage, 1994.

---. *Finding Beauty in a Broken World*. New York: New York: Pantheon, 2008.

Zukav, Gary. *The Dancing Wu Li Masters: An Overview of the New Physics*. New York: Bantam, 1984.

recommended READING

This list, compiled by the author and contributors, is not meant to be comprehensive, but rather a sampling of works that refer to and enhance the subjects raised in *Women Outside*.

Ackerman, Diane. *A Natural History of the Senses.* New York: Vintage Books, 1990.
---. *The Moon By Whale Light.* New York: Vintage Books, 1991.
Adyashanti. *Emptiness Dancing.* Los Gatos, CA: Open Gate Publishing, 2004.
Alcosser, Sandra. *Except by Nature.* Saint Paul, MN: Graywolf Press, 1998.
Anderson, Lorraine. *Sisters of the Earth: Women's Prose and Poetry about Nature.* New York: Vintage, 2003.
Awolalu, J. Omosade. *Yoruba Beliefs and Sacrificial Rites.* Brooklyn: Athelia Henrietta Press, 1994.
Benyus, Janine. *Biomimicry : Innovation Inspired by Nature.* New York: Harper Perennial, 2002.
Beihl, Janet. *Rethinking Ecofeminism.* Cambridge, MA: South End Press, 1991.
Buntin, Simmons. *Terrain.org: Journal of the Built and Natural Environment.* http://www.terrain.org/.
Cabrera, Lydia. *El monte.* Miami: Ediciones Universal, 7th Edition, 1995.
Campbell, SueEllen. *Even Mountains Vanish: Searching for Solace in an Age of Extinction.* Salt Lake City: The University of Utah Press, 2003.
Diamond, Irene and Gloria Orenstein. *Reweaving the World: The Emergence of Ecofeminism.* San Francisco: Sierra Club Books, reissue, 1990.
Duncan, David James. *My Story as Told by Water: Confessions, Druidic Rants, Reflections, Bird-Watchings, Fish-Stalkings, Visions, Songs and Prayers Refracting Light, from Living Rivers, in the Age of the Industrial Dark.* San Francisco: Sierra Cub Books, 2002.
Erhlich, Gretel. *The Solace of Open Spaces.* New York: Penguin, 1986.
---. *This Cold Heaven.* New York: Vintage, 2003.
Gaard, Greta. *Ecofeminism (Ethics and Action).* Philadelphia: Temple University Press, 1993.
---. *The Nature of Home: Taking Root in a Place.* Tucson: University of Arizona Press, 2007.
Gaard, Greta and Patrick D. Murphy, eds. *Ecofeminist Literary Criticism: Theory, Interpretation, Pedagogy.* Chicago: University of Illinois Press, 1998.
Gessner, David. *Ecotone: Reimagining Place.* http://www.ecotonejournal.com/.
Grimaud, Helen. *Wild Harmonies: A Life of Music and Wolves.* New York: Riverhead Books, 2006.
Halpern, Sue. *Four Wings and a Prayer: Caught in the Mystery of the Monarch Butterfly.* New York: Pantheon Book, 2001.
Heinrich, Bernd. *Mind of the Raven.* New York: Cliff Street Books, HarperCollins, 1999.
---. *Winter World: The Ingenuity of Animal Survival.* New York: ECCO, HarperCollins, 2003.

Hinchman, Hannah. *A Trail Through Leaves: The Journal as a Path to Place.* Norton, 1999.

Holmes-Binney, Debi. *Desert Sojourn: A Woman's Forty Days and Nights Alone.* Seattle: Seal Press, 2000.

Houk, James. *Spirits, Blood, and Drums: The Orisha Religion of Trinidad.* Philadelphia: Temple University Press, 1995.

Hubbell, Sue. *A Country Year: Living the Questions.* New York: Harper & Row, 1983.

Hunter, Jo Anna. "Oro Pataki Aganju: A Cross Cultural Approach Towards the Understanding of the Fundamentos of the Orisa Aganju in Nigeria and Cuba." *Orisa Yoruba God and Spiritual Identity in Africa and the Diaspora*, edited by Toyin Falola, Ann Genova. New Jersey: Africa World Press, Inc. 2006.

Hurd, Barbara. *Stirring the Mud: On Swamps, Bogs, and Human Imagination.* Boston: Mariner Books, 2003.

LaDuke, Winona. *All Our Relations: Native Struggles for Land and Life.* Cambridge, MA: South End Press, 1999.

Legler, Gretchen. *All the Powerful Invisible Things: A Sportswoman's Notebook.* Seattle: Adventura Books, Seal Press, 1995.

---. *On Ice: An Intimate Portrait of Life at McMurdo Station, Antarctica.* Minneapolis: Milkweed Editions, 2005.

Matthews, Anne. *Wild Nights: Nature Returns to the City.* New York: North Point Press, 2001.

Mason, John. *Black Gods: Orisa Studies in the New World.* New York: Yoruba Theological Archministry, 1998.

---. *Olokun; Owner of Rivers and Seas.* New York: Yoruba Theological Archministry, 1996.

---. *Orin Orisa: Songs for Selected Heads.* New York: Yoruba Theological Archministry, 1997.

Moore, Thomas. *Care of the Soul.* New York: Harper Collins, 1992.

Morrow, Lance. *Evil: An Investigation.* New York: Basic Books, 2003.

Morrow, Susan Brind. *The Names of Things.* New York: Riverhead Books, 1997.

Norris, Kathleen. *Dakota: A Spiritual Geography.* Boston: Houghton Mifflin, 1993.

---. *The Cloister Walk.* New York: Riverhead Books, 1996.

Oliver, Mary. *New and Selected Poems, Volume One.* Boston: Beacon Press, 1992.

Oliver, Mary. *The Leaf and the Cloud: A Poem.* Cambridge, MA: Da Capo Press, 2001.

Olsen, Rendell, Ed. *How2: Ecopoetics.* http://www.asu.edu/pipercwcenter/how2journal/vol_3_no_2/ecopoetics/index.html.

Plant, Judith, ed. *Healing the Wounds: The Promise of Ecofeminism.* Santa Cruz, CA: New Society Publishers, 1989.

Powning, Beth. *Home: Chronicle of a North Country Life.* New York: Stewart, Tabori, & Chang, 1996.

Rogers, Pattiann. *Firekeepers: New and Selected Poems.* Minneapolis: Milkweed Editions, 1994.

Rogers, Susan Fox. *Another Wilderness: Notes from the New Outdoorswoman.* Seattle: Seal Press, 1997.

Rothenberg, David and Wandee J. Pryor. *Writing on Air.* Cambridge, MA: Terra Nova, The MIT Press, 2003.

Rothenberg, David and Marta Ulvaeus. *Writing on Water.* Cambridge, MA: Terra Nova, The MIT Press, 2002.

Sauer, Peter. *Finding Home: Writing on Nature and Culture from Orion Magazine.* Boston: Beacon Press, 1992.

Shellenberger, Michael and Ted Nordhaus. *From the Death of Environmentalism to the Politics of Possibility.* Boston: Houghton Mifflin, 2007.

Shiva, Vandana. *Staying Alive: Women, Ecology and Development.* London: Zed, 1989.

---. *Earth Democracy: Justice, Sustainability and Peace.* Cambridge, MA: South End Press, 2005.

Skinner, Jonathan, editor. *Ecopoetics 06/07.* 2009.

Slovic, Scott, Kyhl Lyndgaard and Michael Branch, editors. *ISLE: Interdisciplinary Studies in Literature and the Environment.* http://isle.oxfordjournals.org/

Slovic, Scott. *Seeking Awareness in American Nature Writing.* Salt Lake City: University of Utah Press, 1998.

Sullivan, Robert. *Rats: Observations on the History and Habitat of the City's Most Unwanted Inhabitants.* New York: Bloomsbury, USA, 2005.

---. *The Meadowlands: Wilderness Adventures on the Edge of a City.* New York: Anchor, 1999.

Thomas, Elizabeth Marshall. *The Hidden Life of Deer.* New York: HarperCollins, 2009.

Vicuna, Cecilia. *The Precarious / QUIPOem: The Art and Poetry of Cecilia Vicuna.* Lebanon, NH: Wesleyan Poetry, 1997.

Warren, Karen. *Ecofeminism: Women, Culture, and Nature.* Bloomington, IN: Indiana University Press, 1997.

---. *Ecofeminist Philosophy.* New York: Rowman and Littlefield, 2000.

Wujnovich, Lisa and Mark Dunau. *This Place Called Us.* Ithaca, NY: Stockport Flats Press, 2008.

Wynne-Tyson, Jon, Editor. *The Extended Circle: A Dictionary of Humane Thought.* London: Open Gate Press, 1990.

Zukav, Gary. *The Seat of the Soul.* New York: Fireside, 1990.

Zweig, Connie and Abrams, Jeremiah, editors. *Meeting the Shadow.* New York: Jeremy P. Tarcher/Perigree, 1991.

ACKNOWLEDGMENTS

There are many people to thank in the making of this book: first, my daughter Cassandra Valentin and her father Tony Valentin, who provided encouragement and support; Elaine Giguere and the Delaware Valley Arts Alliance of Narrowsburg, New York, which provided an Artists in the Community grant to get started; Kathleen Spivack, who lit a fire under me when I needed one and provided invaluable insight into the structure and flow of the book; Marcia Nehemiah, for her wise feedback and enthusiasm and for my introduction to Tony Soprano; Sandy Conway, whose care over these pages corrected many an error; *The River Reporter* offices, in particular Danielle Gaebel, Jennifer Bitetto, Anne Willard and Connie Kern; Lori Anderson Mosemen, whose keen eye and ear improved the book immeasurably, for her patience with the process and dedication to the project; and most of all the women whose voices are included here, who gave so generously of their time, their hearts and their minds. I hope I got it right.

WITNESS POST Series

In the aftermath of Federal Disaster #1649, a flood along the Delaware River, Lori Anderson Moseman and Tom Moseman created Stockport Flats to celebrate writers and artists whose creative buoyancy builds community. This series, *Witness Post*, features works by those who are dedicated stewards of sustainability. The geological term, *witness post*, refers to a signpost "placed on a claim line when it cannot be placed in the corner of a claim because of water or difficult terrain." Our culture makes reclamation and sustainable land practices extraordinarily difficult. The writers and artists in this series bear witness to this complex task; their claims help us work toward awareness and action.

Designed by Lori Anderson Moseman and Mary Olmsted Greene, this volume was created using Hoefler Text and Century Gothic, printed on recycled paper by BookMobile. This on-demand edition has an initial printing of 151 copies. BookMobile purchases all of its electrical power through Windsource®, which provides energy produced in wind farms in southwestern Minnesota.

WITNESS POST Titles

This Place Called Us by Lisa Wujnovich and Marc Dunau
Women Outside: Conversations about Nature, Art & Spirit by Mary Olmsted Greene

Stockport Flats, 2010
1120 East Martin Luther King Jr. Street   Ithaca, NY 14850   (607) 272-1630